THE HEGEMONIC MALE

New Directions in Anthropology
General Editor: Jacqueline Waldren

THE HEGEMONIC MALE

Masculinity in a Portuguese Town

Miguel Vale de Almeida

Berghahn Books
Providence • Oxford

First published in 1996 by
Berghahn Books

Editorial offices:
165 Taber Avenue, Providence, RI 02906, USA
Bush House, Merewood Avenue, Oxford, OX3 8EF, UK

© 1996 Miguel Vale de Almeida

Library of Congress Cataloging-in-Publication Data
Almeida, Miguel Vale de.
  The hegemonic male : masculinity in a Portuguese town / Miguel
Vale de Almeida.
    p.   cm. – (New directions in anthropology : v. 4)
  Includes bibliographical references (p.) and index.
  ISBN 1-57181-888-X (alk. paper) . — ISBN 1-57181-891-X (alk.
paper)
    1. Men–Portugal–Pardais–Psychology.   2. Masculinity
(Psychology)–Portugal–Pardais.   I. Title.   II. Series.
HQ1090.7.P8A43   1996
305.31'09469–dc20   96-18532
                                                CIP

British Library Cataloguing in Publication Data
A catalogue record for this book is available from
the British Library.

Printed in the United States on acid-free paper.

CONTENTS

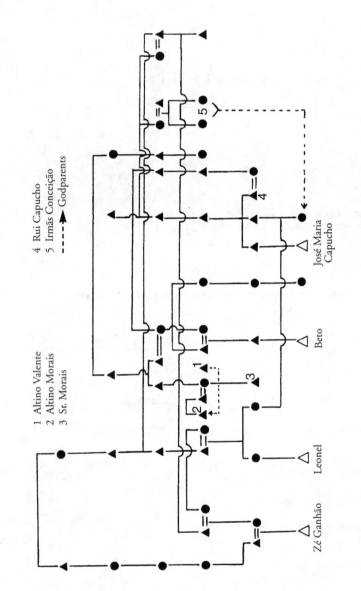

1 Altino Valente
2 Altino Morais
3 Sr. Morais

4 Rui Capucho
5 Irmãs Conceição
----▶ Godparents

FIGURE: GENEALOGICAL CHART SHOWING KINSHIP AND RELATIONS BETWEEN MAIN INFORMANTS

Zé Ganhão   Leonel   Beto   José Maria Capucho

PERSPECTIVES I

*P*eople in Pardais do not talk just about masculinity, gender or sexuality. Far from it. The themes are themselves difficult to address with everyday words, and so they are expressed as embodied practices, in symbols and metaphors. Talk – and writing – about subjects that in one way or another touch upon sex can always be misinterpreted. It is a 'touchy' subject, since it hinges on the very moral ground of life in society and of personal identities, highly visible yet guardedly private. That is why people have pseudonyms in this book. However, the name of the village and those of surrounding towns, are real. Social life is made of real people in real places. Although privacy should be preserved and anonymity guaranteed, I believe that villages belong to the public sphere of culture as a lived dispute and negotiation of the meanings of identity which can have – and do have – social and political consequences. The village life as observed by the anthropologist is public, there to be interpreted and enjoyed by experts and general audiences, as much as to be lived in and by the local population. I do realise, however, that this double strategy (personal anonymity, public visibility) is not wholly satisfactory. I also believe that there is yet to be born the anthropologist who can solve once and for all the ambiguities of these ethical dilemmas.

When I left for the field, I took along with me certain questions. The main one was: how is masculinity reproduced in daily life and interaction? Specifically, how is hegemonic masculinity reproduced, when the diversity of men's experiences and identities suggest that there are several masculinities? These questions multiplied throughout fieldwork, reading and writing. They gave birth to other questions that I have tried to address in the different chapters. After the initial Portuguese manuscript of this essay had been written I came across the 1994 collective work edited by A. Cornwall and N. Lindisfarne *Dislocating Masculinities.* I was happy to find that my work had already followed some of the authors' suggestions for future research on the subject:

> ... anticipate directions that anthropological studies of masculinity may take in the future: these include a focus on the processes of gendering, the metaphors of gendered power, and the relation between dominant and subordinate masculinities and other gendered identities in any given setting. (1994:9)

The initial motivation for my research questions had to do with a personal interest in the broad area of gender studies. Gender studies have been connected with feminist critical theory in the social sciences as well as in the 'real' world. Under the early form of women's studies, they were an attempt to counterbalance excessive androcentrism in anthropology, since ethnographic writing juxtaposed the masculine and the social points of view. Women's studies and early feminist efforts in anthropology studied societies and cultures from the point of view of women. This project, however, presupposed that gender relations were, at the base, relations of power, hierarchy and inequality, not simply dichotomous, symmetrical and complementary relations, as common-sense categories like to put it. Therefore, social relations based on gender became understood as one more set of relations to be added to and intertwined with relations based on age, status, prestige, class and other vectors.

The political position of the promoters of gender studies was initially – and it still is, to a great extent – a peculiar one: their political engagement was seen by the public and by the academic establishment as stronger than that of researchers who focused on other areas, such as social class or race, areas which by their own nature could not avoid having strong political connotations. Part of the problem with gender studies and this misconception of its political bias (connected with feminist social movements) was that it was cornered in a ghetto. One consequence of this was that the commonly held idea of what gender studies practitioners were doing and their actual practice tended to coincide: studies *by* women, *about* women, *for* women.

Fortunately, this has changed somewhat. To not recognise, accept and incorporate in anthropological research and theory the gender variable is today seen as negative as not recognising, accepting and incorporating the variable of social class, for instance. Furthermore, the countries where feminism had its greatest impact – the cosmopolitan societies which are also the centres of anthropological production, like the United States, the United Kingdom and France, unlike Portugal – witnessed the emergence of the gay movement, with its academic ramifications. The gay critical perspective provided gender studies with one further question beyond the questioning of the essentialism of male and female: the essentialism of hetero- and homosexuality. If until then male and female, masculine and feminine were critically and sociologically questioned in their relational aspect, now each of them could be questioned *per se*. The notion that there are several femininities and several masculinities has thus been gaining recognition. Actually, in modern societies, once culture achieves the control of the natural process of human reproduction, gender and sexual identities are increasingly becoming something 'one has' or something 'one chooses' – a malleable, manipulable aspect of personal identity.

A few honourable exceptions aside – most of them focusing on non-European contexts – the analysis of social processes defining masculinity have focused mostly on homosexuality as an object of enquiry, similar to the way that women's studies had focused on the female universe. I like to define my work as an effort to make explicit social processes and relations that constitute hegemonic masculinity, the central model that attempts to subordinate alternative masculinities (of people, groups or societies), and which is the model of male domination, compulsory monogamy, heterosexuality and reproduction. This is what is truly exotic to me, the object of awe, the 'Other' that needs translation.

Thus, the initial questions unfolded into a myriad of other questions: is hegemonic masculinity more resistant to change in oral culture contexts, as opposed to modern, urban ones? Is this distinction of any value for us? To what extent has feminist theory and gender studies been based on an Anglo-Saxon, individualistic view of Man and Woman, incompatible with a context such as the Portuguese? Can we really talk about male domination, and up to what point are the agents of domination victims of it too?

I was initially convinced that this type of research needed the double strategy of fieldwork with participant observation and theoretical, bibliographical and comparative research. I was also aware of the trans-disciplinary nature of gender studies, since gender cuts across other types of social identity. That is probably why this book constantly oscillates between the ethnographic register and the theoretical pursuit.

Fieldwork confronted me with one main methodological problem: the non-existence of an available model for data gathering on masculinity.

Being a man is something that becomes 'visible' mostly at the level of discourse and at the level of discourse as practice. Since this is a field of dispute of moral values, in which the distance between what one says and what one does is great, I have opted for a strategy of insertion into a group of men in conditions of sociability. This has conditioned my work to aspects of *homosociality*, more than relations between genders.

Once I had chosen Pardais as the site for my stay, I moved to the village and lived there for one year. The choice of fieldwork site was triggered by the will to compare differences and similarities between models of masculinity geographically close to, and inside the same linguistic universe of a common Nation-State. The province of Alentejo was chosen because it is an almost virgin ethnographic field and the Portuguese extension of southern Europe, culturally classified as 'Mediterranean'. However, I looked for a context that, instead of being remote and forgotten, was a region undergoing transformation. Therefore the choice fell upon the marble production region, characterised by this post-agrarian economic activity with strong ties to world economy and culture. Once in the village, interaction with the men led me to understand that if I was ever to understand masculinity, I would have to pay close attention to discursive and performative aspects: the expression, whether verbal, embodied or ritualised, of moral evaluations about what it is to be a man (and a woman), based on a classification of the world that uses human sexual dimorphism as the basic metaphor.

Sociability was the ideal context of interaction, space and time for pursuing my research which, together with the impossibility of working in the marble quarries, led to the development of a double strategy: during the day I interacted mostly with children, women and the elderly; in the evenings and on weekends, with men. I have always tried not to bias my data by confusing expressions of masculinity with moments of leisure, which I believe becomes obvious in the subsequent work.

I also found myself in the field – and while writing – without any defined paradigm. Unlike in studies of social stratification, kinship or material culture (and still …), studies of masculinity (themselves a sub-area of gender studies) demand experimentation with several perspectives. I have tried to include all throughout my written work, as an indispensable element of anthropological reflexive experience, these crossroads of theoretical and methodological experimentation, as well as the process of living and discovering throughout the year in the field. I do not define my work as Marxist, Weberian or Durkheimian (or any of their respective offshoots), since I believe that the notion of culture which we have today needs the concurrence of the three lineages, in both harmony and confrontation.

This book revolves around one main hypothesis: that hegemonic masculinity is an ideal central model which, unattainable by practically any single man, exerts over all men a controlling effect, through embodiment, ritualisation of practices of everyday sociability and a discursiveness that excludes a whole emotional field considered as feminine; and that masculinity is not symmetrical with femininity, inasmuch as the two relate in a hierarchical, asymmetrical form. Furthermore, masculinity is to be seen as a constructed, fragile and surveilled process of cultural construction, as peculiar to all forms of claimed social precedence.

The chapters in this volume were planned to be rather independent, allowing for different rhetorical strategies in each. They are connected, however, by a common narrative thread that follows the process of discovery in the field experience together with the unravelling of the research problem. There is implied the notion that what one produces in anthropology is a text. This book represents neither the real experience I had in Pardais, nor the 'real' life of my informants. It is an interpretation: a subjective one, because I am the author, and one that is based on the discourses (interpretations) of my informants. Its objectivity can only lie in the comparison with what has been written on the same topic, in the objective elements of context, and in the internal coherence of argument.

Interpretation, however, is not folly. It is a responsibility towards my informants, who know better than anyone how to conduct their lives. It is a responsibility towards the academy, which judges on internal coherence and plausibility of an interpretation. I do not intend to make value judgements on the values of my informants, but I can not either pretend that when one talks about gender one is not being political. One is political, because relations of power and domination, pleasure, freedom, family, morality and reproduction are at stake and these are in permanent discussion in our societies. James Clifford wrote in his influential *Writing Culture* (Clifford and Marcus 1986), that the authors in the collection

> see culture as composed of seriously contested codes and representations; (...) assume that the poetic and the political are inseparable, that science is in, not above, historical and linguistic processes. (...) assume that academic and literary genres interpenetrate and that the writing of cultural descriptions is properly experimental and ethical. (1986:2)

This does not mean a total acceptance of some of the exaggeration of post-modern trends in contemporary anthropology. The field which

Writing Culture opened up has sometimes been misinterpreted. It is true that ethnographic interpretation has led to a terminology that, occasionally, fails to distinguish the latter from theoretical concepts, thus creating the epistemological confusion referred by Sperber (1981); however, it is true that the anthropologist's text largely betrays the experience in the field, and intervenes in society in a political way. I have tried to show the meaning of being a man for my informants, but this does not mean full-fledged relativism, since I can admire notions such as honour, straightforwardness and pride, but do not accept manifestations of male chauvinism or homophobia.

In order to convey those meanings – and my own – I have relied on narrative. Human beings tell stories, even scientific ones. Anthropology has the advantage of being one of the last human sciences that still values the description of human condition *per se* (Nader 1989:19). Besides being a narrative form, anthropological production should also be critical of social issues. When new questions arise, methods need to be innovated too. These, as well as theories, undergo experimental periods, particularly so when there are no standard paradigms at work, as is the case today:

> A period of experimentation is characterised by eclecticism, the play of ideas free of authoritative paradigms, critical and reflexive views of subject matter, openness to diverse influences embracing whatever seems to work in practice, and tolerance of uncertainty about a field's direction and of incompleteness in some of its projects. (Marcus and Fischer 1986: x)

Chapter 1 addresses what I have called 'the outsider's look'. It corresponds to the first period in the field and tries to rationalise on the village's structural elements, providing some objective data that may set the context for the lives of my informants: population structure, social and professional structure, geographical and socio-economic characteristics of the region. I have also tried to confront this data – particularly that which concerns domestic groups – with recent alternatives in the study of family and domestic groups. Sex and gender approaches come out as one of those alternatives.

Chapter 2 outlines the levels of social identity and the contexts in which the discourses and practices of masculinity are expressed and by which they are shaped. I introduce the reader to the main informants, while characterising their social incorporation in terms of age, civil status, social stratification, work and so on. This group of key informants is further complemented by some emblematic characters from other social identities and masculinities: the president of the *Junta* (the local authority) and the influential families. Masculine and feminine are presented as classificatory principles, attributable to men and women, which are used for the definition of the sexual division of labour, the division of sexual labour and the sexual dichotomy in the world view.

Chapters 3 through 5 continue the ethnographic approach of Chapter 2. Chapter 3 concentrates on the world of work and work relations. It then elaborates the wider category of power and focuses on the understanding and management of conflict. The discussion includes hierarchy in the work place, social stratification, the notion of respect, the symbolic aspects of money and consumption, the notions of sacrifice and strength, among others. The purpose is to outline the relations and the mutual construction of these notions in the constitution of masculinity and wider social relations.

Chapter 4 includes three case studies. The first focuses on the café as a time and space of homosociality, a metaphorical 'men's house'. The second is a description and analysis of an evening out – a male nocturnal excursion – as an example of ambivalent sexual morality. The third one is a cultural analysis of the symbolic and performative universe of bulls and bullfighting as a text and representation of gender relations and masculinity.

Chapter 5 concerns emotions and sentiments. The central case study is that of the poems by a local oral poet, in which those emotions that are considered as culturally feminine are expressed by men and among men. The chapter also includes an approach to the female strategies used to face male domination, as well as the process of incorporation of masculinity by male children.

Finally, an *Excursio* was added to provide a systematisation of theoretical influences on my work. I elaborate on the notions of symbol and meaning, discourse and practice, social construction and reproduction, and on the theme of hegemonic masculinity and embodiment.

The conclusion – which I have preferred to call 'Perspectives II' – synthesises and intertwines the stronger arguments in the book and outlines the main avenues for exploring masculinities and for bridging some gaps that I feel to be evident in contemporary gender studies and anthropology at large.

1. A Home for a Stranger
The Anthropologist's Construction of a Community

Anthropology faces alternate and sometimes opposing attitudes towards including or not an anthropologist's personal and reflexive experience in the field as part of the ethnographic text. One attitude posits objectivity as its aim and thus neglects the subjectivity of the 'other' and of the research experience. Another attitude tends to see subjective and intersubjective experience as the very substance of anthropological narrative.

These attitudes are both extreme. In this chapter I wish to find an equilibrium between the two. It is important to recognise the epistemological relevance of the anthropologist's personal experience. However, this should not preclude attention to the relative objectivity of the social reality under study. In this chapter, it is my intention to narrate and reflect upon 'first contacts': those periods of time prior to settling in the village, the choice of the site of fieldwork, and the political strategies for integration and acceptance of a stranger called 'anthropologist'. In this phase of the research process, 'community' is something one understands as a collective entity, a structure, a set of statistical data, comparable with dozens of other ethnographies and understood in a typological fashion as established in academic tradition. The obvious trap is that communities are to a great extent ideological constructs, corresponding, in the researcher's mind, to administrative divisions and human population agglomerates.

This entails what I like to call an 'external vision', one that is qualitatively very different from the sort of 'vision' one acquires as days and weeks in the field go by. Slowly, specific people, and relationships established with and between them, mark the subjectivity as well as the objectivity of anthropological fieldwork. Before writing about specific people, I would like to provide answers to some basic preliminary questions: what is the population of Pardais, what do its inhabitants do for a living, what does the village look like, why did I choose it?

A starting question could be: why doing fieldwork in Portugal, in my own country? The difficulties of limited time and money for the pursuit of fieldwork in an 'exotic' context are largely responsible. This is an issue of the political economy of scientific research, where divisions between centre and periphery are quite obvious. Still, my purpose was to study the social construction of masculinity, not a specific culture from a monographic, holistic point of view; this rather more anthropological than ethnological project allowed me to study any context, regardless of cultural specificity. Nevertheless, the issue of 'anthropology at home' (see Jackson 1986) was at the time of research quite relevant. My belief remains that 'nations' do not account for cultural variety and are not the level at which distinctions can be made between 'anthropology at home' and 'anthropology abroad'. In the territorial space of the Portuguese nation-state, cultural homogeneity and heterogeneity coexist. State structures and linguistic homogeneity have their counterpart in hetero-geneity of forms of social reproduction. This can be perceived at a regional level (the stark differences between northern and southern Por-tugal), at a developmental level (the abyss between coastal urban areas and inland deserted areas), and also at a broad social level – namely the stark difference between the academic, trans-national anthropologist, and the marginal and illiterate strata of the population.

Now that the field experience is past, I wonder if all would have been easier if I had been a 'total' foreigner learning a new language, and how much my gender played a role. My status as a male (and, officially, sin-gle) jeopardised my chances of access to the female world.[1] My status as an educated, urban, bourgeois man placed me on a specific rung of the social ladder previously established by local categories. I was almost never able to use the excuse of cultural ignorance or lack of proficiency so useful for anthropologists. However, this might have contributed to the richness of my field experience. It made me see my own 'national' culture as a strange object. I was able to see how different the cultural patterns of Pardais were from my own as a member of Lisbon's suppos-edly educated and cosmopolitan academic elite.

The choice of the Alentejo region as the broad site of fieldwork had to do, in a first instance, with the fact that this province is usually classified as belonging to the broad cultural area of the 'Mediterranean' and 'southern Europe'. This is a cultural area about which monographs supply a great deal of material on issues of gender and sexuality. The reason for this rests mainly on the idea that southern Europe has a 'male chauvinist' culture, simultaneous with a strongly marked sexual division. These ideas have been systematised in Mediterranean ethnographies with the concept of 'Honour and Shame' complexes. However, part of this is also the remittance of sexuality and sexual urges to the south by northern-European scholars, in what has been a true remake of the scholarly opposition between 'Civilised and Exotic', or even, in the worst case scenario, between 'Nature and Culture'. This book does not follow these lines, but partly because of them it seems to me that researchers on the Mediterranean concerned with the constitutive power of the honour and shame morality have never really succeeded in establishing a 'Sex and Gender' approach. That has been the *apanage* of more exotic contexts, predominantly Melanesian ones. I believe that the excessive juxtaposition of cultural areas and theoretical themes is prejudicial for anthropology.

Having chosen the Alentejo province, the next question was: where, in Alentejo? It was most important not to be tempted by the nostalgia for the ideal-type Alentejo: that of *latifundia*, depopulation, unemployment, demographic recession, Agrarian Reform, Communist Party influence, as well as the whole array of linguistic, ritual and gastronomic folklore. Neither did I want to choose a research site that would be too marked by local specificity, usually of a vaguely exotic and touristic allure. Portuguese anthropology has already suffered too much from this attraction. I searched instead for a context that would be marked by a strong social dynamic, a place undergoing transformation with rural-urban inter-penetration as well as global-local links. In sum, a place where *ancien régime* structures would meet 'modernity'. During an exploratory tour, I came across the marble-production region of Estremoz and realised that the very opposite of stereotypical Alentejo was in existence: greater demographic concentration, employment, urbanisation, change (or should I say, destruction) in the landscape.

The so-called 'marble triangle' is composed of the municipalities of Estremoz, Borba and Vila Viçosa. Its social and economic specificity has been recognised by the state's Alentejo Region Co-ordination Commission (CCRA) which has published a series of development projects for the territorial unit composed by those three municipalities. This specific reality can be perceived by the most distracted of casual travellers: when one crosses to neighbouring municipalities like Elvas, Alandroal or

Arraiolos, one is crossing the border to a physical and human landscape that has characterised the Alentejo – great plains, the cultivation of dry cereal crops, oak woods for cork extraction, every now and then an iso-lated farm (a *monte*) can be seen on top of a low hill. Generally, one has the feeling that no one lives there any more.

In the 'triangle', one feels that one is witnessing the birth of a future urban area: the towns of Estremoz, Borba and Vila Viçosa are so close together that they could easily become one. Alongside the roads con-necting them, new neighbourhoods are on the rise. It is however, the marble quarries which most strikingly mark the landscape. They are chaotic, gigantic. The land is as if it had been recently bombed. The quarries have pushed away wheat fields, olive groves, cork-tree woods; these have been replaced by bulldozers, cranes, debris piles, holes and craters. Here one rarely sees the traditional horse carts and donkeys of the Alentejo, they are replaced by swarms of proletarians going to work on their noisy motorbikes. Although cars belong mostly to quarry own-ers, engineers and white-collar workers, all connected with the industry, even car traffic has become heavy. Still, one can find a few small villages, the apparent remains of an old world and an old order. However, upon a closer look, they are really residential satellites housing quarry workers.

Within the 'triangle', the municipality of Vila Viçosa was my choice for reasons that I later abandoned. During the preliminary stages of research I was interested in exploring the relationship between the knowledge and action of Church and aristocracy on the one hand, and the peasantry on the other, with regard to sexual morality. The project then had a strong historical component. Vila Viçosa was the ideal place for that since it has for centuries been the headquarters of the House of Bragança – the Portuguese royal dynasty. Around the Paço (the palace), monasteries and convents had flourished, alongside court life. I pro-ceeded then to choose a residence from among the three villages in the municipality. Bencatel and São Romão are two large Alentejo villages. The former's economy depends on marble extraction, the latter depends on large estate agriculture (being on the border with the Elvas plains and outside the marble area). Pardais is the smallest. It depends almost totally on the marble industry, and is located on the southernmost tip of the municipality, one kilometre away from Alandroal, a typical municipal-ity of the 'deep Alentejo'. Pardais has the southernmost and last of the marble quarries. It struck me as such an exemplary case of social change that it even led me to abandoning my initial historical and archival research interest and opting for studying more closely the relation between gender construction and social, economic, labour and cultural changes connected with processes of modernisation. Pardais converted me from research of archives and written texts to living people, with their discourses and practices in everyday life.

Facts and Figures: Knowledge of the Field

The CCRA defines the municipalities of Estremoz, Borba and Vila Viçosa as a sub-region with specific characteristics. The 1983 Development Project provides the broad picture for the sub-region. In this document, sites with less than ten homes are defined as 'isolates'. Thus, from the sum total of 35,219 inhabitants in the sub-region, 7,162 lived in isolates, that is 20.34 percent. The higher percentage being in Estremoz, and the lowest in Vila Viçosa (27.80 and 9.57 percent respectively). In Pardais, the total number of isolates was then 222 inhabitants, in a total of 750 (1980 census) inhabitants in the *freguesia*.[2] The percentage of isolates was, thus, 29.60 percent, while for Bencatel and São Romão it was respectively 11.59 and 8.49 percent. The *freguesia* had but one site with more than one-hundred inhabitants – the village of Pardais proper, with a population of 528 (70.40 percent of the *freguesia*).

The number of isolates had been decreasing ever since the 1950s. The characteristic population concentration of the Alentejo was already strong, with seventy-six percent of the population living in places with more than one-hundred inhabitants (in the sub-region); the percentage living in places with more than 1,000 inhabitants was also high: 64.47 percent. The case of Vila Viçosa was outstanding, since 90.43 percent of the population was living in the four places, all over 1,000 inhabitants, the only one with less than 1,000 being precisely Pardais. The same developmental model outlines the main aspects of population evolution for the *freguesia* of Pardais: 594 in 1911, 688 in 1940, and 815 in 1960, 862 in 1970, and a decrease in 1981: 750 inhabitants. My data from 1991 adds up to 659.

As for geographical characteristics, the CCRA project stresses two aspects: low-quality and low-productivity soil; and the existence of large natural deposits of marble. The occupation of agricultural soil at the time was mainly dry-crops, but also some olive-tree and cork-tree plantation. Wet farming, with irrigation, was scarce and limited to the small areas of *hortas* (vegetable gardens) and orchards near the streams. In comparison with the rest of Alentejo, however, the sub-region has a relative abundance of water: underground water is itself a by-product of the geological characteristics of the sub-soil. That is why the exploration of the sub-soil for the marble industry can trigger changes in the water supply, making more difficult any hypothetical return to agriculture in case of crisis in the marble sector.

Let us interrupt this preliminary data on population and geography. After all, this is not the anthropologist's speciality. Seven kilometres south of the town of Vila Viçosa and one kilometre north of the town of Alandroal, Pardais presents itself to the traveller, almost hidden on a slope leading to the Pardais stream, an affluent of the Guadiana river. Seen from above, the village is almost square-shaped: four main streets around the Quinta dos Passos. This square is drawn on a slope: the top part of the village, near the church, is locally known as *a aldeia* (the village), and the lower part as *a ribeira* (the stream). Living in Pardais means a constant back and forth movement, going up-hill and down-hill between the western top part and the eastern lower part. Northwards, there is the Bairro das Pedreiras (Quarry Neighbourhood); southwards, the small road that winds along the *hortas* and orchards close to the stream. As people say, 'it leads nowhere'.

Early Days in the Field

Upon arrival at his or her field site, the ethnographer's first temptation is to rationalise all that he or she sees. Aerial photographs, maps and charts, statistics, all these are forms of appropriation, of objectification (and 'domestication') of a real world. A world that, because it is unknown, causes confusion and a certain amount of anxiety. As a matter of fact, one day I realised that I was practically the only one who had this 'external' vision of the *freguesia*. When I showed several people the maps and aerial photos, they simply could not identify any features at all: that flat depiction of their reality had no translation in terms of the 'high' and 'low' attributes of a terrain that was lived with the feet and breath. South and north did not correspond to the pragmatic use of points of reference such as quarries, types of vegetation and *hortas*; the rows of houses seen from above in a map had nothing to do with the social marking of space by means of neighbours' names and relationships. Only the president of the *Junta* immediately understood what those representations depicted, since after all he was the 'translator' between the local population and the state administration.

I first approached Pardais a few months before fieldwork began. I still recall a child I talked to at the time. I did not know then that he would later become one of the most enthusiastic guests in my house for the drawing sessions that were to take place there. The first contact with the village was physical and very impressionistic: I was attracted to the sensuousness of the whitewashed houses, the intensity of light, the sky as blue as in a slide, the orange orchards threatened in their integrity by the piles of debris from the quarries. Then I met the president of the *Junta*. *Senhor* (Sr.) Morais was very reserved. He understood quite rapidly that my work could be advantageous for the *freguesia*. A few days later I sent him a letter stating that I had chosen Pardais for my fieldwork, a letter to which he wrote a prompt and enthusiastic reply. A few weeks later I travelled to the village in order to find a residence. It was a frustrating move: according to Sr. Morais there was not a single vacant house.

The fact that I was to live in the village was an unprecedented event. Therefore, there was no precise formula for dealing with this new fact. Without family in the surroundings, not being anyone's client, furthermore being a man and single, I did not seem to fulfil any socially acceptable requisite, other than the fact that I was a 'doctor' (in Portugal, people with university degrees are immediately called 'doctors', thus acquiring a great deal of status) and that I was going 'to write a book on the village'. As such, he suggested that I should look for an apartment or small hotel room in the town of Vila Viçosa; this was actually seen as more appropriate for my status. The notion of 'wanting to live with the local people', which I repeated endlessly, seemed to him somewhat absurd. I insisted so much that I even 'threatened' to chose another village for my fieldwork. Then, Sr. Morais remembered that the Capucho family (which later I realised was the most powerful local family) had a vacant garage that had been renovated into a sort of reception hall for parties. It was inhabitable and nobody was using it. I did not even visit it: I wanted a real house where I could sleep, work, welcome guests and cook. This notion of 'cooking' added an extra flavour to my socially bizarre status. He did however promise to keep on searching. And so I drove back to Lisbon.

Many weeks of anxious waiting followed. Finally, a telephone call came through: 'It seems like there is a house after all. It belongs to an old woman who is currently living at her daughter's'. I left for the village almost immediately, where Sr. Morais explained to me that the owner of the house – Maria do Só – did not want to rent it out. She had said that she had her plants there and all of her belongings. The house had been on a sort of stand-by ever since her husband had passed away. One day she would go back home: probably never, but nevertheless it was important for her existential peace to know that she had a home she could go back to. Sr. Morais suggested that I approach her daughter and son-in-law. They also turned me down in a euphemistic way: the rent was to be extremely high. Once more I drove back to Lisbon – having left Sr. Morais in charge of negotiating a lower rent – and waited.

A few more weeks went by. At last, Sr. Morais called saying that they had accepted my rent proposition, as long as the *Junta* took charge of building a small hut in the patio to store Maria do Só's plants. Happy but nervous, I left for Pardais on a bright autumn day.

Maria do Só was an eighty-year-old woman who complained about several ailments and illnesses. After her husband's death, she had moved to her daughter's house, in Fonte Soeiro, a settlement one kilometre away from Pardais. Her daughter runs a *venda*, a small grocery store in the front part of her house. Her son-in-law is an electrician, working for the marble industry. He has secondary-level education and his father is a rather famous local character, a self-made librarian in the Ducal Palace in Vila Viçosa. What was now 'my house', was a renovated old house: the new rooms had walls of brick and concrete that could not keep the cold and the heat out. The chimney had disappeared, and instead there was a gas stove. The whole house was decorated throughout with all sorts of knickknacks; I asked permission to store them away in boxes, claiming that I wanted to safeguard them, but the truth was that I had a rather difficult aesthetic relationship with them.

I was finally settled. I let myself fall back on a chair. I tried to calm down. The chirping of birds helped. A whole year was ahead of me. I trembled with fear and enthusiasm. How would I ever manage to get entry to the village? That was how I started the compilation of maps and statistics and published information. The look from without: the slow construction of a real and metaphorical home for a stranger.

The physical village, that which I first observed during fieldwork was the houses themselves. There is a striking opposition between the old houses and those that have been built after the 1960s. The former have lath-and-plaster or brick walls and are all whitewashed. The latter, made of brick and concrete, are two-storied and painted in colours or covered with ceramic tiles. Whether old or new, they are lined up along the streets, in the very urbanised manner that has become a characteristic of Alentejo: since most residents in the past were landless, houses and villages are places of residence, not of work. Today, most houses are rented, they do not belong to their dwellers, so urban space is tight, there being very few houses with patios or vegetable gardens. In the case of Pardais, however, streets do not constitute a net, an urban web on a small scale. The village seems to have grown around the walls of *Quinta dos Passos*. This is a *casa de lavrador* (estate owner's house); a rather small one, although bearing the signs of social precedence and even pretensions to nobility. Attached to it is a large orchard and garden, entirely walled in. Along the outside of these walls one can find the older houses in the village, built in terraced-house fashion, like barracks. These were the dwellings of landless workers, each home being distinguishable only by means of individual chimney and door number.

The more recent houses have been built along newer streets. The oldest nucleus of the village is basically the terraced-houses along Rua das Escadinhas or Rua Padre Espanca, facing the church. The church was built in 1910, when it replaced the cemetery chapel, outside the village. Another early core is a row-house complex adjacent to the main entrance of *Quinta dos Passos*, in Rua dos Passos; lastly, there is the Praça, the only real square in the village, although not the traditional central *praça* or *plaza* of southern Iberia.

Most of the houses in *montes* and *hortas* (small homestead and homes with space for vegetable gardens and/or fruit trees) are also very old. The origins of the *freguesia* actually have to do with the high concentration of *hortas*, originally holding water mills for grain grinding. The more recent sections are located in Rua da Igreja or Rua do Lavadouro, in Bairro das Pedreiras, and Rua Nova da Igreja. The street named Casas Novas (New Houses) misleads the observer with its name: it is actually a name that refers back to the nineteenth century, when the village first expanded to the Ribeira area. One hundred forty-eight houses were built before 1919, thirty-four between 1919 and 1945, forty-two between 1946 and 1970, thirty-nine between 1971 and 1980, and twenty-five after 1981.

Even before one starts going inside people's homes, just walking along the streets helps one build a sense of local history, of social stratification, and of changes in taste. Older houses are occupied either by older people or people with lower incomes. The more recent ones show signs of prestige such as ceramic tiles, a second story, verandas and garages. They depict the social climbing that resulted from selling land for marble exploration, from trade, or even from the wages earned in the quarries. One of these streets was begun in the late 1980s. Its houses are single family homes, with their own private gardens, in which specialised workers, such as machine operators and electricians from the marble industry, live. The president of the *Junta* has an ambitious plan of expansion and urbanisation for an empty space near the village. The blueprints show a preference for a criss-cross street display around a central square, which can eventually replace *Quinta dos Passos* as the symbolic focal point of an *ancien régime* society.

Besides the *Quinta dos Passos*, the village has also another 'lordly' house, the *Quinta do Panasco*. Apart from these references to nobility, there are a series of public and official buildings: the *Junta* of the *freguesia*, which holds also the Day Care Centre for the elderly; the *Casa do Povo*[3] (civic centre), which includes the small medical centre. The village has three stores: one is still of the *venda* type (family grocery store run out of someone's house), while the other two, referred to as 'mini-markets', emulate the supermarket model and are dependent on a national wholesale grocery distributor. To these one should add the two bakeries; the village also has an elementary school, a kindergarten, a Church, a public laundry tank, two public toilets and baths, one *touril* (bullfight arena), and two cafés. There are no longer any *tabernas* (taverns) and there are not yet any restaurants. The cemetery, with its chapel, and the football field complete the public facilities of the village.

Besides the village of Pardais proper, the people identify three other settlements in the *freguesia*: Fonte Soeiro, Azenha Cimeira and Monte Claro. The remaining population lives in *hortas* along the stream and in a few scattered *montes*.

Facts and Figures II

In the census of domestic groups which I conducted, I identified 246 groups in the *freguesia*. Two of them, however, should not be included in the count: one was composed of two families from Ribatejo province who were temporarily (for a few months) camped on a tomato field that they had hired for planting and harvesting; the other was myself. My data is mainly qualitative, including names, date of birth, profession, children's school or job situation, kinship ties with other groups and so on. This data was later compared with the results from the State's official census of 1991. In this official statistic, the number of 'Classic Family Questionnaires' (the closer category to that of 'domestic group') is 252. There is a discrepancy of six units; this has to do with the inclusion, in the official census, of the two Ribatejan families and of some groups that

dwell in houses which actually do not belong to the *freguesia*. The official population was 661 (330 men and 331 women), whereas in my data
it is 323 men and 336 women, adding up to a total of 659 people.

Some aspects of the structure of population and social stratification
can be extrapolated from this data, specifically those related to aspects of
gender. Thus, regarding sex and age structure, an age pyramid would
depict the general tendency common in the Alentejo: an ageing population. Pardais, however, shows a relative strengthening of the young
strata, a trend more typical of larger administrative centres than of rural
villages. This is probably a reflection of a recent population settlement
due to jobs in the quarries.

As for the evolution of the population since 1864 (the year of the first
national census), the population decrease after the 1970s is due mainly
to change of place of residence from the village to the town of Vila
Viçosa, rather than to emigration abroad. Migration to the suburbs of
Lisbon and Setúbal was a common strategy in the 1950s and 1960s, and
temporary emigration to Switzerland has become a common trend in
São Romão, but not at all so in Pardais.

According to Nazareth (1988), the province of Alentejo had a decrease
in population from 770,965 in 1960 to 585,000 in 1980, that is 24.1
percent fewer in all places with under 10,000 inhabitants; population
increased only in the higher echelon towns and cities (31.9 percent more).
Places with more than 2,000 inhabitants decreased by 14.8 percent.
Places between 2,000 and 5,000 inhabitants decreased by 38.1 percent,
corresponding to rural centres that went, between 1960 and 1981, below
the threshold of two-hundred inhabitants, that being the reason why the
decrease in places between one-hundred and two-hundred inhabitants
does not seem to be high (8.9 percent). The maximum decrease was in
isolates with less than one-hundred inhabitants: 55.5 percent.

Therefore in the period of highest national emigration (the 1960s),
Alentejo had relatively low rates, since leaving the land meant mostly
going to Lisbon or Setúbal. This does not however, contradict the generalised idea that Alentejo has been going through a process of depopulation. The age pyramids for Alentejo regularly show a narrow base and
a large top. Those for 1980 show a diminishing importance of the young
active population of both sexes. Return was not important, considering
that emigration had not been important either. For the region of Alentejo in 1980, 20.7 percent of the population was between ages 0 and 14,
63.2 percent between 15 and 64, and 16.1 percent over 65 (Pardais,
1991, 0–14: 18.20 percent; 15–64: 64.33 percent; 65+: 17.45 percent).

In sum, the Alentejo is the Portuguese region with the lowest percentage of young people and the highest of elderly people.

Unemployment statistics for 1984, the most recent available at time of fieldwork (C.M.V.V. 1985) showed that the total number of people unemployed in Pardais was 116. Of these, however, only eleven were men, and 105 were women. Twenty-two of the total received unemployment aid, and they were all women. This gender division of unemployment is an important factor, since it shows a situation of almost full male employment – a result of the marble industry; but it shows a blatant female unemployment – a result of agricultural decadence. Data can deceive; however, one has to take into account that women's agricultural activity is seasonal (olive picking, working in the vineyards, eucalyptus planting, tomato crops etc.), and they tend to apply for unemployment aid during the periods between tasks. Also, in many cases (especially those of couples where the man is a semi-specialised skilled worker in the quarries), female unemployment has become a twisted form of social climbing, by means of the incorporation by the women of a new bourgeois identity – that of *doméstica* (housewife).

Let us now take a look at my classification of jobs and occupations of the adult population. The official statistical criteria include young people who have abandoned school and started working after the age of fifteen. However, there are young men of thirteen working in Pardais, but I will follow the standard criteria used in demography. As for men, 136 were directly attached to the marble industry in one way or another. As I shall demonstrate elsewhere in the book, the sector has its own hierarchy at work, meaning different social identities. At the bottom of the hierarchy there were, in 1991, three apprentices and sixty-eight *cabouqueiros* (literally 'diggers', but I shall refer to them henceforth as 'workers'). There were fifteen machine-saw operators (although they distinguish blade, diamond, and sand-saw operators); and twenty-four machine operators. At the top of the hierarchy, there were eighteen foremen (whether quarry foremen or personnel foremen). In trades directly connected to the marble industry, there were three locksmiths, one mechanic and two electricians and, finally, in white-collar jobs, three office clerks.

Also not connected with agriculture, the other main sector of employment is the construction business and diverse types of jobs: there were ten bricklayers, two machine operators and four cleaning or gardening workers in the municipality. Only sixteen men were somehow in commerce or services: one taxi driver, ten merchants (in bakeries, butcher-shops, coal selling and cafés), one auto-shop owner, two office clerks, one secondary-school teacher, one policeman and two butcher apprentices. The agricultural sector mobilised a total of twenty men: one estate owner, eight farmers, two cattle owners, two tractor drivers, three agricultural foremen, two shepherds, two grooms and one horse rider. Finally, the total number of retired or invalid men was seventy, amounting to twenty-six percent. Women employed in services and commerce were: one elementary-school teacher, three office clerks, two civil servants, two kindergarten teachers and one laboratory assistant; three café co-owners (with their husbands), four in grocery stores, four in bakeries and one as a shop attendant. Sixteen women were housemaids, thirteen cleaning and kitchen workers in shops and municipal offices.

The agricultural sector employed a total number of seventy women. However, only two declared their activity as 'polyvalent farmers', that is people who actually live off their own land. Of the remainder, thirty-eight were permanent workers on vineyards and eucalyptus plantations, and thirty-two had declared a 'last seasonal activity', whether in grape, tomato or olive picking. Apart from one worker in a tripe factory nearby and one woman who had been employed in a now shut-down copper mine, ninety-two declared themselves to be 'incapable' and/or retired, and thirty-three did not declare any occupation. The percentage of invalid or retired women was 33.82 percent.

I had, from a certain moment on, a structural image of the village life. There was an almost exclusive dependence on the marble industry, in which the majority of workers have no specialised activity. In that sense the old landless workers tradition was being followed. The difference however, was that this new occupation was now a steady one, a year-round job, even though company and employer mobility was high, due to the great number of enterprises and the relative scarcity of labour. If landless workers were not somehow proletarians themselves, one could talk of a proletarianisation process. However, from a symbolic point of view, being a form of extraction of something from the land, work in the quarries has some characteristics of agricultural work. Much of the peasant world view has thus been kept; a lot more has been lost, or probably was never there among people who never owned land. I believe that the lack of land ownership, the fact that it is was not the property of those who worked on it, and that it did not constitute a resource for inheritance and the focus of the reproductive strategy of domestic groups, greatly facilitated the change towards marble extraction.

21

The anthropologist's critical use of statistics can be demonstrated in a small exercise that helped me see how important it was to understand the meaning and practice of relationships rather than the eminent structure behind numbers. If we take the commonly held idea that a family is made up of a married couple, a father and a mother in the biological and social sense, living together with their single children, it is very easy to realise that this is also the ideal model in the village. Furthermore, its perpetuation has been helped by the fact that in the historical socio-economic structures of the Alentejo, the nuclear family has been the main reproductive strategy. There has thus been a fortunate overlapping between folk, state, and church models of the family. However, from an anthropological point of view, studies on the developmental cycle of domestic groups or on bachelorhood, to mention only two examples, have provided us with a rather more dynamic and heterodox picture of people's practices. Let us see how many domestic groups in the ethnographic present in Pardais did not correspond to the commonly held model, as well as the variety of situations identified. I have excluded from this exercise those cases where the couple, due to old age, does not have children living at home, a situation which local morality accepts.

In a sum-total of 246 domestic groups, there were eighty-seven cases outside the model, that is thirty-five percent of the total. Many cases of elderly widows fit the local morals of acceptability, and they amount to twenty-three cases. If we exclude them from the exercise, the number of atypical cases drops to sixty-four. Widowed men living alone are not acceptable in many contexts, since they are supposed to live with their children, preferably with a married daughter. However, if we do assimilate them with their female counterparts, the number of atypical cases drops further to fifty-seven. One should at this point exclude the special cases of the anthropologist and the two families from Ribatejo, thus leaving us with fifty-five cases. Of these, we have: eleven single men and six single women; nine men and women who are either separated or divorced; three young couples living with the man's parents and two living with the woman's parents; four couples living with the father or mother of the wife; one case of second wedding; one case of co-residence with an employee; six declared cases of unregistered marriage (*juntos*, i.e., a situation of unmarried couples); four cases of a wedding registered only after the birth of the first child; two adoptions; eight cases of sons and four of daughters living with their parents beyond the age of fertility; two cases of co-residence between single brother and single sister and one case of three single sisters residing together.

All these cases contradict, in one way or another, the model of the family supported by folk, state or church (and indeed by many an anthropologist too). They represent twenty-one percent of the domestic groups. This is by no means a small percentage, which leads us to think about how practices do not always (if ever) correspond to preferential rules: to marry forever and faithfully before thirty, to live in one's house, to have legitimate children, to take care of parents in their old age.

Past Present

When I was looking for a house in the village, one of the possibilities presented by the president of the *Junta* was that of boarding at Altino Valente's house. According to Sr. Morais, Valente lived alone in a large house and the fact that he was Sr. Morais's godfather could facilitate the approach. Theoretically, that is. The hypothesis suggested by the president was little more than rhetorical. The list of Sr. Altino's faults was immediately presented to me: he was supposedly a grumpy old man, who strangely liked to live alone, he did not like to share things too much. I was told it would be very difficult living with him. Throughout the year of fieldwork this same opinion was to be conveyed to me by both young and old. The heart of the matter, as I soon was to find out, was his status as a single man, who had a fair amount of savings accumulated from the time when he had been a *seareiro*, a sharecropper.

During my first days in the village I had my meals at one of the cafés. That was how I met Sr. Altino, who is the only person in the village who takes his regular meals there. He seemed like a very affable, generous and loving man. He was always eager to supply me with all sorts of information and was the only person who actually cried with emotion when I left the village and said good-bye to him. The exclusion of which he was a victim, inflicted on him by his neighbours (namely the children who were afraid of his fury when they played football in front of his house, banging the ball against his walls and, indeed, windows), was to become one of the threads that I followed to discover the codes of masculinity. Sr. Altino's 'problem' was composed of a set of culturally negative traits: he was a bachelor; he spent too much time at home; that time was spent alone; he attended church regularly; he ate at the café but did not drink or take part in commensality; he was a client of the two powerful families. However, this did not preclude Sr. Altino from being the man with the largest number of godchildren, both of baptism and wedding.

I spent several afternoons in the first weeks at his home. In the living room – an uncommon room in local houses – the setting included a central table, with four ornate chairs around it; a few other chairs were located in the corners of the room. A large, framed photograph of himself hung on the wall: it portrayed him as a child, dressed as a girl. He said that was how his mother liked to have him dressed, although it is known that such was a common practice in the turn of the century. The whole atmosphere of the house interior had an old feeling to it, as if social status had been thoroughly objectified in furniture, pictures, and other objects.

During those first weeks, when I was not with him, or otherwise strolling around the village to make myself seen and get acquainted with as many people as possible, I would be diligently taking notes from Padre Espanca's *Memoirs*. Padre Espanca was a Catholic priest and Vila Viçosa's local sage and historian. He lived during the second half of the nineteenth century and was for a time Pardais' resident priest. He wrote several volumes on the history of Vila Viçosa, the royal House of Bragança, critical commentary on the liberal and anti-church policies of his time, and a few but incomplete portrayals of rural life in Pardais. I would also take notes from the *Róis de Confessados*, the censuses that priests carried out in order to find who had paid church contributions and who had confessed during Easter – a precious source of historical information in Catholic countries, since these *Róis* (i.e., 'log-books') mention land, property, occupation, kinship ties etc., for the entire population. Somehow – although I had already abandoned the 'look from afar' and the sociological and geographical generalisations – I was still refusing to plunge into the world of the quarries, the cafés and lively interaction with and among people. I was letting myself be seduced by history, by the old world of landless workers, large estate owners, sharecroppers, rural foremen and the constant state of unease and revolt involving state, church, and social classes. The same kind of world so vividly described by Picão (1983 [1903]) and still identifiable in Cutileiro (1977 [1971]).

Sr. Altino's life story is an emblem of a type of social identity closely associated with agriculture and relations of production motivated by the structure of land ownership. It is an interesting tale to follow, since it links both with local social transformations of historical importance, as well as gender and masculinity. I will allow Sr. Altino Valente to speak for himself, even though the translation into English makes it impossible to convey the flavour of the local dialect and archaic expressions. Still, I have kept the rhythm and 'mistakes' in syntax:

24

Sr. Altino was born in 1913. 'When I was a child, my parents lived with no difficulties ... and then I grew up. I studied until I was twelve, I was always dumb with letters, I did not learn, and so my father (may he rest in peace) – and since my brother had completed the fourth grade – wanted me to have the fourth grade too. We had to go to Évora, sixty years ago, the exams were there, but I fell ill and did not take the exam. I asked my father not to make me study. I wanted to work along with his employees that he had. So they put a mare in my hands, and I went and did the sowing with one of the workers. And that is how I started in that life.

'Then one day, I was twenty, my father (may he rest in peace) passed away. We had that property over there rented [*Quinta do Panasco*]. I stayed there with my mother for four years. And then, I do not know why, the property owner became cross with us, he threw us out. We left the place and came to that house down there, my [female] cousin's, near where *senhor doutor* [literally "mister doctor", he is referring to me] is, and we stayed there for a few years. From there I moved to this house. Then I rented *Fonte da Moura* and entertained myself with that during the day, while in the evenings I would work at the *Casa do Povo*, on Sundays that is. I was there for thirty-five years and eight months, in the *Casa do Povo* that is. That's where I get my retirement money from.

'My parents were from Alandroal. My mother was born in a *herdade* [large estate], a big one – it's the *Conjeito* – on the way to Redondo. My grandfather paid rent for those *herdades*, both *Conjeito* and *Val do Pio*. Or was it not? Well, anyway, my father was from the region of ... I don't even know the name of the *monte* [isolated farm house in a large estate, where sharecroppers lived] where he was born, but he was from Mina do Bugalho. They married when they were twenty-something, or thirty years old, something like that. That was ... my mother, it will be now twenty-eight years on May 19th that she passed away, in this house. My father and my brother passed away there at *Panasco's*... and I was born in 1913. My brother was four years older than me and my mother was yet to have a girl, a stillborn or something like that, so, maybe in 1905, something like that, maybe they were married. I think that my father, when he married, he went straight on to live at *Torneiros* and – what was the other *herdade's* name? – *Igrejinha*, that's it. Nearby Vila Boim. My brother was born there (...).

'From there they came to Vila Viçosa. My father bought a plot, a large plot of land and rented this farm. The *Panasco* farm; and he paid rent for *Nave de Baixo* also. The *Quinta do Panasco* belonged to a sister of Sr. Manuel Joaquim da Costa. He administered all that, since his sister was not sane, poor thing, she had some mental disease. Then he passed it on to his nephews … it was Dr Botelheiro. So it was that Dr Botelheiro's daughters got it for themselves. It was Dona Virgínia, who was Dr Botelheiro's wife. Today it belongs to that Ferreira do Amaral. I think he is Minister of Public Works, I think…

'So I was alone with my mother. We would pay the rents, I would work on the farm and a servant, a hired hand, would come and we would do all the work there. Everything. My mother was administrating the house, of course. She had a woman working there. First she had a permanent housemaid, but then … she didn't. We stayed there for four years and something. It was then we came to my uncle's house. This [female] cousin of mine, you know, that was her father's inheritance. That house and a *courela* [small plot of land] further down and plus I do not know how much, forty *contos* in cash? It was a lot then. My cousin's husband, he was from here [Pardais]. And he went and married her in Alandroal. Then, since he had some property here … his and his brothers'. It was his father's, of course.

'When I went to my cousin's house, I had nothing. I was just doing a small plot of land out there and… I was a *seareiro* [sharecropper], I became a sharecropper. I stopped having a larger *lavoura* [farming; as a noun it means land, utensils and the activity itself], and had now a smaller one. Then I moved here, my mother was still living. When I rented *Fonte da Moura*, my mother did not last long (…). *Fonte da Moura* belonged to the Conceições. They lend me this house too. *Fonte da Moura* is a four *moios* [ancient measure] of wheat land. They were average lands. One can not say they were good, but they were not bad either. After I left it – or should I say after they took it away from me, to explore the quarries? – I never rented anything else. I became attached to the *Casa do Povo* until I retired.

'When they took the land away from me, there were some holes opened already. And then, when I left, there were seven or eight quarries working, to such an extent that some of them were not profitable, the stone was no good. It was not enough to cover expenses and to pay the rent, so they closed them up. I, when they took the land away from me, I still asked the ladies [the Conceição sisters] to give me a bit of land there, to let me do a bit of farming. But they told me they had already given away everything. They had given it to their godchildren, first to Fernando. Then Quim and his brother opened up another quarry. Then the Galrões did too. Then the Saloios. That one there, Pardal, the father of the one who has the bakery down there, he opened one too. That huge quarry from Marmetal company, it was two small quarries when I was still renting the place (...) Godchildren! Ah! They weren't really godchildren. One of them was, the eldest he was Senhora Gertrudes' godson, the eldest of the ladies, but they really were cousins. Second cousins, those Capuchos were. Their father, he was the ladies' first cousin. The father of these three brothers. The four, I should say, they are three boys and a girl.

'At one time I had my marriage arranged with a lady. Here in this house. And this lady, when there was just one month to go until the wedding, she gave up. I was sore at the time, because my wedding god-mother (the godfather was one of the Conceições, I had no trouble invit-ing godparents because it was them who volunteered) was my cousin from down there, the one who passed away. She was to be my god-mother, on my side. On the lady's side it was to be her brother and sis-ter. But she backed off and sent a boy here, the husband of one of her goddaughters, to say that she was willing to marry again. Then I sent a message saying that this time it was I who was not willing! I never thought about marriage again. I still courted some girl out there, but it did not look right, I was already fifty. It looked ugly. I still thought about marrying another girl, but then her family didn't want me to court her.

'My first fiancée I met her... Well, Sr. António Simões, I worked a lot with him. For twenty-something years. And he had an accident over there in Lisbon. I went there to see him. And when he came back home, I went to see him again. The lady in question was a seamstress in the house. I do not know why, but I felt a certain sympathy towards her and so I came home and wrote to her. So we entertained ourselves for a few months, maybe one year, exchanging letters and not making any deci-sion. One day in Vila Viçosa I said "well, this can't go on like this, writ-ing to each other". I was forty. Almost fifty. So one day I came across her, went up to her and said: "This can't go on like this. I would appreciate a decision, yes or no?" I wanted to organise my life. So she came to visit my place, to see what was here, what was lacking, and so we arranged for our wedding. A month before, she wrote me a letter saying she did not want to go through with it.'

Aspects of the Old Society

Alentejo is part of the Mediterranean area of *latifundia* property and land organisation. Great landowners possess all the goods pertaining to all agricultural categories (grazing land, pastures, wheat land, woods, vegetable gardens, vineyards and so on). In some cases the assets had a large geographical distribution, as was the case with church properties or some aristocratic houses. Another kind of property was that of municipalities, *misericórdias* (mutual-help religious societies) and the royal family (namely the House of Bragança). Most properties were rented out, the tenant paying a *foro* or *cens*, a part of the *emphitheusis* relationship. The contracts were either perpetual or lasted three lifetimes. The variation was mostly regarding inheritance. On the one hand there was sharing, and on the other hand the person designated received the totality of assets. *Herdades* belonged to either one proprietor *in solidum* or to several *pro indiviso*. In the latter case there were frequent inconveniences. One of the proprietors (the landlord) was responsible for the cultivation and was in charge of drawing up the renting contract. The others only received their proportion of profits. This was due to the division of inheritance, to the fear of dividing one *herdade*, thus making it difficult to cultivate.

The usual contract was that of renting, but there were also places where those who cultivated the land had to pay a percentage of the crop (from one sixth to one ninth) to either the king or a concessionaire. The situation of those peasants was analogous to that of *seareiros*, who were the real equivalent of the English sharecropper. The *seareiro* only had a right over the crop. The great transformation and opening up of wild land in the late nineteenth century was really their work; they would cultivate second-rate land; but the name *seareiro* is also used to refer to any farmer who rents a small piece of land. *Herdades* were either rented in whole or in small fractions to *seareiros*, in exchange for one quarter, one fifth or one sixth of the production.

For centuries, the typical farmer in Alentejo has been the *lavrador rendeiro* (tenant farmer). Tradition established that renewal of the tenancy agreement was automatic, unless either the tenant or the landlord renounced it, in May. Rent was paid in cereal, but in the late nineteenth century cash payments were introduced, amounting to twenty-five to thirty percent of net production.

The resulting social class division was between large landowners, *lavradores*, *seareiros* and *jornaleiros* (wage earners, workers). Properties belonged mostly to *morgadios* (*morgados* were the eldest sons of landowners; the institution was abolished with the Liberal revolution of the mid nineteenth century) or religious institutions, and the profits were transmitted to Lisbon, where the absentee landowners lived. This situation generated the existence of a great number of intermediaries contracted by the absentees, who sub-let the land. There was also, however, direct exploration, in which the owner cultivated his land via a manager, which was not quite the same as a tenancy situation.

Lavrador only applied to those who actually conducted an agricultural enterprise of considerable dimension. Thus, the *lavrador* was one who had a lot of land, and the *seareiro* one who had less. The notion does not depend on land ownership. *Lavradores* were not a truly homogeneous social class, since there were great differences in scale. What distinguished them from the *seareiro* was the fact that they owned ploughs and farm-work animals. So the *lavrador* occupied a *herdade*, the *seareiro* a *courela*. Size was important. The *seareiros* had a historical connection with the distribution and division into *courelas* of the *herdades* belonging to the House of Bragança and the Order of Avis, and were also favoured by the regular cultivation of *baldios*, the municipal communal land. The *seareiros* also had a historic role in the late nineteenth century of cultivating the last untamed land in the area. Eventually as the farming of cereal began to require large amounts of capital and machinery, it became too intensive for the *seareiros* who had only ploughs and oxen at their disposal. Thus began their decline.

Workers have always been the symbol of Alentejo. The saga of famine and social revolt has always been associated with them and, since the Second World War, with the strong support for the Communist Party in Alentejo. The labour force had become too numerous by the time that mechanised agricultural processes were implemented. The relationship of production established between the owner of the means of production and the direct producer was of a capitalist nature. The worker's ambition was to have a contract, to have steady employment, but most of all to become a *seareiro* by means of buying a couple of work animals. In general, though, workers were a true 'labour reserve army'. The workers were among the most politically active in the period after the fall of dictatorship in 1974, occupying land and establishing labour co-operatives. Agrarian Reform was implemented, with nationalisation of the large estates by the pro-Communist government. By the late 1970s, with the establishment of regular democracy and Portugal's adhesion to the EEC, it was over.

The social and economic history of Alentejo can thus be summarised. The first period, between the twelfth and the fifteenth centuries, was the result of the re-conquest of the south from the Arabs, during which the original *foral* law (concession of local administration by the king) prevailed. The second period, from the bourgeois revolution of 1383 and the period of Discoveries on, was characterised by the action of the centralised mercantile state; this continued into the early nineteenth century. Thirdly, in Portugal's first attempt at entering the industrial revolution and advanced democracy, the parliamentary state, based on commerce and industry, started with the Liberal revolution of the first half of the nineteenth century. Finally, it should be added that between 1928 and 1974, the dictatorial regime conducted a policy of political repression and protection of the interests of the *latifundia* owners.

The greatest changes occurred during the third period. These changes were witnessed at the local level by Padre Espanca, and which were written about in his *Memoirs*. In 1832, all feudal legal remains were abolished, including the crown assets. In 1863 religious orders were abolished as well as the *morgadio* status. In the south, the consequences were the strengthening of land concentration, by means of transfer of massive amounts of land from the old dominions to the hands of the bourgeoisie that purchased them in auction, so that the indirect exploitation of land continued, based on renting, sharecropping and *emphitheusis*.

Eventually the system was eroded due to migration, unemployment, raise in wages and diminishing number of *seareiros*. This resulted in intensification of land cultivation and the abandoning of lower quality land. The Portuguese anthropologist José Cutileiro carried out fieldwork in a village not far from Pardais in the 1960s. Land ownership, in his account, was still the cornerstone of social stratification. Around the village there were groups of small properties whose owners were local residents. They were the result of the divisions of *baldios*, public municipal land, in 1874. Wheat was still the main crop at the time of fieldwork. *Lavradores* were extremely dependent on governmental agricultural policies, and generally the intensification of wheat production stimulated by dictator Salazar was failing miserably, and forest plantation was becoming an alternative. Cutileiro's *freguesia* had a population of 480, of which only twenty-six had property large enough to allow them to live without looking for work on other people's land as *seareiros* or wage earners: they were the *proprietários*, who owned twenty-one percent of the land. Twenty-five percent belonged to small land owners who also worked as *seareiros*. The main social groups included the *latifundia* owners, characterised by a strong class consciousness; the *proprietários*, who invested greatly in symbolic distinction and who, as opposed to *latifundiários*, had no foremen or overseers mediating between them and the workers; the *seareiros*, based on family labour and paying one-quarter or one-fifth of their crops to the landowner; and *jornaleiros*, who were constantly looking for yearly, monthly, weekly or daily jobs.

The intense exploration of marble in Pardais, which started in the late 1960s, mobilised the local labour force, preventing it from becoming a revolutionary potential. Property structures were also changed. Most land was rented out for quarries, and profits soon made the rents worthless. Agricultural activity was soon abandoned and replaced by the 'marble economy' or the 'white gold', as the local trope goes. The present image of abandonment in the Alentejo is not so obvious in Pardais. Elsewhere, and since the post-revolutionary agrarian reform has failed to redistribute land, Alentejo is both depopulated or undergoing an unemployment crisis. European agricultural policy has made the Alentejo virtually unprofitable, and land has been converted either into huge tourist hunting reservations or for the ecologically negative eucalyptus forest plantation (for the paper industry).

In Pardais, at the cost of total land excavation, there were jobs at the time of fieldwork. However, the dependence on the world markets for marble, the absence of a processing industry, and the lack of planning so often characteristic of fast profit making enterprises could at any moment generate a crisis similar to the rest of the region.

NOTES

1. Gregory (1984) says that the difficulty arising from the gender of the anthropologist is a myth and that with personal effort and methodological precision one can obtain access to the 'female world'. That could be true, but it does not preclude that – in contexts of extreme gender division – few occasions exist for inter-gender contact. Also, when such occasions are available, women informants do not necessarily sexually neutralise the anthropologist. The field experience in Alentejo reported by some female colleagues indicates that it is easier for women anthropologists to gain access to the masculine world. This is of course related to gender stereotypes that associate gender and the division of labour, thus masculinising scientific work. One should, therefore, be very careful about reaching conclusions on this topic: class may be a more relevant variable than gender, as anthropologist Diana Hill (with fieldwork in the Alentejo) remarked in personal conversation.

2. Portuguese administrative and political divisions: 1) Districts (total number of eighteen); 2) These are divided into *Concelhos* or municipalities. Each has a *Câmara* (Town Assembly) with a *Presidente* (Mayor). There are over three hundred *concelhos*. Vila Viçosa is a *concelho* in the *distrito* of Évora; 3) Each *concelho*

is divided into *freguesias* (townships). These are the equivalent of the old parishes, and they also have an assembly and a *Junta* (Board) with a President.

3. *Casas do Povo* were civic centres established in each village by Salazar's dictatorial, corporative regime. They were supposed to be the peasant's corporation, providing medical assistance, insurance plans, retirement plans, and also held cultural events and, of course, propaganda sessions. The system has been deactivated but the buildings remain, being used as town halls for assemblies, elections and *bailes* (dances).

2. Blood, Sweat, and Semen
Masculinities in the Village

The Baile

*M*y interaction with a group of working age men started during a *baile* (dance).[1] When I entered the *Casa do Povo* (the local Civic Centre), at about 10 p.m. I couldn't find anyone that I had already met. Only two couples were dancing: a man and a woman, and two women. In the bar next to the dance hall I found Altino Morais (uncle of the President of the *Junta* and godson of Altino Valente, whose name he carried). He wore a beautiful, slightly scornful smile, a sad expression and a traditional rugged three-layered woollen cape with a fur collar. Being more at ease with the elderly, I joined him. He told me how dances used to be in the old times; then, *concertinas* (a squeezebox) and *gaitas* (harmonicas) were played, people sang the *saias* and danced in circles, exchanging partners endlessly. Dances were always held in private homes and thus were not open to all.

More people started to arrive. The bar – a male preserve – was becoming crowded. In a sort of preparatory stage for going to a dance, many men had already been drinking at the café. One of them, an obviously drunk heavy-built young man, fell on the ground next to me. I helped him stand up and asked the young man who accompanied him whether it would not be better to have the other drink some water. I bought him a bottle of water and persuaded him to drink it. He was quite obviously grateful as he muttered incomprehensibly to me. His companion, Leonel, immediately started talking to me.

Leonel is twenty-eight years old and works in the quarries owned by one of the Capuchos, a powerful local family. He went to school until the eighth grade, making him somewhat special in the local milieu and, according to him, he would have liked to have studied further had it been possible. His parents are old and retired and had been poor landless workers. The house where he lives with his parents, brother and sister, is paid for by himself and his younger brother, who works as a stable hand for one of the Capuchos, an equestrian bullfighter. The younger sister takes care of the domestic chores and only occasionally works outside the home. The elder brother works as machine operator in a quarry which affords him and his wife comfortable means as well as their own home. Leonel would like to dedicate more time to two hobbies he enjoys: drawing and reading science-fiction novels. He is one of the few people who uses the Gulbenkian Foundation travelling library. Following my initial conversation with Leonel and his friends I was to be identified by many people as a writer, thus replacing a previous identification as a priest....

Leonel wears pointed cowboy boots, jeans, a necklace, and a denim jacket with lapel pins from rock bands; his favourite depicts a skull, a symbol very much associated with a trend in rock known as 'heavy metal'. Heavy metal is very popular among working-class and petit-bourgeois youth in the suburbs of Portugal's bigger cities. His motorcycle, although not an expensive model, has the looks of one. It is a good imitation, and stands out from the more utilitarian motorcycles used by most of his colleagues. He did his military service in nearby Beja and in Amadora, a suburb of Lisbon. In Amadora his duties frequently included standing guard at the barracks's entrance. Apparently, this situation allowed him to look and to be looked at, in a game of sexual possibilities. I eventually became used to the boastful, but ultimately more rhetorical than judgmental, manner in which these things were talked about. As Leonel warmed up, he recounted how he and forty of his comrades had sexual intercourse with a specific girl one night. In the conversation that followed, and many thereafter, 'women' were the central theme. 'Women', however, was not used in a neutral sense, but rather took on the meaning of *gajas* (chicks, broads) – the very opposite of girlfriend, wife or mother. Following this conversation I was invited to join in the circuit of discos and *boîtes* (sexually oriented night-clubs and bordellos): I was invited for an excursion into the world of 'those' women.

This was my introduction and entrance into the village's masculine world. Leonel, rhetoric aside, would eventually reveal himself to be an extremely sensitive and sympathetic person, and was a good friend until the end of my stay. Since the *baile* is in itself a very special situation of interaction, very different from everyday life, I will continue with that evening's recollections.

Zé Safado walked in, with his bright blue eyes defying his old age (he is Raposo's father; Raposo, already a father himself, will be mentioned again later on as he became one of my key informants on the world of work relations). Zé Safado did not wait too long to explain his philosophy: he is married, but since he earns 150 *contos* (150,000 escudos, approximately US $1,000) a month (a rather high salary for Portugal), it is not hard for him – in fact, he says that he 'can and must' – to spend twenty *contos* for a night out on the town. He spends the money on women, since for him 'all women are whores' (once again, women as a general category, not including specific wives, mothers, daughters...) and supposedly there is not one woman in the surrounding area who has not 'passed through his hands'. Sometimes he even goes to Badajoz, in Spain. He says he always asks his wife if she wants to join him on the trip; but 'since she always says no', he tells her that he is going with friends, and ends up coming back only the next day. Actually, what he does is telephone a certain number in Badajoz and 'they [the women] drive to the border to pick you up'.

Being a man, single, at the dance, and in the company of other men, seemed to lead the conversation to themes of sexual predation. It also allowed the scope of informants to broaden significantly and added human richness to my relationships in the field. Through Leonel, I met Beto. He would become an ever-present companion throughout the year. This situation was difficult at times as he became possessive of my time and company. In fact, a few months later I became the pawn in a dispute over my friendship between Beto, Leonel and Zé Ganhão, a third privileged companion in the field.

Beto starts his conversation with me by describing how hard it is to work in the quarries, but stressing that is no impediment to dedication to *borga* (having fun). There is no doubt about that. My head was already spinning, as it would spin endless times, in the face of what I can only classify as 'alcoholic excess'. There was excess in the circulation of drinks, in the volume of voices, in the juxtaposition of conversations, excess in the late hours, in stories told, in friendly and playful patting, hugging, joking and tender gestures.

As Beto starts talking, Zé Seco Jr. and his son come in. Zé Seco Jr. is very drunk. He immediately starts praising his father, the poet Zé Seco. His son (an angelic creature of fourteen, beer in one hand, cigarette in the other) was obviously bored by his father's repetitious declarations that I was the person who was to type up the poet's *décimas* (formulaic oral poetry) when he remembered to bring them to me. Furthermore, Zé Seco Jr. had to vie for my attention with Camilo, from Fonte Soeiro, who wanted desperately to offer his help in telling me the names of owners of different houses, fields and farms in the outskirts of the village.[2]

The night goes on. As dawn approaches it is time for fighting scenes to start, if they are to happen. At this dance, it happens between a man in his forties and a young man. Zé Seco Jr. wants to protect me, while he explains that the older man is a giant, 'strong as a bull' (I had seen him previously demonstrating his strength by lifting up another quite heavy looking young man), 'but a good person'. The so-called giant, according to Zé Seco Jr., is from Caldas da Raínha (therefore a total outsider to the region), 'a loner, no woman, no nothing', and I had to be protected from any accidental aggression. I could not help thinking how similar that man's social description was to my own.

The scene fades out. A group of young men in crew cuts come in: they are soon to go into military service and had organised the dance previous to this one, the *baile das sortes*.[3] As soon as the word *tropa* (military service) is mentioned, some older men proceed to show their tattoos. Leonel does not hesitate. He describes an old army buddy's tattoo that portrayed a snake that crept up from feet to chest and back down again, with the snake's head coinciding with his penis.

The following morning, 25 November, was the patron saint's day, Saint Catherine of Alexandria, although the annual festival is held in the summer. The village was swarming with cars: all with Portuguese license plates. They were the cars belonging to people from Pardais who had migrated to the big cities, mainly to the suburbs of Lisbon, such as Odivelas, Ramada and Caneças, or to the municipality of Almada also within commuting distance from Lisbon. I went into the café and ordered a drink; when I asked how much it was, the owner pointed to a young man at the other end, meaning that he had already paid my tab. I had met him at the dance. Although young, he is an *encarregado* (foreman) in a quarry, and drives a Volkswagen Golf, which is very much admired and envied by others. He and I never became friends. Today I understand why: Leonel, as well as Beto and Zé Ganhão, belong to the more modest social stratum, both in terms of their genealogy and in terms of their being non-specialised workers. The 'guy in the Golf' happened to be one of the targets of their criticism for he was suspected of ingratiating himself with his boss, one of the Capuchos. Still, his gesture of commensality was an interesting one, mainly because he did not approach me, did not try to start a conversation, but instead went straight ahead to the next room where the billiards and table football were. He had welcomed me; and at the same time he had become a creditor of my esteem.

In order to outline the context for the discourse of masculinity, two sets of data need to be addressed. The first is a look at the people (mainly men) with whom I established relationships both of close contact and information gathering; they, ultimately, shaped my image of masculinity in Pardais. The second is a mapping out of the levels of social identity and the social contexts in which the discourses and practices of masculinity are expressed and shaped. Together they give meaning to the information gathered and to the relationship established with these partners in the field. These elements will be the object of ethnography in Chapters 3 through 5 and analysed as a symbolic system of masculinity.

Leonel

Leonel, Beto and Zé Ganhão were undoubtedly my privileged friends and informers.[4] Leonel, as I have already mentioned, is somehow the 'bachelor' *par excellence*. For the outside observer, his family situation seems the most obvious reason: since he and his brother support the household financially, it becomes more difficult for him to establish a separate domestic group. On the other hand, however, Leonel – not unlike many of Pardais' young men – says that 'there aren't enough girls for the boys in the village'. If one is to do a rapid count by age groups and matrimonial status, it becomes apparent that reality discredits this statement. However, if one includes the variable of level of education, the gap between young women and young men becomes very real. Different educational levels correspond to different reproductive strategies: a young woman who has completed the twelve years of schooling does not wish to marry to a young man with elementary school education.

Let us look at an example: Filomena – who was my fieldwork assistant in gathering archival data at the Civil Registry – is the same age as Leonel. She lives with her mother, a widow and seasonal agricultural labourer. She belongs to the same social stratum as Leonel's family. Nevertheless, Filomena has completed her twelve years of schooling and only contemplates the possibility of marrying a man with the same schooling, or at least one whose socio-professional status is equivalent to her high educational capital. Since such a potential partner can only be found in the town or in the large cities, girls who go to high school in the town are expected to find their future husbands there. If that does not happen, they might find themselves in Filomena's situation, that is, 'over-quali-fied' for the village's matrimonial market.

Let us return to Leonel: besides the two facts already mentioned (his family's dependence on his work and the status imbalance in the matri-monial market) – or because of them (or, still, due to intimate reasons which are not socially explicated and are beyond the scope of the anthro-pologist's ethnographic capacity), Leonel has constructed for himself an identity which includes an insistent eulogy of the bachelor's life, a certain mocking of the institution of marriage, and the cultivation of symbolic and performative elements which he interprets as characteristic of the heart-breaker (my words). Leonel learned many of those elements dur-ing his stay in Lisbon while drafted in the army; others are local cultural elements; others still are media emulations. In Lisbon he realised, for instance, that a man can be desired. In fact, local notions on relations between the sexes portray women as attractive beings who set male desire in motion; men are portrayed as desiring beings. Men are also supposed to enact actions and strategies for the conquest of female favours. Under-lying this – and because women are also seen as ambiguous creatures – there is a male suspicion that women also have strategies for conquest. These strategies, however, are never visible and obvious (furthermore they are not supposed to be visible). In terms of social visibility, the man always has the public responsibility for triggering a process that may lead to a love relationship.

Leonel says that in Lisbon, however, not only was he regularly harassed and/or desired by other men, but above all, by a woman, with whom he eventually established a relationship. According to his narrative, she was a middle-class and middle-age woman living alone; she invited him to her home, helped him buy a motorcycle and several items of clothing that he could not have bought otherwise, all in exchange for his com-pany. This situation could easily be interpreted by many men in Pardais as unprestigious (Leonel being in a 'passive' and submissive situation, being 'bought'), but it is reinterpreted by him as the result of his cun-ning, as his ability to take advantage of the woman's sexual need.[5]

Local cultural elements have to do, mainly, with the predatory sexual-ity that is expected from men in general and from young single males in particular. If the former should behave according to rules of equilibrium (since excessive predation is seen as endangering family stability, a nega-tive fact for masculine prestige), the latter should make that behaviour obvious; in a way, they should 'wear off' their predatory behaviour before marriage. What Leonel did was a sort of cultural invention based on the available cultural codes: instead of wasting his predatory behaviour and becoming a mature and complete man (i.e., married, with children, and responsible for a household), he appropriated this behaviour as an element of his identity that he now displays as a choice (by means of saying that he does *not want* to get married) and even as a token of his moral superiority: he does what all married men do anyway without having to do it undercover.

This type of Don-Juanesque character is not, however, a possibility in the local cultural script. Leonel calls on extra-local symbolic elements of what he interprets as 'modern': urban pop culture as portrayed in the media (cinema and television) and in rock music. This is obvious in the way he dresses, in his slow, yet self-assured way of walking, in his self-conscious monotone style of speech. It is also apparent in the way he looks at people; he never lets his sight wander, but is rather, poised. His self-assurance itself is in a style that can only be described as pop-culture 'cool'. Furthermore, Leonel is able to play this game because he has more schooling than his fellow companions in the village, because he articulates his discourse better, and because he is assertive in explaining his life choices. As such, he is respected; he is, of course, seen as a case apart, but not a marginal character.

Beto

Beto is different in many aspects, the most important of which is probably the fact that he is married. After a few years of courting (*namorar*)[6] he married a girl from the nearby town of Alandroal at a very young age. He describes the courting period as one of 'great passion'; but as in most cases in Pardais, he does not talk in passionate terms when referring to the present or to his wife. He is the son of a sharecropper who tends to a farm that produces some of the best oranges in the region. Beto's parents, although 'humble people', did not need Beto's labour: Beto's brother is a *cabouqueiro*, (quarry worker) and his sister still lives at home. Beto, who is the eldest, married and established his own home, much in the same way that Leonel's older brother did. At twenty-five, Beto already has four children, all under six years old. He works in the quarries, but actually throughout my fieldwork I came across him working at all sorts of different tasks: sometimes as a lumberjack, cutting down cork trees in a large estate (*herdade*), sometimes as a bricklayer in construction work. The common denominator in all these activities was his boss, one of the Capucho brothers, who allocated Beto's labour to either his quarries or the mending of buildings and farms. Beto's relationship with the Capuchos was one of the patron-client type: he received plenty of gifts from his employer, praised his entrepreneurial capacities, his charitable kindness, his humble social origins, even his sometimes dubious *esperteza* (smartness, cunning) for business. He could, nevertheless, criticise his employer's power and discretionary authority.

Like Leonel, Beto often went out in the evenings. As with most men, he was hardly ever at home. When he came back from work, he would go home to wash and change clothes, only to go straight out to the café to have his afternoon *aperitifs*. He would interrupt this activity to go home for dinner and, once over, would be back at the café where he remained until 11 p.m. or even later. Once or twice a week, and always at weekends, he would leave the village for a *festa*, a *baile*, a disco or a *boîte*. When I talked with his wife about this, she told me that it was all right with her, provided that he came back home every night and shared the bed with her, since she actually preferred to have her man outside the house: men 'get in our way', ' make things a mess', 'do not know how to behave at home', 'their place is in the streets'.

Beto did not have the cool, vigilant attitude so characteristic of Leonel. He was more anxious: he was more prone to talking about women, about sexual prowess of dubious credibility; he was cruder when describing his desires and predatory wishes; yet, he was also more troubled about his inner life. He found in me someone with whom he could elaborate a sort of discourse that was not possible in the village: about dreams and nightmares, states of soul, melancholy and sadness, dissatisfaction and impotence. Also, his sexual bravado and self-pitying complaints – always stimulated by a great propensity for drinking – were counterbalanced by his reiteration of being a good provider for wife and children, of the love he felt for them, and by his tendency to demonstrate his financial capabilities (showing money, talking about commensal expenses, narrating sumptuary expenses with his family, such as meals in restaurants, gifts, clothes, etc.).

Zé Ganhão

Zé Ganhão was my third important friend and informant. I met him about six months into my fieldwork. Until then, Leonel and Beto were very much together, and I with them. Slowly, Beto became very posses-sive towards me and Leonel – elegant and forlorn – started to distance himself. Something was cooling off between the two: Beto wanted my exclusive attention, whether during evening sprees away from the village, or around the café tables, and also visited my house frequently. When I met Zé Ganhão, who was introduced to me by Leonel, I was told that Leonel thought that Beto was lying more and more often (i.e., his exag-gerated statements about sex, commensal expenses, and honour in con-flicts and disputes were crossing the established limits for fantasy), was drinking too much and was becoming a character difficult to cope with.

Zé Ganhão was altogether different: already in his mid-thirties, he was divorced. He had two daughters from that marriage and the eldest was living with him. His ex-wife had fled with another man, originally from Vila Viçosa, where she was living with the youngest daughter. For Zé Ganhão, she was a *perdida* (literally 'lost', meaning a victim of moral decadence), the victim (to a point) of the man with whom she was now living. Her leaving the village was seen as a recognition that she was guilty, and the fact that the other man was not from Pardais, both con-tributed to keep Zé Ganhão's honour almost intact. Zé was now living at his father's, a widower, together with Zé's single sister. His father had been an agricultural labourer and also a *cabouqueiro*; his sister worked in a eucalyptus plantation, but had nonetheless concluded the twelve years of schooling and was courting (*namorar*) a young man from another vil-lage who called on her everyday driving his brand new car.

Zé had once worked in the quarries but he had found that kind of work to be alienating and dangerous. Actually, he had an almost poeti-cal fascination with country life and his life plans and his emotional energies were very much focused on the flock of sheep that he had man-aged to buy and breed. He worked as a tractor driver in an agricultural estate (*herdade*) that belonged to the equestrian bullfighter (*cavaleiro*) Capucho. Zé was very critical of him, characterising him as 'vain', as someone who thinks he is 'more than others'. He dreamed about the possibility of becoming financially independent, while looking at his growing flock, which he kept in the *Horta dos Apóstolos*. This small farm was tended by his friend Mariano, a 'young farmer'[7] subsidised by Euro-pean Union funds.

With neither Leonel's nonchalance, nor Beto's anima instability, Zé Ganhão was always smiling. He was the kind of person that did not seem to be acting out a role, or to have a *persona*. Like most men I met in Pardais, he also talked a great deal about women, but he did so with a fresh and positive attitude: sex for him was something pleasant, women were attractive creatures and one talked about these realities in a matter-of-fact way, as with any other good things in life. Rarely did I hear him use degrading expressions, statements of power or narcissistic bravado, unless in a sarcastic tone. His conversation would quickly shift to subjects such as agriculture, sheep, bulls or – in a more emotional tone – to the daughter who lived with him.

Comparing Men: Levels of Social Identity

Leonel, Beto, and Zé Ganhão. What united them? Certainly two aspects did: age and social stratification. However, differences were obvious regarding other aspects that seem to me to be central in understanding the heterogeneity of masculinity: their marital status (Leonel was single, Beto married, Zé Ganhão divorced); personality (Leonel was introspective and rational, Beto extroverted and sentimental, Zé Ganhão balanced and caring); their relationship with work (Leonel earned his money so that he could comply with his family obligations and have fun – he was functional; Beto was more prone to idleness and was very involved in patron-client relations; Zé Ganhão had a life project).

The age factor can be approached from two perspectives: the first, in the ethnographic present, has to do with different concepts and practices of masculinity by different age groups; the second, in the individual life cycle (associated with the developmental cycle of domestic groups), has to do with the learning of different social roles that follow the rules of the various age groups (although not always, as in the case of people who are single). My key informants, those with whom I had a close, day-to-day relationship, were almost all in their twenties or thirties: they were the group of young bachelors or newly married men. This may have caused some bias in my interpretation of masculinity; but I still consider it to have been a happy chance and choice; as a generation, they are the ones who are located at the hinge (a social, not temporal, one) between the 'old society' and the modern integration of the village in the national and global spheres. With regard to the life cycle, they were all in a tense situation between male adolescent permissiveness and the responsibilities of productive labour and family reproduction.

Some of my informants were children, adults and elderly people, both men and women. Children provided me with the possibility to observe some aspects of socialisation, especially how masculinity is constituted in the family, in games and playing. In school, masculinity was incorporated into a process of learning ideological standards elaborated by the state. Adults between forty and fifty years old were mostly sources of information on work related aspects: they were men in overseeing jobs in the quarries (the *encarregados*), the president of the *Junta*,[8] the owners of cafés. That is, people who had to balance their personal interests with the political equilibrium of social stratification. Elderly people were the ones who had lived through the strongest structural change in the village's history, due to the decline of agriculture and the penetration of gender values different from those of rural society. They also had witnessed new forms of sociability (cafés, discos, travelling facilities, media and democracy) which altered the construction of gender and which contributed to their vision of the modern world as a 'mess' or a 'shameless' thing.

As for social stratification, as I have mentioned in Chapter 1, the large majority of men are *cabouqueiros* and even those who are *encarregados* are so thanks to practical experience and not due to any higher level of education or a different social origin. In a certain sense, I thus interacted with what constitutes the overwhelming majority. However, social differentiation (of class, prestige or status) is not a matter of percentages: it is a relation of power and inequality. I was confronted with a limitation of my scope in relation to the 'disinherited of the earth'. Regarding this, three points need to be made.

First, a significant exception was my relationship with the president of the *Junta*. Second, I did not have a personal, direct and regular access to the quarry employers, particularly the Capucho family (which I will address in Chapter 3). Third: locally, people do not differentiate themselves socially with the same categories as those of the observer; what for us are small differences can be insurmountable gaps for the people of Pardais. As in the case of a young man who, being of the same social provenance as Leonel or Beto, and having also been a *cabouqueiro* at one time, suddenly became an *encarregado*, bought a car, started to wear fashionable clothes and all this supposedly due to the fact that he had entered a privileged patron-client relationship with his boss. Let us take a closer look at each of these aspects.

Sr. Morais is the paradigm of a type of social identity that falls short of constituting a social group: as president of the *Junta* he is the elected representative of the people in its relations with the state. Besides this political post, he belongs to a small and diversified group of people who work in white-collar jobs, which implies a level of schooling considered

43

high in local terms. Mostly it means distance from manual, physical labour, as well as access to elements of literate culture such as law, newspapers, political and institutional debate, and so on. His life trajectory is exemplary. His father – whose funeral was the main event on the day of my arrival in the village – was born in Terrugem, in the nearby municipality of Elvas. At a certain point in his life, he moved to Pardais as an agricultural labourer in the *Quinta do Panasco*; Altino Valente (whom I talk about elsewhere in the book), whose parents were sharecroppers of that farm at the time, was Sr. Morais's baptism godfather. Sr. Morais was born in Pardais. His father would eventually start his own business, a small tavern that no longer exists. However, his new life as a shopkeeper elevated him one step on the social ladder. Opposite the building where the tavern once was, today one can find Sr. Morais' house, one of the few two-story buildings in the village. It has been built adjacent to the *Quinta dos Passos*, since the Conceição sisters allowed Sr. Morais' father to build four houses there. In the school registers from the time of Sr. Morais' childhood, he stands out as the only student with honours, amidst a sea of school failure, and is the only one registered as a shopkeeper's son. He continued studying, while becoming more involved in the management of his father's business. At one time he had plans to open his own café, when there was none in the village, but his prospective partner and cousin continued with a butcher business in town.

Sr. Morais is an office clerk in a metallurgical company, located in town, that provides machinery for the marble industry. Simultaneously, he owns a grocery shop (what is locally called a 'mini-market'), a franchise of the national grocery franchiser Grula. The shop is on the ground floor of Sr. Morais' house. The store also serves as *Posto Público* (village public telephone), and Sr. Morais is also the local insurance broker for a large national insurance company. He is married and has one son, who is already working in Sr. Morais cousin's butchery and who will become a partner in the expanding business (meat consumption being one of the most outstanding indicators of the rise of standards of living). After 25 April 1974 (restoration of democracy), Sr. Morais was elected president of the *Junta* as candidate of the Socialist Party, and has been always elected ever since, regardless of the fact that in national elections the Communist Party has strong representation in Pardais.

He is an enthusiastic man, who loves to talk about politics and who taught me a great deal about local political compromising. He is also fascinated by organisation and new technologies (the *Junta* was buying and installing computers at the time of fieldwork; Sr. Morais is also the local television repairman). However, he is outside male commensality and his discourse contains no elements of sexual bravado whatsoever.[9] He is a family man, who stays at home in the evenings, organising his paperwork or watching television. The prestige that he has accumulated from politics and economic success largely compensates for any eventual loss of sexual prestige: his masculinity is anchored on success and overlaps (as almost always) with that of respected *pessoa* (person).

As for powerful or prestigious families, there are only two that have ties with the village (as the property system implies that the land-owning bourgeoisie is not local, sometimes people do not even know who the proprietors are): the Capucho family and the Conceição family. The Conceição own the *Quinta dos Passos*. The family name is visible far back in time in the civil registers and *róis de confessados*.[10] It becomes apparent, by consulting these archives, that up until the nineteenth century they were a family of sharecroppers (the *Quinta dos Passos* was property of a noble absentee family from Lisbon) who, step-by-step, became actual owners of the land whose produce they shared. Before the democratic regime the president of the *Junta* was appointed by the central state authorities and for decades was a member of this family. By the time the 'marble age' had started the family had become richer and richer as marble was discovered in their lands. The *Quinta dos Passos* was inhabited until twenty years ago by the Conceições (as the local idiom goes, using the plural for Conceição), who were seven single siblings (although, according to Sr. Altino Valente the brothers all had mistresses in the area), of which only two sisters are living today. These sisters took as a protégé (who became a virtual goddaughter) a girl who was Leonel's relative; the girl is now the potential heiress. She is a character in a local 'moral story' about a physician from the town of Alandroal who broke his marriage commitment to a poor girl from Pardais in order to marry the potentially rich heiress. The two elderly sisters live today in Alandroal, with their goddaughter and the physician.

The father of the Capucho brothers was a cousin of the Conceição siblings. His sons were, therefore, modest sons of a sharecropper who eventually became quarry owners, either through marriage or inheritance strategies. The three Capucho brothers are Rui, Fernando and Quim. The first is the true 'lord' of Pardais, the proprietor of several quarries and patron of church, priest and annual festivals. He is Beto's employer. Sr. Morais has a difficult relationship with him, due to his support for the Social Democratic Party, in power during the ethnographic present. Rui lives in a luxurious house in town. Fernando also has his own marble company and owns cattle estates. Finally, Quim – the only one who lives in the village – owns the vineyards in the village where some women work; he also has some quarries. The three brothers do not get along well; in a recent judicial dispute, Rui managed to get hold of more land and quarries.[11] Fernando is the father of Zé Maria, a nationally known equestrian bullfighter who is also an owner of quarries and a local entrepreneur. Fernando once was Leonel's employer, and Zé Maria is Zé Ganhão's employer. All Capucho brothers are excluded from local masculine commensality, from interaction in the cafés, from going out in the evenings in the male groups. Their masculinity is as if imbedded in their social precedence. The equestrian bullfighter has the extra advantage of practising an art which is in itself a complex symbol, very much marked by a gender ideology (see Chapter 4).

Relationships between employers in general – but specifically these proprietors and entrepreneurs – and workers are a semantic field for the expression of masculinity. The key words of many conversations on the subject are: 'money', 'work', 'rich and poor', and 'laziness'. This semantic universe has been analysed with regard to Mediterranean societies, but mostly this has been done regarding social stratification and patronage. Seldom have they been analysed in terms of masculinity. I believe that, if work and social status are important for the definition of social identity, so too are they important for the definition of masculinity. Furthermore, that the pairs of relations, laziness / work, richness / poverty, and others, also define continuums of greater and lesser masculinity. There seems to be differential investment in different characteristics of masculinity, depending on which end of the scale particular men are located. Let us take a closer look.

In their lives my informants deal with an apparent paradox, one that is also salient in discourse. First, there is a moral obligation to work, provide for the family, and sacrifice the body; all these are prestigious elements in the symbolic capital of masculinity.[12] One finds, however – and this is the second point – that there is a utopia of laziness and leisure, of abundance and plenty as a result of richness, and of the cleanliness of non-physical labour. Thirdly, underlying this, there is an idea that unequal distribution of wealth is an injustice and a result of a wrong moral behaviour of the rich, called *ambição* (ambition); this implies that, antithetically, poverty confers honour. However – and this is a fourth point – one also praises cunning, the capacity to develop strategies of patron-client relations, and the ability to accumulate wealth as prestigious.

This is a complex world of meanings and actions, in which a great deal of the symbolic capital of masculinity is at stake. A case in point is the young man I have referred to previously. By means of friendship or patron-client relations with a quarry owner of his generation, he managed to secure a better salary and job, thus provoking envy, respect and spite all at the same time. Envy, because he gained access to goods that are seen as added value for the masculine image; respect, because his symbolic capital of masculinity became higher, as a result of correct strategy; spite, because by becoming closer to the world of the rich he was showing that lack of morality that is supposed to be at the root of wealth.

The transformation from *latifundium* agriculture to quarry work enhanced the process of proletarianisation. It guaranteed for the first time stable and relatively well-paid jobs for men, although higher rates of unemployment and more domesticity for women. The cultural androginisation of modernity did not entail a substantial change in inequality, since men have seen their role as family providers reinforced and obtained even more mobility. The greater domesticity of women is, however, interpreted by many of them as acquisition of prestige by means of the emulating figure of the 'housewife' (*dona-de-casa*), a bourgeois and urban category.

Following the local logic of organising everyday life – i.e., the division between work time, leisure time, and family time – the latter was my privileged time-space of observation and interaction. Sociability, which will be further analysed in Chapter 4, using the example of the café as 'men's house', is understood as interaction outside the tasks of work and domestic life. At this point, a distinction should be made between inter- and intra-sexual sociability. The former include *bailes*, *matanças* (pig slaughter) and *festas* (festivals), both in their religious and profane aspects; the latter include mainly two arenas: the café and/or tavern, and the evening outings (groups of men who go out together in the evenings to *bailes*, *festas*, discos and *boites* outside the village).

If the café is an exclusively masculine space, the *baile* and the *festa* are not. Nevertheless, the gender division is established. In *festas*, religious ceremonies are attended mostly by women, and the profane ceremonies are divided into a time for families and, after the family returns home, a time for men. The mobility of men also reproduces the gender division: men cover a wider geographical space when it comes to *festas*, whereas women usually attend only their own village *festa*. As for the domestic world, dominated by women throughout the year, exceptions do occur, as in the case of baptism parties, wedding parties, anniversaries or *matanças*, occasions in which men play domestic roles (as fathers, husbands or hosts); in some cases it is actually women who select and invite them, as in the case of the *matança* (see Lawrence 1982).

Concerning family life, some problems of observation arise for the male ethnographer due to the closing off of homes to strangers. Homes are female territories, in which even the family men stay only for short periods of time other than sleeping hours. The home is a space of exchange and mutual visitation between women, especially between mother and daughters who live in separate households, but also between sisters, cousins, sisters-in-law, and neighbours.

Masculinity, however, is not constructed and reproduced solely by means of the division of labour, socialisation in the family and school, or by ritualised forms of sociability and interaction. The domain of the notions of person, body, emotions and sentiments, and of all that constitutes the dynamic between personality and cultural rules, is an area of human experience that constitutes and is constituted by gender categories. Chance allowed me the privilege to meet an extraordinary elderly man who is the local oral poet; he allowed me to trace out a whole field of poetic expression that not only reinforced my understanding of the symbolic system of masculinity, but also allowed me to understand how fluid it is, how capable of change it is, and how much, I think, it results from a 'social pact' with femininity in men – a femininity that is channelled, contained, regularised by poetical rhetoric (see Chapter 5).

Symbols and Meanings of Gender

Let us try now to trace in broad terms the system of cultural symbols and meanings that operate in discourses and practices that contribute to the reproduction of gender categories, particularly masculinity.

For the people in Pardais, the world is divided into masculine and feminine, two principles that are – in an anthropological interpretation – of an essentialistic nature. That is, the division by means of a sexual dichotomy is as much an essence of the world and of life as the division between animal and human, for instance. The body is the site for the masculine / feminine division, and since the body is seen as the *locus* of the person, the sexual division is inescapable as a constituting element of identity and of two sets of human beings: men and women. What we understand as sex and gender, are here juxtaposed. As an extension of the body, human activities and their products or outcomes also follow the same principle. This is visible in the sexual division of labour and in the division of sexual labour, on the one hand; and, on the other hand, it is visible in the genderisation of objects, such as the house, its internal divisions and spaces for different types of social interaction, and so on. Analogically, the same occurs in nature and two levels of human experience: social relations at large, and emotions and sentiments. This genderisation of the world and society is reinforced in the Portuguese case with the fact that the Portuguese language genderises almost everything ('house' *is* feminine, 'work' *is* masculine, for instance).

In everyday practice, things are not so rigid: masculinity and femininity are lived as sets of qualities that can occur in the opposite sexual half. Thus, people acknowledge that men can have certain kinds of behaviour, emotions and activities that are catalogued as 'feminine', and vice versa. That is, provided that they do not possess or enact them exclusively, a situation that would make them anomalous persons. In order to define, for instance, the masculinity or femininity of an emotion, action or situation, the notions of activity and passivity are central concepts. These notions operate at yet another level of complexity in the sexual dichotomy: a man is never just that, but rather someone with a specific social role and moral conduct, a role which changes over a life span, or during a day, and may coexist with other roles. That is how a man can be a husband, a father, a son, a boss, a worker, rich, poor, and so on. So the classificatory principles are always being challenged by contradictory everyday practices and the essentialistic nature of one's sex is complicated by a certain recognition of what anthropologists would call constructed gender.

Female children may learn to be passive, as boys may learn to be active, by means of a process of embodiment[13] of these characteristics as *habitus*.[14] This is visible in boys' games, which are mostly based on the constitution of teams and extended groups, that engage in a sort of physical activity that covers wide public spaces and enacts competition for leadership. It is, usually, a matter of using the body 'outwards' (*para fora*), something that is later in life made explicit in the phrase '*encolhe a barriga, estica o peito*' (belly in, chest out), a hallmark of military service training. Some examples of this are: kicking, throwing, fighting, hunting, chasing, running, and even the exploration of exterior space (exterior to the house, the school, and even the village). One could include here masculine play involving the domination of lower forms of life, often involving cruelty to animals, that actually are forms of training for hunting, an exclusively masculine activity that is much appreciated in the village.

As for girls, their playing activities focus on a circular physical dexterity within the confines of limited space. Sometimes this space is actually drawn on the ground (as in the game of *macaca*, a sort of hopscotch), or symbolic markers are established, as the *coito* (hiding place). Many feminine games reproduce family life and motherhood by imitation. In the latter type of games, it is perfectly acceptable that a girl plays the role of father, whereas it would be virtually impossible for boys (younger ones take part in these games too) to play the role of a mother. Girls also learn, as a distinctive quality of their gender, to talk quietly, to *segredar* (tell secrets), to walk in pairs in the street. An ideal of intimacy, complicity and display of modesty is thus learned, as opposed to boys' public performance.

Nevertheless, there are games that serve the purposes of interaction between the sexes: *cabra-cega* (a blindfolded hide and seek game) and *escondidas* (hide and seek) are two good examples. In these it becomes possible to touch in order to identify individuals by body features and clothing, in an anonymous situation. Until the age of seven or eight, girls and boys discover each other, but they will not do it again before adolescence and then in a different sort of encounter – that of *namoro* (courting).

Deviance[15] is clearly looked for and identified in childhood. Often innocent situations are granted excessive meaning and salience, which in effect largely constructs the very deviance itself. It is the case of Gabriel, an eight-year-old boy, who is known for being shy, a good student and a well behaved youth. He wanted to learn needlework at school. Needlework classes, however – and contrary to any official state specification, which says nothing about gender specificity – were classified by the two female school teachers as 'just for girls'. The boy insisted, and the teachers did not know what to do. However, the other children started calling him *maricas* (sissy). He soon gave up his ambition, but continued learning his needlework at home, thanks to his tolerant mother, one of the two women in the village who work in a factory in a neighbouring town.

Boys also learn that they are allowed to get dirty and to ruin their clothes. Mothers do scold them for this, but the scolding is in itself a source of prestige among the group of boys. Often fathers boast (although using the rhetorical device of complaint, but betraying their meaning with a scornful smile) about how 'wild' their sons are (on the other hand, they express their pride of how 'sweet' their daughters are). Girls tend to despise these aspects of masculinity, and repress the tendency to be *maria-rapaz* (a tom-boy). This refusal is compensated by gratification in the competition for good looks. Good looks in clothing, hair, and neatness are stimulated in girls by their mothers, in what is virtually a competition between mothers.

It is by the end of the elementary-school cycle, when children are approaching puberty, that the signs of the boy's separation from his mother become evident – an attitude that will generate the split notion of Woman, with the virgin mother on one hand and the dangerous seductress on the other. There is no symmetrical split in women's conceptualisation of men. With puberty, boys take their first steps in 'going out', physically leaving two strongly feminised spaces: the home and the neighbourhood (which can be a common patio for several houses, a stretch of street, or a network of houses with kinswomen or even a *monte* – a farm outside the village). Girls, on the contrary, learn how to co-dominate these spaces with their mothers. In fact, the tie between mother and daughter is almost never severed, even after the daughter's marriage (this is also connected with a tendency for uxorilocality); the father-son tie is not symmetrical to this, the severance in the mother-son relationship not entailing a substitution with a father-son tie. Emotional relations between sons and fathers actually become authoritarian and then avoidance prevails. The activities of adults confirm the state of things in the child's perception: father leaves early for work, returns in the late afternoon to wash and eat and typically goes out again, for the café. The mother – if she does not work – stays home or goes out shopping, to the washing tank, or to the homes of relatives. If she works on seasonal agricultural tasks, she does so as part of a group of women controlled by a man in charge. It is quite common in this case for mother and daughter to work in the same group.

The preferred residence rule in Pardais is neolocal. The family is a nuclear group, revolving around a house, where the family sleeps and eats, even when several houses (of the children of a couple) are built together around a common patio. The house has a particular symbolic importance for gender category definition. Apart from the roof – which is a man's job to maintain – the woman cleans, whitewashes the house walls, sweeps the street area outside her door, starts the fire (before gas stoves became common), takes care of the garden if there is one, and accomplishes quite a lot of the maintenance work, including painting and some bricklaying. The inside of the house has the kitchen as the central space, directly connecting with the street. Decorative objects of prestige, including electrical appliances, are displayed in what apparently is a theatrical rather than utilitarian form. Actually, it is both simultaneously, because the setting of appliances in the corners, for instance, is part of a circular use of space, very different from the rational grid lines and quadrangular shapes of modern urban settings. The door is always open: while looking in can not intrude too much, neighbouring women can still approach, call out and talk.

The master bedroom is the second most important room, often occupied by furniture centred around the bed: this is often the most expensive furniture bought and that to which most emotional investment is made. As long as these two rooms – kitchen and master bedroom – are guaranteed, all other functions are provided for according to possibilities. In many houses, the children sleep in the kitchen-cum-living room, if the house is small. Children's toys are part of a whole collection of paraphernalia bought during trips, visits to sanctuaries, or offered on important occasions. Children hardly ever touch these items. The last two decades have introduced a new part of the house that now has a strong meaning for social prestige: the bathroom.

For a stranger, houses in Pardais sometimes look like mausoleums. Most of the dwellers seem to be constantly expelled from the premises. Girls are sent to the adjacent patio or stretch of street, boys are practically expelled into the village streets, men to the 'street', meaning the outside world generally. That is probably why elements of popular architecture that have survived in other parts of the country, such as fireplaces – which play a relevant role in keeping family sociability and cohesiveness – were so easily abandoned and replaced by stoves. Women appropriate the house and home as their realm, in a social situation where the peasant house (meaning fields, inheritance and lineage) does not exist. In Pardais, houses are not referred to by family name, house name, or the man's name, but rather by the name of the woman who lives there.

The roof in a traditional house is held up by a large beam made of a single tree trunk. It is the symbolic backbone of the house. It can either have *viço* (liveliness, fertility) or its negative excess, *vício* (vice),[16] a feminine ill. Vício comes from (menstrual) blood. There is also a masculine vício, but it refers to a moral judgement of behaviour (to drink too much, to spend too much), being a result of bad influences exerted by other men or of the wife's incapacity to control him. The positive side of women is milk, a nourishment that reinforces the positive side of motherhood. Male semen can also be glossed as milk and is equally positive. However, semen is seen as a limited good, that can be wasted due to the vicious side of women (their sexual appetite and the enchantment they exert over men, who 'can not resist them'), this being partly why it should not be mixed with menstrual blood. The other meaning of sangue (blood) has to do with reproduction, in the sense of heredity: the blood of man and woman when joined in the sexual union have result in a new human being.

Men verbalise their uneasiness about being at home. To stay at home *faz mal* (is bad for you), *amolece* (makes you soft). It can be a sign of unemployment (therefore of a man's incapacity to provide), a sign of laziness, a sign of dependence on the wife. In brief, domesticity feminises. A man will invite other men to his house only on ritual occasions (the christening of a son, a wedding, or on village festival days), during which he is host to others, capitalising on his wife's domestic effort with regard to household chores and conservation, cooked food and calculated accumulation.

The masculine space *par excellence* is the café. The main activity at the café is alcohol consumption following rules of commensality and reciprocity among men. This is complemented by card games, eating the products of hunting, fishing, and gathering (fowl, fish, mushrooms and wild asparagus). But the dominant event is conversation. In this time and space of leisure, conversation is made in loud voices and accompanied by codes of gesture that contrast with the functional control of the body at work. The tired body, disciplined by hierarchy and tasks, gives way to open gestures, banging on tables, excessive volume, reiteration, and narratives of self-praise.

Sex is an important theme of conversation. Other themes are work and relations between workers and bosses, money, comments on situations of drunkenness, fun, and conflict during nights out. When it comes to sex, it is mostly exaggerated stories about sexual prowess and joking invitations to homosexual intercourse – expressed in touching other men's buttocks, lighting a lighter on a rear end, inviting someone to sit on one's lap, gesturing kisses, or grabbing another man's testicles. Another element is the objectification of women, since they are talked about without reference to names and particular situations, but rather as archetypes: parts of their bodies, particularly breasts and buttocks, and reference to sexual practices that are locally considered as out of the ordinary: oral and anal sex, and love triangles.

Alcohol can allow for and stimulate sentimentality. This allows for the expression, by means of poetry or song, of emotions normally classified as feminine, such as love, charity, pity, compassion, nostalgia. If the situation is particularly festive, the atmosphere can verge on the carnivalesque which, during Carnival proper, can take the form of transvestism. Other social spaces in which men prevail include: the workplace, urban and rural areas outside the village (cafés, *boites*, brothels, *festas*), and the 'great outdoors' (in activities like hunting, fishing and gathering). Only during the village annual festival are the gender barriers lifted. One can then feel a strong feminine presence in the streets, not only because it is women who organise religious activities (another trait of masculinity is the uneasiness about entering the 'house' of God), but also because they display their family's status by means of clothes – theirs and their children's. It is, however, during the religious ceremonial that they take over the village as a symbolic house, conducting the procession, carrying the saints on their shoulders in the circumvolution of the village's territory. At the local *bailes*, held precisely for the gathering of the sexes, the gender division is ritualised in the visual control exerted by older married women who sit around the precinct, and by the searching look of bachelor men – standing and moving about – until they find a girl who will accept to dance once she has acknowledged a coded blink of the eye.

As I have said before, the masculine/feminine division is not linear or straightforward. It goes through mutations according to age, social class, work relations, subtle changes of status, accumulation or loss of prestige. In general, one can say that masculinity is always being constructed and confirmed, whereas femininity is seen as a permanent essence, 'naturally' reaffirmed by pregnancies and births.

While a boy, one is not man in the true sense of masculine. In order to achieve masculinity, the boy has to sever his emotional dependence on his mother. This is not simply a psychological perspective (and a contested one, for that matter); it has been expressed verbally by many local men. Severing ties with the mother means severing ties with house and home and family. It means doing more and more 'manly things' with other young men – and with more intensity than older men do. Youngsters leave school as soon as possible in order to have access to the remuneration of work. This is of course part of the domestic group's reproductive strategy and a consequence of wider political economic realities, but it is understood and lived by boys as their own choice. Most of the money they earn at work goes to the house, the mother being the person they give the money to (she also administers her husband's wages), but he keeps a fund which he will invariably use to buy a motorcycle. With the motorcycle, young men acquire mobility, thus visiting *festas* and bars in surrounding towns, where they learn how to handle alcohol and can have their sexual initiation with prostitutes. A cultural object as (apparently) insignificant as a motorcycle has, after all, a salient significance. As opposed to other regions in Portugal, girls and women in Pardais do not have or ride motorcycles. Their mobility is thus reduced, at the same time as it is their supposed immobility that justifies their not buying motorcycles. The object then becomes exclusively masculine, as well as the behaviour it permits. No wonder, then, that motorcycles are such an important theme of conversation among boys and young men. They are the object of a whole aesthetic, of classification and competition, one that talks about status and prestige in close association with masculinity.

Military conscription completes this learning. It implies leaving the village and going to a different region of the country; it involves a connection with a masculine group as such – not only according to local identity. It means a regime of the body based on discipline and preparation for war; and it promotes the identification of masculine with national, as already prefigured in school-books' stereotypes on national history (Vale de Almeida 1991). Military service is the closest form we can find to a rite of initiation or passage to manhood; this idea is reinforced by (today less common) ritual practises in Portuguese villages, called the *sortes*: boys of the same year of recruitment had a special bond and promoted *bailes* in their honour.

Marriage is seen as necessary for entering adult status, and the conflation between 'adult' and 'man' is quite common. The choice of spouse is seen as free, with a preference for village exogamy. The percentage of men who leave the village to marry is higher than that of women, but it is not the result of a rule. Another practice is that of *viver juntos* (living together), which allows for the starting of matrimonial sexuality and cohabitation even when economic and material conditions are not fully met. It is a form of elopement: the first night together is supposed to be secret, but normally the woman's mother is informed by her daughter about what is going to happen. The relationship is then institutionalised, the new couple dwelling usually at the woman's parents household.

With regard to the specific field of sexuality, a clear distinction must be made between what is said and what is done. Access to the latter is of course very limited during fieldwork. The local norm divides men and women internally. The virginal, protective mother woman is antithetical to the 'lost', sexually active, 'wild' woman. Female ambiguity, and the notion that women are submitted to an inferior social status out of which they might want to escape by means of shrewd manipulation, stimulates the construction of images of female physiology as something secret and mysterious. This is clear in the supposed dangers of menstruation, to

55

which taboos apply, ranging from whitewashing to food preparation and *matança* activities.

The antithesis of the predating male is the wise man, who cares about providing his family and takes care not to engage in too many vices, such as drinking, smoking and gambling. A victim of an ever-present libido, his body is not questioned, but rather seen as clear, visible, external, a non-question. At the sexual level, the genitals are understood to have autonomous will. This paradox results in the fact that women know their physiology very well, since part of their social importance concerns reproduction, which men consider to be obscure; on the other hand, men know very little about their own, although they portray it as unproblematic, due to the 'exterior' characteristic of male organs. Many men, for instance, are fascinated by the erotic techniques displayed by prostitutes. These techniques have to do with the prostitutes' experienced learning – they know men's bodies and sexual physiology. However, since men do not question their own bodies (for instance, there was not one who knew that pressure on the prostate could stimulate ejaculation), they take it as relating to moral characteristics (in this case, transgressional ones) of the prostitutes. The commonly held idea that 'peasants' know all about sexuality because they 'see animals doing it all the time' is wrong. What people see in animals is reproductive copulation, not physiology or sexuality, much less eroticism.

One of greatest fears held by men is adultery by their wives or lovers. If a woman is adulterous, the man becomes a *cabrão* (literally, a billy-goat, see Chapter 4). He must be wary of other men's predation, and so he lives ambiguously with the trust of friendship and the mistrust on others' predatory virility. Similarly, his wife is supposed to have a reduced sexual appetite that he can fully satisfy, with moderation and at the appropriate times. The other element that has to be taken into account is that he can obtain some prestige among men if he sees the 'other' type of women, spreading his semen, spending it in excessive, fantastic practices; but this can lead to physical weakening and excessive financial expenditure. If he spends the money he is supposed to give his wife for the administration of the home, it is his prestige as a provider that is jeopardised. So it is the wife who is supposed to control him, to manage the household money including the man's salary, and to allot him enough money for him to partake in masculine commensality and sprees – which may occasionally include access to 'other' women. It seems to be clear that conditions of ideological male domination can coexist with a strong matrifocality and informal authority.

The danger of adultery apart, women are supposed to domesticate their libido by means of becoming pregnant (an example that shows men's ignorance of female physiology, because pregnancy does not necessarily diminish the libido); and they are supposed to channel their need for social contact towards female friendships. Men regard female friendships as based on gossip, insincerity, the attempt to control men, and religious beatitude. Women, however, explain their relationships as an escape from solitude and a way to create solidarity that will empower them to *fazer chegar a água ao seu moínho* (literally, 'to lead the water into their mill'), to obtain want they want while leaving untouched the status quo of male prestige and female modesty.

Among men, masculinity is strongly grounded on specifically sexual elements. Internal divisions among men are also established, in analogy to divisions between men and women. Masculinity being a fragile process, in sexual terms there is nothing visible one can show to others. The most common fear and form of aggression is present in the idiom of homosexuality, understood as a passive category, symbolised in the image of anal penetration, thus feminising men. This strategy is used in all competitive and conflictive relations between men, whether at work, business or play. On the other hand, homophobia situates and exorcises the immanent danger of homosexuality in homosociality. One of the central characteristics of hegemonic masculinity mentioned in *Excursio*, besides the definition of female inferiority, is homophobia.

I have previously mentioned the utopia of social equality. This is in contradiction to the desire for social climbing and wealth. These, in turn, conflict with the negative image of the rich as ambitious people and of the poor as honoured people. In certain contexts, smartness and capacity to manipulate others are prestigious, and work (seen as an ennobling sacrifice) is seen as less important than laziness (normally seen as a result of passiveness). Everything happens as if men lived in a constant attempt to once again find an adolescent being-in-the-world: egalitarian, homosocial, without mother or wife, in the pursuit of pleasure and without economic responsibilities. In Freudian terms, this would be called 'regression' or escape from the 'reality principle'. This utopia can be most visible in leisure activities, in commensal practices and in reciprocity: drinking, playing, gambling, being in the café, going out in the evening, having casual sex.

Women, through the privileged and continued relationship between mother and daughter and their control over the home, do not express a similar kind of existential ambiguity and do not elaborate on a feminine homophobia symmetrical to that of men. Reproduction is said to grant them a sort of ontological security as productive, transcendent human beings. However, I have little doubt that they have a desire for public autonomy and intervention, as well as for the pursuit of pleasure, which is denied to them by male domination. They do though, 'echo' the dominant ideology, since their consciousness, raised in conditions of male domination is, on the whole, not truly free (see Mathieu 1991).

NOTES

1. The title is taken from a sentence by Gilmore: 'Men nurture society by shedding their blood, their sweat, and their semen' (1990:230). In Pardais, blood shed in warfare was replaced by accidents and deaths in the quarries. As for sweat and semen, they continue with their task as metaphors for production and reproduction.
2. See José Seco's *décimas* in Chapter 5. On the character from Caldas da Raínha (Guedes), see Chapter 3.
3. *Sortes* (literally 'luck') means medical inspection for the military service. It comes from *tirar à sorte* (to sort out): those who are chosen celebrate their passage to manhood in the home village. This tradition has significantly faded in Portugal.
4. In order to understand the kinship ties that do and do not exist between the different people mentioned in this and other chapters, see the Genealogical Chart.
5. Actually, one is not 'bought' in this situation: money is a recognition of the value implicit in the *phallus*, the latter meaning the symbolic image of the penis, the principle of masculinity and a good belonging to masculine symbolic capital.
6. The noun *namoro* and the verb *namorar* cannot be translated into English. They refer to 'dating', 'going out', 'courting' and even on occasion to the period of engagement.
7. The *jovem agricultor* ('young farmer') has become a common social character in the Portuguese countryside. It refers to young people who have undergone professional training and received European Union subsidies to improve the market potential of their farms' produce.
8. Portuguese territorial administration comprises three levels: districts, municipalities and *freguesias*. Municipalities (counties) are administered by an elected *Câmara Municipal* (city of town council). *Freguesias* (parishes) are administered by an elected *Junta* (board). Pardais is a *freguesia*.
9. I should note that fieldwork coincided with Sr. Morais' period of mourning for his father's death, which prohibited him from going out to the cafés or socialising too much. However, either before or after mourning, his habits were not considerably different, other than the absence of dark clothes.
10. Civil registers of births, baptisms, marriages and funerals, which can be found in each municipal archive in Portugal. *Róis de Confessados* are village statistics

once written by priests for the purpose of defining the financial contribution each household should make to the Church and whether the members had complied with the mandatory yearly Easter confession. They can usually be found in the local church authorities.

11. In a newspaper article prior to the 1993 local elections, the relationship between Rui Capucho and the *Presidente da Câmara* (mayor) was explored. The mayor had been elected in the Socialist Party lists but in 1993 he was running for the Social Democratic Party. Sr. Morais is also mentioned in this article in a national newspaper: he accused Rui Capucho of refusing to pay the costs for a new road in exchange for expanding the area of one of his quarries.

12. I use here Bourdieu's definition of symbolic capital: 'Capital économique et capital symbolique sont si inextricablement mêlés que l'exhibition de la force matérielle et symbolique par des alliés prestigieux est de nature à apporter par soi des profits matériels, dans une économie de la bonne foi où une bonne renommée constitue la meilleure sinon la seule garantie économique' (Bourdieu 1980:202).

13. By embodiment I mean the unconscious, non-reflexive process of learning by means of imitation, gestures, postures and somatic reactions, that have a meaning in social interaction, establishing hierarchies – among which that of gender – and which form one of the most resilient forms of social memory. See Bourdieu 1980, Connerton 1993, Csordas 1990.

14. This is Bourdieu's concept: '…habitus, systèmes de dispositions durables et transposables, structures structurées prédisposées à fonctionner comme structures structurantes, c' est-à-dire en tant que principes générateurs et organisateurs de pratiques et de représentations qui peuvent être objectivement adapttées à leur but sans supposer la visée consciente de fins et la maîtrise expresse des opérations nécessaires pour les atteindre' (Bourdieu 1980:88).

15. I do not use 'deviance' in any scientific sense, as in studies of deviance, but rather in the generic sense of non-conforming behaviour as it is understood locally. I do not, of course, consider 'deviant' the behaviour of the young boy used as an example. But it is thanks to the identification of deviance that the process of stigmatisation is triggered: one is accused of 'being' something (a sissy) because of an action (needlework). See Goffman 1988 (1963).

16. Cutileiro (1977:128) says that *vício* is the 'predisposition which is responsible for the potential social dangers that stem from (…) the active social life of women'. Pina-Cabral (1989) adds that the word also refers to anti-social and self-destructive tendencies, and that the merging – in popular usage – of *viço* and *vício* sheds light on the analogy between body vigour and fertility, sex and sensuality, 'and that these qualities have a morally negative connotation' (1989:126).

3. From Land to Stone
Work, Power, and Conflict

*C*hapter 1 defined the region in which Pardais is included as economically dependent on the marble extraction industry. The change from agricultural activity and the relations of production characteristic of *latifundium* land ownership to this recent activity has triggered social changes from which gender and masculinity are not excluded. In this chapter I will try to trace the outlines of the system of production and the social relations it involves, by means of paying particular attention to how discourses and practices of work constitute and are constituted by the cultural categories of masculinity. The local cultural themes of 'work', 'rich and poor', 'respect' and others will be analysed together with social relations such as patron-client relations, political power, the hierarchic world view, the dependence on the world economy, and the tensions and dynamics resulting from these.

More than statistics, poetic interpretation expresses the local understanding of the importance of quarry activity and its importance for local identity. The following is a *décima*, a local form of poetry, the creation of an illiterate improvising poet; in Portuguese the verses rhyme, which is difficult to imitate in an English translation:

> From Pardais to Sousel
> it is one single quarry
> many gather capital
> others lose their lives.

Oh, what great richness
Alentejo has
it has enough stone
for Portugal and Spain
for France and Germany
for Egypt and Algiers
the stone from Bencatel
is very much praised
there is so much stone extracted
from Pardais to Sousel.

With the drill and a pointer
with the crane pulling up
they can pull out
stone for the whole world
wherever it is bought
stone both short and long
stone of all sizes
I don't find it strange
it is one single quarry.

There's blue and tainted stone
White and pink too
which is most profitable
after it's been produced
even when well calculated
no one knows how much it's worth
they could go to court
in front of three judges
the unfortunate die there
many gather capital.

The Italian he says
that the stone of Alentejo
goes into all colleges
shines throughout the country
torn from its roots
where it was produced
after the stone is cropped
there is stone everywhere
many have become rich
others lose their lives

José Seco, poet

Three aspects should be stressed in this *décima*. First, the awareness of local economy's insertion in the world economy; second, in spite of the process of industrialisation and machine implementation, the extractive, crop-like nature of this industry makes it somehow similar to activities connected with the land; third, the description of the activity is inseparable in the narrative from value judgements about how some 'gather capital' and, on the other hand, some 'lose their lives'. These elements will always be present simultaneously in what follows, since social inequality is defined by a juxtaposition of the two. It becomes particularly obvious in the existence of patron-client relations, incomplete proletarianisation, and the rich-poor dichotomy as an alternative to 'class consciousness'.

The national Mines and Geology Services states that there is a high concentration of marble extraction in the Triangle sub-region. Eighty-five percent of the national total of this ornamental stone is produced here; 2.4 percent of the enterprises produce forty percent of the marble extracted in fifteen percent of the existing quarries. In 1986, only nine percent of the companies had more than fifty workers and eighty-one percent had less than twenty employees. This places all companies in the category of small or middle-size enterprises; the largest has less than three hundred workers (Neves 1991). According to Neves' study, there has been a considerable growth in the extraction industry in the last decade: the average rate of growth in total production was 7.7 percent between 1977 and 1984, and the average rate of growth of established equipment was ten percent. In the same period the labour force in the sector grew by an average rate of three percent. It should be made clear at this point that the stone processing and transformation activity is almost insignificant. It is carried out in other regions of Portugal, but mostly abroad, particularly Spain and Italy, where – it is said – Portuguese marble replaces Carrara marble. Therefore, my informants' activity is located at the very bottom of the production chain as extractors of raw materials.

A first visit to the quarries is an unforgettable experience. The landscape on the way to Pardais, if one comes from the north, is almost moon-like. The earth has exploded and necks of the cranes punctuate the horizon like strange birds of prey. Piles of debris grow in height and size, to such an extent that agricultural land has been bought at extremely high prices for the sole purpose of being used for more piles of debris. Pardais, since it is the last and southernmost village of marble production, was for a long time immune to this landscape attack; however, throughout fieldwork I witnessed the growth of an immense pile of debris. It was piling up on the horizon like a slow-moving mountain; when I returned to the field one year later it had tripled in size. As for the quarries themselves, one only realises how deep they can be when approaching the rim of the precipice. They are like photo negative images of buildings, carved out in steps that can go down for forty metres or more.

Beto and a friend took me on my first tour of the quarries. We paid particular attention to the oldest which belongs to Marmetal company. It is located in Fonte da Moura, property of the Capucho family who eventually purchased it from the Conceição family. It was hard to believe that was the same place where Sr. Altino Valente had once led his mules for the cultivation of wheat (see Chapter 1). Quarries produce blocks of marble stone that must fit certain requisites in size and quality for commercialisation. They are dispatched to other companies that take care of transformation and/or export. Quality is defined by the type of fracturing and by the *vergada* (non-homogeneous colour, with lines and spots of different colours and shades). Since local marble is too fractured and *vergado*, only thirty percent of the stone extracted has commercial value.

The extraction of stone starts with the outlining of the area of extraction and the removal of soil. Then the directions of primary cuts are defined, so that great masses can be detached from the rocky formation. These are then reduced in size to smaller blocks, an activity called *desmonte*. This is done with instruments like the *guilho*, block-cutters and pneumatic drills; the masses are then removed with cranes from the quarry and reduced to even smaller blocks with blades.

Hierarchy in the Work Place

Beto is a *cabouqueiro* (literally a 'ditch digger'), as are most men in Pardais (see Chapter 1). The local hierarchy at work recognises the following strata: *cabouqeiros*, whom I shall call workers, non-skilled and non-specialised workers; machine operators, who work with tractors, cranes or cutting blades; and foremen. Outside of the context of daily work at the quarries, a category apart is that including all those not engaged in manual, physical labour: these include office clerks, engineers, and the employers. As Zé Seco (son of the above-mentioned poet) once said:

> First comes the boss, then the engineer, as well as the accountant, who measures and sells; then comes the foreman, he makes the men work.

Only then come the man who work in the *barrancos* [ditches]: first, the machine operators, including those who work with the cranes, but these make more money than the others. At last, you have the workers [*cabouqueiros*].

Before returning to the workers – the majority – there are some aspects in the Neves' study that will be useful in defining the intermediary characteristics of foremen. Neves' work is about a group of enterprises operating in the neighbouring *freguesia* of Bencatel in 1984. Foremen there amounted to ten percent of those working in the extraction industry (in Pardais, they are eighteen percent). In the period between 1977 and 1984 the average rate of growth for workers was 2.4 percent, but 4.8 percent for foremen (data for the whole Alentejo).

Usually, a worker starts his career at the quarry with no formal training, with very little schooling, and basically learns his job through practice. Among my informants, the prototypical male life-story starts with dropping out of school around the age of thirteen (when one can no longer stay at elementary school, which, were it not for the high rates of school failure, should be finished by the age of nine). One then becomes an apprentice worker, while living at the parental home. By the time of marriage the apprentice has become a full worker. As Beto said: 'There I was, a thirteen-year-old in third grade at school, my body was already that of a complete man, but I was surrounded by kids! Damn it, I said! I took off for the quarries!'

Workers do not have a defined, fixed job at work, just like the machinery, especially the diamond and sand chain saws that can be moved from one end of the quarry to the other, and used in both horizontal and vertical position. Work tasks vary greatly and decision making relies on experience alone.

Experience is acquired throughout a lifetime. The worker can adapt to any quarry thanks to his knowledge of 'stone work'. Throughout his life, after starting as an apprentice, he becomes a 'practitioner', then a full worker and, eventually, a *mestre* (foreman) or *contra mestre* (substitute foreman). The passage from one degree to the other depends on a kind of general acknowledgement of the improvement of his capabilities. This acknowledgement comes from the *mestre* or foreman, but also from his colleagues: it is as if they 'elect' him to lead small groups that are organised around the cutting of a block. Since these groups are not permanent – mobility is high inside the quarry – it is skill, personality and the embodiment of these qualities that make the others say 'you lead now'.

Age is, of course, an important factor, but the crucial element is the culture of experience. There are no courses, professional training, degrees, or examinations. In that sense, specialisation or skilling are not total. Therefore there is not such a tremendous difference vis-à-vis the parameters used in peasant relations and work. The characteristics that lead to the 'election' of one man as more apt to climb in the hierarchy are quite often tied to extra-quarry factors, such as kinship, friendship, prestige, respect, correct behaviour in commensality or sociality. In sum, those elements that are common to the definition of what it is to 'be a man' (in Portuguese, *ser um homem às direitas*, to be a straight man, a righteous man).

The foreman – as in the case of Caralinda, for instance – is a man who has the capacity, demonstrated in practice, to organise work and make decisions. His social origin is exactly the same as that of the workers, as is his schooling. The difference is that he has managed to succeed in the long and repeated process of trial and error and contextualised learning. Another important aspect is the capacity to incorporate experiences that relate to power relations in the work place – the absorption of a set of values, of an ethic (Neves 1991). The whole process of socialisation leads, in the cases of most foremen, to a situation of 'respect'. This characteristic – which is central in the definition of a person's prestige – is also acquired and checked outside work, whether in the village, or the sub-region, since workers in a quarry come from different neighbouring villages. As Neves says, 'individual qualification in this context is clearly a collective production. The professional knowledge to which the apprentice has progressive access belongs to the workers both individually and collectively' (1991:11).

Caralinda started his career at seventeen. After a trial contract for two weeks, his boss 'liked him': he has been in the quarry for ten years now, that is 'the time it takes to cut three levels'. According to him, a foreman is chosen for his *esperteza* (smartness, cunning), which he sees as the capacity to create harmony among the workers. In order to achieve this, it is necessary for the workers to feel that they too are respected for their sacrifice, embodied in manual and physical activity – and not despised. Caralinda says that he does not even know how to write and read well; all the necessary written work is done by others, under his direction. This adds to the idea that it is not a written (in the sense of scholarly) professional specialisation that contributes to a foreman's worth. Furthermore, his sons, who also work there, replace him when need be, which indicates how the life strategy of a foreman is also the reproductive strategy of his family, and the knowledge passed on to the sons is of the same kind as the knowledge required previously in the peasant world: learning by imitation, trial and error, embodiment and practice, and all relying on a moral sense of doing the right thing.

In a videotaped interview with Caralinda, he compares the 'old' working methods with the 'modern' ones: the former are seen as 'slavery', the latter as 'easiness'. Progress in machine use, in fact, has been significant ever since the 1930s, but particularly after the late 1960s. Physical body strength has lost the importance it previously had. Sr. Altino Morais, for instance, describes 'old work' as 'hand work' (manual labour); his assessment of today's work process is very radical: 'It isn't as hard, otherwise how could they all dress up nicely and go out for the evening?' In 'the old times' (that is, the 1950s), working in the quarries meant the possibility of a steady job, even if one had to bicycle all the way from villages as far as Juromenha. Manual labour used to be all that men had to offer, whereas now a greater number are associated with machine work. This becomes obvious in the answers to the domestic groups' questionnaires, in which the item 'occupation' is answered with fine detail of distinction, using expressions such as 'first-class machine saw-operator'. The transient and ambiguous character of work in the quarries is also analysed by Neves:

> In spite of changes in the workers' qualifications, he remains a working-class type, possessing a polyvalent skill, as a whole, mastering the art of stone by means of tools and machines that have been used for generations. Workers in the quarries are part of a work team, with the *mestre* and *contra mestre* as organisers and distributors of work tasks. The authority of these direct leaderships is not contested – and the social organisation of the quarry has not undergone much change. In general, team work has remained more important than fixed jobs, since workers often get together to assemble and operate a piece of machinery, to prepare and create the conditions for moving a block.... (Neves 1991:14)

Discontinuity with an older rural world does not seem to be great, since, as in *latifundium* agriculture, journeymen sold their physical labour to several employers, for multifaceted, unspecialised tasks. At the turn of the century the foreman was responsible for all areas of production: he hired employees, paid their wages, fired them. As machines became more important – and also with foreign capital investment in some of the enterprises – an increasing number of production engineers and technicians intervened in these areas. Still, formal technical, engineering, and geological knowledge is not enough to raise production and profit. Foremen, as well as workers, have achieved in practice the capacity to 'read', as they say, the stone and the terrain, which is a capacity similar to that peasants have in estimating the potentials of a tract of land. Zé Seco once made this very true and poetic statement: ' If you look at a stone, you see as little as I do if I look at your writing. We folks look at the stone like you look at your writing'.

On the whole decisions are reached by foremen and technicians together. The former thus has two aspects to his activity: a technical and organisational one, which deals with planning, preparing and distributing work in the quarry, and a social one, which defines him as the hierarchical intermediary and leader of men. Foremen are expected by employers to fulfil deadlines, maintaining the work rhythm, guaranteeing discipline. These demands relate to making equipment, men, space and time profitable. That does not mean that the foreman has completely entered the culture of profit and economic calculation; he is not the entrepreneurial manager. That is probably why Caralinda can be seen, on the same day, fraternising at the café both with the engineers and with his fellow workmen.

So workers 'do', and foremen 'make them do'. The capacity to 'make someone do' needs to be acknowledged as legitimate by those who receive orders. Since in the local ethos the hierarchy of age as synonymous with 'knowledge achieved by practice' is still very much alive, the age of foremen can be an important factor. The foreman has regular contact with the foreman-general who supervises all the quarries belonging to the same company. He becomes a liaisor, and creates ties that help him stay in the same company for many years, something that does not happen to the workers.

Each foreman usually supervises an average of ten men, as well as a *contra-mestre* who replaces him when he is absent. His authority is bounded by the ethics of mutual respect, he must be vigilant, but in a limited way; if he over-steps the line he may create all sorts of conflict, because 'men do not like to be treated like servants or children'. He is an expert in safe working techniques which he has embodied and which he can show to his men. In this sense he is also an educator of bodies. What he ultimately seeks to obtain from his workers is 'respect'. He can legitimately expect respect due to his position but, first and foremost, respect must be earned and deserved, it must come as a spontaneous attitude from the workers. This is what respect is all about: you can achieve it through innate status (a father is respected by his son, an employer by his hierarchical inferior, a teacher by the pupils and so on), but one must constantly 'prove to be worthy of respect' (*dar provas de respeito*). It means one has to be honest, straightforward, know how to deal with threats, master the rhetoric of language, have a sense of equilibrium in expenses, excesses and pleasures, and be a good provider for the family. As in 'honour', 'respect' is an unstable good, either because of others' threats (the bad behaviour of those who depend on the respected person), or because of one's vice and temptations. At work, foremen expect to find in some men certain traits of personality such as 'dedication', 'engagement', 'pleasure in work' which can trigger and accelerate the process of learning and ascent of the hierarchy.

At the quarry where Zé Seco works – a quarry that has been running for thirty years – his boss was emotionally moved on only one occasion. That was when he said good-bye to his foreman. 'We could make an average of six-hundred cubic meters with him, now we only make one hundred and fifty'. The foreman was described as someone who knew how to command: he was efficient, he was fair, he never scolded his men in the presence of others and he did not gossip. As if to give a final touch to the moral superiority of this man as someone who could even afford to be a little heterodox, Zé Seco said: 'And, mind you, he wasn't even married. He was *junto*' (literally 'together', living with a woman but unmarried).

Social Stratification, Work, and Respect

So far I have referred to hierarchy in the work place. The emphasis could easily have been placed on social stratification or social classes. I would not like to be accused of paying little attention to this topic, as was the case with the literature on 'Honour and Shame' and its common confusion between status and class.[1] If the criteria used for the definition of social class is the classical 'ownership of means of production', then we are faced with a clear division between quarry employers and all the workers, foremen included. However, it seems more interesting to try to understand the local folk theory about social hierarchy and inequality, situating it in the context of the local work processes, and intertwining it with other social meanings and practices. I wish to focus on those aspects in particular which draw upon gender ideology or influence it. It seems to me that this is the true anthropological contribution even to the study of class. The social division outlined by Cutileiro (1977) between 'rich and poor' may be a good starting point which one can clearly apply to Pardais.

Cutileiro's interpretation is useful in two ways (besides the fact that his is, unfortunately, the only anthropological work on Alentejo so far). It refers to a social reality similar to that of Pardais a few decades ago, and in his work one can find the outlines of a cultural system of symbols and meanings that prevail in Pardais, even if moulded into new circumstances. In relation to social stratification, in Cutileiro's Vila Velha there were four representative groups: *latifundia* owners, *proprietários*, *seareiros* (sharecroppers), and rural workers (*jornaleiros*). The first did not live in the *freguesia*, they were absentee land owners, whose kinship ties spread well beyond the municipality – they actually had a nation-wide character. They had inherited their land and were strong supporters of a system in which one is born with a high status, as opposed to workers who, owing nothing to their ancestors, have only their labour as capital: according to Cutileiro, it is the nobility of work that confers a certain status to the worker (1977:62).

The group of *proprietários* was composed of people from the *freguesia* who managed to live exclusively from the profits of the land they owned and managed. They were physically and interactively closer to the workers, they had no overseers in between, and their social group had originated on the division of public municipal land in the turn of the century. Cutileiro says that as a sign of respect, workers would always address them with the prefix Senhor. *Seareiros*, on the other hand, were an uneasy group, afraid of social decline through down-marriage with workers, and were the most prone to emigration. For these three groups an important distinction is made between those who are self-sufficient and those who are not. Those who own or rent land, whether they work it themselves or hire others to, are self-sufficient, whereas the journeymen, who must hire themselves out yearly, seasonally, weekly or even daily, are not.

Cutileiro pays particular attention to a cultural trope that in Pardais is equally salient – that of *trabalho*, work.

> *Trabalho* includes all agricultural tasks that are done for a salary, as well as the conditions in which they are carried out. Thus it excludes the remaining forms of earning a living. Artisans are 'artists'; their work is an 'art', not work. Shopkeepers, attendants and travelling salesmen do not work either (...) *lavradores* [farmers who own their land] obviously do not work. (Cutileiro 1977:76)

In the workers' opinion, the *lavrador* has achieved man's selfish ideal: to live without working, but nevertheless without losing prestige. Cutileiro adds that after the opening of a factory in the *freguesia*, the new category of the 'factory worker' arose. Since rural workers suspected that factory worker's standards of living would be much higher than their own, their activity was not initially considered as 'work'.

Things are different in Pardais. Partly because of the 'extractive' nature of work in the quarries, and partly because the people of Pardais have re-interpreted their social condition by making it homologous with the old notion of work. Most of all because what is at stake in the cultural definition of work is the fact that one has to sell one's labour, plus the manual, physical nature of the activity. Up to a certain point Cutileiro confirms this: the fact that agricultural work is opposed to praised values such 'standing straight', 'chins up' (*cabeça erguida*), 'straight man' (*homem às direitas*) (Cutileiro 1977:80), thus – I would add – connecting, through embodiment, physical posture, body techniques and moral rectitude. This is why work is an ambiguous semantic field. In Portugal, Alentejans are the victims of jokes in a similar way that Poles are in the United States and Belgians in France. The main negative attributed characteristic is laziness. The proverbial Alentejan laziness has an ironical justification in reality: the mute resistance to alienation and exploitation; the remainder – the essentialistic notion of laziness – being no other than ethnocentric prejudice.

Another aspect stressed by Cutileiro relates to patronage and patron-client relations. He states that patron-client relations stem from needs which are the result of an awareness that things one has access to in life are scarce and can be obtained thanks to privilege; and that you can only be privileged via the protection of someone placed close to the source wherefrom comes the desired good (1977:271). So personal relationships of exchange of favours are established; but they are in their nature unbalanced. The client has to offer objects and services of less significance than those he or she obtains from the patron. The underlying idea is that society is not well organised and that individual effort, much more so than collective effort, can remedy the situation. Davis (1977) defined patronage as a relationship that occurs whenever a man shows deference to the more powerful, thus succeeding in obtaining access to certain resources, and he drew attention to the fact that patronage was not a mere extension of friendship or of 'spiritual kinship' (god parenthood), but rather the procedure by which the autocracy of local magnates is controlled by the weaker members of society (Davis 1977:132–135).[2]

The kind of classifications which we as social scientists may outline for social stratification do not necessarily correspond to those used locally. The latter follow a dichotomous principle, that of 'rich and poor'. They are like two poles, two opposed extremes on a scale, and are a classificatory principle in the same way as 'masculine and feminine' or 'active and passive'. In addition, they have interesting mutual translations between them, since poverty tends to be passive and passivity tends to be feminine (i.e., all of them unprestigious), and vice-versa for wealth (although as in all symbolic systems of hierarchy inversion may occur at the two extremes).

'We are poor. That is, we live well, but we are poor because we work', Beto told me, using a rather commonly heard phrase in Pardais and one that probably says a lot more than entire chapters in a social science manual. Even when earning relatively high wages compared to those he would earn were he a rural journeyman, the worker includes himself in the broader category of 'poor', he sells his labour, his work is physical, his power – understood as the social capacity to autonomously control the conditions of one's existence – is limited. Note, however, that if on the opposite pole are the 'rich' or the employers, the foreman is nevertheless 'part of the poor'.

The local political utopia (and a common one in Alentejo, Andaluzia and the south of Iberia in general) speaks about 'equality'. Equality supposedly does not exist because 'the rich' possess in their 'nature' a moral fault – 'ambition'. It is ambition that enables the rich to set out personal selfish strategies for obtaining the control of scarce resources. Rich and poor are thus morally opposed. This is what generates the fact that at work – in a similar fashion to friendship relations and male sociability – there is a stressing of equality of circumstances, leading to the utilisation at work of the same ethical principles that guide friendship. Beto, for instance, would talk a lot about the friends he had made at the work place and the mutual construction of 'respect'.

Respect can in some circumstances – between social opposites – mean social distance. Distance and proximity are linguistically marked by terms of address, in European Portuguese *tu* means 'you' in an informal sense and *você* a formal 'you'. The other meaning of respect is respect as the result of moral and ethical characteristics among social equals which make them trustworthy. 'Truth' and honesty are its pillars. These are tested in the lesser or greater capacity of individuals to balance out their selfish interest (which can only be positive if used to trigger patron-client relations) with the equalitarian utopia of all-male groups.

The *cabouqueiro* worker of Pardais is not 'quarry-hungry', to use a similar expression to that of 'land hunger' that has been used to characterise

71

Alentejo rural people. A comparative (both ethnographically and historically) example can help us make this point. In Almeria, in Spanish Andaluzia, and unlike Pardais where quarries were never communal land, quarries were privatised in the mid-nineteenth century (Alcantud 1990). The *canteros* (marble workers) of the village of Macael who were interviewed by Alcantud confessed to him that they did not consider themselves as 'miners'. They thought that mining was harder work. The Macael *cantero* felt an ambiguity based on the fact that on the one hand he earned a salary – which made him different from the peasant – but on the other hand he wanted to overcome the characteristic working-class 'equalitarianism'. Unlike the Andaluzian rural world, in which *jornaleros* had a clear notion of their condition and objectives (they did not have land, they wanted it and they knew who to take it away from), among *canteros* real property and rights of use of the sub-soil were confused, since nominally it had been theirs ever since the Muslim occupation. None of this occurs in Pardais: if anyone feels that ambiguity it is the quarry owners or the company owners, divided between those who actually own land and quarries and those who – although owning companies – have to rent the rights of use of land for marble extraction. Alcantud's example shows how social movements in rural areas can be regionally specific, because they are not simply clear-cut social class struggles, but rather a web of interests involving law and history, patronage and clientelism, kinship and proximity and so on.

Thus work in quarries appears in places to be some sort of logical continuation of the rural journeyman's work: no specialisation, workers doing all sorts of tasks, choosing their working schedules according to their financial objectives, calculating when to work on weekends and holidays or extra hours throughout the night. This also corresponds, of course, to the employers' strategy for obtaining, controlling and containing the work force and its claims. Of course, the most important difference continues to be the fact that there is work available, whereas previously one could be in a situation in which work literally had to be begged for.

Young men in Pardais who are working are somewhat privileged. The previous generation, and particularly those who were *seareiros*, had to migrate to the great cities, and women are experiencing severe unemployment. Also, any change in market values for marble abroad can have catastrophic consequences locally. In the eventuality of an end to the marble industry, not only have the landscape and the ecology been destroyed, but agricultural work opportunities are gone as well as the knowledge of agriculture. As one young man told me once, 'I was lucky to have learned how to handle a plough; but most of the guys don't know how to do anything other than quarry work'.

Returning now to the notion of 'work', which also contains the elements of 'sacrifice' and 'risk'. These are ambiguous, since they are not desired, but they reinforce prestige for the man who has undergone tribulation, in a cultural universe in which masculinity invokes physical strength.[3] Palhinhas has already retired, he is an old man, and he worked for twenty three-years and nine months in the quarries, and succeeded in becoming a foreman. The first thing he recalls when talking to me is that he was run over by a *vagona* (a small wagon on rails), sustaining ten broken ribs, injuring one leg and – which was worst of all for him – damaging his left testicle. Beto too, told me that ever since he had seen a man die in an accident in the quarry, he has dreamt that the same will happen to him and always wakes up crying after the nightmare. Since the deceased man died on his birthday, Beto now refuses to go to work on his own birthday and concludes with a popular saying '*Anos é festa*' (a birthday is a festive day).

Dangerous work conditions are part of the reason why there is such strong desire for one's children to have access to a higher standard of living. A man told me that thanks to his hard work he had managed to provide his children with *ofícios* (trades) as mechanics and marble polishers. He once had a *fazenda*, a small farm that he sold 'for almost nothing', in order to start working in the quarries; later, the same land would be sold for a lot more money – 'you can see the cranes there today, to prove it'. As a foreman, he makes one hundred and forty *contos* per month (the equivalent of a teacher's salary) and an extra sixty *contos* for draining the water whenever it rains. He also told me that even in agriculture it is around Pardais that the highest wages are paid (which obviously relates to a labour shortage in the sector), six *contos* (6,000 escudos) daily 'plus some eats to ease things out'. This is the male salary, for women have a hard time finding jobs and have traditionally been paid considerably less than men. However, according to him 'they now all live off their husbands' pay'.

Zé Seco Jr, using the rhetoric of *sorte e azar* (good and bad luck), says that there are plenty of accidents in the quarries. He described one occasion when a man fell from a height of thirty metres: his head ended up far from the body and 'his brains were scattered all over the place'. Throughout fieldwork, news of accidents became an ever-present feature, a sort of parallel emotional life of the village, and their effect was only second to that of suicide attempts, mainly made by women.[4] The maid of one of Pardais' elementary school teachers – who lives in Vila Viçosa – lives in permanent fear when she hears ambulance sirens, since she immediately thinks it means her husband might have had an accident in the quarries. I personally met a young man of twenty-four who is wheelchairbound as a consequence of a quarry accident, and the school teachers say they have had plenty of 'quarry orphans' among their students throughout the years. This dramatic sense of life, work and luck has a true enough grounding in reality – I have myself felt anxiety about my friends' safety on many occasions. The danger reinforces the work's sacrificial overtones, something which is simultaneously frightening, undesirable but also like a trophy of 'respect' which can be awarded to those men who pass through such tribulations. Maybe it is not by chance that marble extraction is an exclusively masculine activity.

Power, Patronage, Politics

Power has various dimensions of interaction: from power in interpersonal relations, particularly obvious as an object of dispute in male relationships, to power in family and conjugal relationships, to the more salient social dimension of power in social difference and the management of collective life. Let us try to understand this web with three local examples that seem to be particularly meaningful: the cultural value of money and consumption in stating the prestige of the 'poor'; patronage and the example of the powerful Capucho family; and the play of local political power.

Zé Seco Jr is a heavy drinker, but says that he knows how to control himself. One evening I met him in the café and he told me that on the previous day he had received sixty *contos* of holiday pay, had deposited it in the bank in Vila Viçosa in order not to spend it and so be able to hand it to his wife the next day; then he proceeded to, as he said, 'get loaded' and until the moment we met he had not returned home. His wife was probably worried, he said, especially because he could be spending his money on drink or … and he proceeded to gestually describe the sexual act. At the time of this episode, many conversations expressed concern with the Gulf War. Besides general moral considerations on the issues of human 'evil' and 'ambition' – personified by Saddam Hussein, although many good communists would also put Bush in the same bag – the War was having direct consequences in Pardais: many work contracts were being cancelled and there were threats of unemployment, since Arab countries in the Gulf region (Iraq included) are the main purchasers of Portuguese marble. A Lisbon intellectual who lives near Pardais had told me that according to the law, quarry owners should pay ten percent of their profits to the Municipality, but instead established their official headquarters elsewhere in order to escape this tax. Of the three hundred quarries in the municipality of Vila Viçosa, the majority are on rented land, with rents of over a thousand *contos* a month, which is just the price of one single block of marble. This is why some poor old men who owned small tracts of land and rented them for quarries suddenly became quite affluent. The Lisbon intellectual even said: 'There are no poor people anymore, neither is there class consciousness. As soon as there is more money people trade the Communist Party for the Social Democrats [the conservative party in government at the time of fieldwork]'.

These are but a few examples of 'money talk'. One of my friends in the field was Raposo. He is a *cabouqueiro* worker in his twenties. He has been married for a short time and has a son who attends kindergarten; he lives in a brand new house in the brand new *Rua dos Covões*. Raposo is an expert practitioner of the arts of irony and sarcasm, especially when applied to issues of social inequality and competition. For quite some time he tried to convince me that I should become friends with Rui Capucho, the owner of the largest local quarry, entrepreneur, and his boss. Raposo's line of reasoning was that I would thus have access to all the aspects and secrets of the economic activity, provided, however, that in exchange I led him to believe that I would somehow (my influence in the outside world was very exaggerated) promote his enterprises. Raposo said – confirming the Lisbon intellectual's opinion – that if I were to check on the Treasury archives I would find out that all quarries are non-profitable. That was his sarcastic way of saying that dishonest practices were used in income-tax statements. Parallel to his accusations of 'rich people's scheming', he complained bitterly about the low levels of trade-union participation and the fact that workers were always trying to 'fuck each other in order to make more money'.

Perhaps a small parenthesis is needed here: trade-union enrolment has traditionally been high in Alentejo, but only at the level of rural workers, whose social movements for agrarian reform have traditionally been strong and organised by communist trade unions. The low trade unionism of quarry workers indicates two things: strong company mobility and the fact that these workers were initially born into the marble economy, not the rural one. Raposo worried about the fact that he and the others always felt the dilemma between choosing steady working hours and a fixed salary and, on the other hand, what they call 'a by-the-hour schedule' and its floating salary. This freedom to choose work schedules and employers is not, of course, the right atmosphere for trade unionism.

I did not have one meeting with Raposo in which he did not raise the same topic of conversation, and most of the time in a way that always struck me as ambivalent. For him, Rui Capucho was the rich man's paradigm, and he was always both saint and devil. That is, while he accused Capucho of uncontained ambition and dishonesty, he admired his cunning, his aptitude for business, his expertise in manipulating people's allegiance to him. Only later did I realise that the same ambivalence applies in judgements of masculinity: the prestige obtained by the fact that a man works hard to provide for his family can have its opposite in spending a lot of money outside the family particularly with women other than one's own. Or, between the praised capacity to exert self-control (not spending too much on drinking and being able to 'keep one's head cool') and the praising of the man who knows how to 'get really loaded' and act like a care-free adolescent.

For Raposo, marble means money, but the Portuguese government does not know the extent of these riches because the company bosses submit false tax declarations claiming losses. He feels that the sub-region 'is covered with a black cloak, no one knows about it, no one speaks about it'. And I was supposed to uncover these things, to tell the world about the riches and how they were all in the hands of foreigners, or *saloios* (people from the other marble production region, near Sintra in the outskirts of Lisbon), or a very few locals – the Capuchos and few others. In sum, as Raposo says, 'we are all idiots, with all this under our feet and not knowing how to get a hold of it'.

As I have outlined in Chapter 2, the recent history of property, of the economic success of the quarries and of political patronage, is connected with two families: Conceição and Capucho.[5] The former does not excavate any quarries directly or own any companies. They basically rent or sell land for the purpose, and are now practically disconnected from the life of the village. Their *Quinta dos Passos* is now vacant, and only two spinster sisters are still living. The family fortune is administered by their goddaughter and heiress, and her husband, a physician in Alandroal.

The latter, the Capucho family, is a different case. Firstly because they do not really have a past history of land ownership, they do not claim a social identity of *proprietários*. Secondly, because they are a family from Pardais who only one generation ago was living in poverty. Two of the three brothers, Fernando and Quim, although quite affluent in the marble business, have kept a low profile in local social and political life. Rui, on the contrary, has been more successful in both business and personal promotion. One of Fernando's sons, Zé Maria, is also a prominent local character, since he is a well known equestrian bullfighter. I shall pay particular attention, then, to Rui Capucho and Zé Maria Capucho.

Raposo was quite blunt when he referred to Rui Capucho: 'He is the greatest gypsy, but he is also the greatest benefactor in the village. He steals, all right – only he who steals can become rich – but not from the poor'. The use of the expression 'gypsy' is quite common as a description of cunning, and business capacity, understood as something fundamentally immoral but still the only way to achieve a significant economic status. Gypsies, however, are also seen as pariahs, as people who do not 'work', and as marginal to the social order. Gypsies are not integrated in communal sedentary life and are seen mostly at liminal, extra-social contexts such as fairs and markets. Rui Capucho's businesses are seen by most people in Pardais as necessarily dubious. His strategy begins with the manipulation of kinship ties. The three brothers, as godchildren of the Conceição family, have tried everything to get a hold of 'the largest slice of the cake'. Their capacity to use kinship beyond moral limits is also a motive for awe: recently the three brothers were involved in a judicial dispute regarding inheritance, and Rui came out as the winner. He expresses and does what everybody knows is implicitly done in all kinship relationships: the levelling out of emotions and interest, self-interest and moral obligations. It is important however, that Rui Capucho is referred to as someone 'who used to be poor'. His life story is that of a self-made man, which confers upon him a special kind of prestige ('he knew better than others') but also jealousy and the suspicion of devious behaviour.

Since Rui Capucho is a son of the land and boss to many people who actually played with him as children, interaction with him has a strange, awkward overtone: as if the ideals of intrinsic equality among men as members of the same gender had been somehow betrayed. As if that were not enough, Rui Capucho also invests a great deal in paternalism and patronage. This applies to several levels of social life: to individual workers and their families; to the collective life of the village (improving buildings, with donations and, most specially, in religious and festive activities); to the level of municipal political life and also – as a project – national political life. Therefore he is dangerously powerful but a generous benefactor and patron.

Let us give an example: he is the landlord of a couple, Emílio and Purificação, and Emílio is one of his employees. When I gathered this item of information, someone told me that he is also the landlord of two other adjacent houses. In one of them lives a woman who is paid to take care of an old uncle of Rui's wife; yet another woman takes care of Rui's elderly in-laws. 'They are very rich, but they give a lot. Everything by the cart loads. Look, look, there goes a whole cart-full of firewood for the woman who looks after the uncle', said a woman I was talking with at her doorstep. The stories of direct support for employees are numerous: T-shirts and key chains with company logos are given out to all employees and their children for Christmas; *bolo-rei* (an expensive Christmas cake) is given to all families on Epiphany; everyone can go to him and ask for a loan or for a good word to be put in at the doctor's or a civil servant; it is common gossip that driving licences (which are quite expensive in Portugal) can be obtained without the cost of lessons and exams if one is his employee and he needs a driver.

'Rich people get mad with each other but then they have lunch together. Poor people, when they have a fight, it's for life. What a shame', said Raposo. At the core of this morality is the strategy for keeping and reproducing capital, in other words, 'money'. When I first met Rui Capucho, who was introduced to me by Sr. Altino Valente, he said (after he had asked quite sarcastically why I was studying 'his village') that he did not like money. I had not asked him anything, but this was the first thing he said. He gave some examples of how much trouble can come from money: after his aunt died, his entire family demanded part of the inheritance and sent the funeral bills to him, regardless of the fact that he had had to pay someone to take care of his aunt before she died.

Rui Capucho's most direct form of patronage is exerted over local religious and ritual life. Pardais did not have a priest (resident or otherwise) for several years, a situation which was prolonged by inertia due to the fact that church attendance is very low – a common characteristic of the Alentejo. Only a few women relate closely to church life, especially Mariana do Couto, an elderly spinster who has in charge church maintenance, as well as quite a number of children, since parents feel Sunday School to be an important experience for children. A few weeks after starting fieldwork, Pardais obtained a new priest. He is of Spanish origin and was a missionary in Brazil. Father Aragão is a young dynamic character. He organised religious-education classes at the primary school, conquered the affection of children, stimulated Sunday School, and innovated liturgy by introducing new songs and guitars. He convinced

Rui Capucho and his wife to let him use a pavilion in one of their houses to hold guitar classes; the teachers were two young Brazilians, one of them an ex-Franciscan, who were living in Alandroal. In the next chapter I will say more about my relationship with him, via the children. For now the important fact is that the religious order to which the priest belongs is highly subsidised by Rui Capucho.

Vila Viçosa has a strong institutional religious tradition. It is like an island in the middle of the very anti-clerical Alentejo. This tradition comes from the influence of the royal house of Bragança, whose headquarters were there. The tradition has been renovated by the more conservative sectors in the last few years, particularly by the brotherhood of Our Lady of the Conception. One of the local old convents, that of the Capuchos (the religious order, not the family...) – around which an important pilgrimage was held in the past – was abandoned until it was loaned to the Order of the Holy Cross to which Father Aragão belongs. Most members of the Order are not Portuguese. The Order was expelled from Portugal and re-founded in Austria by – so the gossip goes – sectors connected with the Opus Dei; the order bloomed in Spain, centred around the revival of Marianic cult of the figure of Our Lady of the Conception. This invocation of the Virgin is also the patron saint of Portugal, so declared by King John the Fourth in 1640, first king of the Bragança dynasty, after the restoration of Independence. The priests from the Order of the Holy Cross are engaged mainly in missionary work in Alentejo, a region that the Church has declared as 'in need of re-evangelisation'. Through his wife, Rui Capucho has contributed to the rebirth of the Catholic cult in Pardais. His wife organised the entire party to celebrate Father Aragão's ordination; the religious part of the ceremony took place in the Church of Our Lady of the Conception in Vila Viçosa, and the profane celebration took place in the old garage that had been one possible residence for myself.

Pardais' annual *festa*, which takes place in July, has lately been paid for by Rui Capucho, the new president of the organising committee. The rest of the committee is made up of men from Pardais who are Capucho's employees, most of them specialised workers, like electricians and machine operators, as well as by young single women with higher level schooling, such as Filomena (see Chapter 2). Filomena does not hide the fact that she knows that Capucho's strategy is to heighten his prestige, but she accepts (although with some irony) that it is after all 'pennies from heaven'. She was one of the women who carried the altar with the saints in the procession, an event that is mainly a female occupation and

women's symbolic appropriation of the village public space; Rui Capucho's wife lead the procession.

Patronage can also be displayed in Vila Viçosa. Mariano, the young
farmer subsidised by European Union funds and friend of Zé Ganhão's,
once commented 'the things one has to do for the rich!' when, with a
feeling of scandal, he related to me how the philharmonic band in which
he plays had to play a special tune in front of the Capucho residence in
town, dedicating it to him. However, someone who overheard our conversation said: 'What else do you expect? Who do you think paid for
your uniforms?' I know very little of the Capuchos' participation in the
virtual 'corporations' of marble industrialists. But I do know that his
political life is notorious. He is a strong supporter of PSD, the Social
Democratic Party, in power during the ethnographic present, and does
not conceal his wish to become an MP in the near future.

Sr. Morais, president of the *Junta* of the *freguesia* was elected on the
Socialist Party ticket; he has a difficult and tense relationship with Rui
Capucho. Apparently, the latter tried to assemble a PSD list for Pardais,
'so that he could do whatever he wanted with the *freguesia*'.[6] Sr. Morais
is an obstacle to the indiscriminate use and growth of piles of debris in
the immediacies of the village and complains about the destruction of
municipal roads by heavy trucks. Once he told me that the Mayor – then
also a socialist – had warned him that Rui Capucho 'never gives anything
for free', in connection to the offer he had made to build a new road.

If Sr. Morais is an intermediary between the local municipal power
and the *freguesia* level (and he has been very efficient at that, for he has
won all elections ever since the restoration of democracy in 1974, even
though there is a strong Communist influence among voters),[7] Rui
Capucho is an intermediary between his client *freguesia*, economic decisions at municipal level, and the national structure of classes and political power, tied to the global economy in which the marble industry is
embedded. This is ideologically reinforced by the aristocratic and religious aura that Vila Viçosa has in national symbolic identity. Class structure and symbolic distinction are very clear cut in the municipal capital,
Vila Viçosa. For instance, different cafés correspond to meeting places
for different social classes (and sexes): the café for the upper class, which
used to be the *latifundia* owners' café, the café for ladies or pastry shop,
and the cafés for male workers in general. Public ritual depicts the
importance in local identities of an overlapping of symbolic domination.
The first of December is a national holiday, celebrating the restoration of
Independence in 1640. Besides the nationalist discourse proffered in

monumental venues such as the Royal palace and the Castle, Prime Minister Cavaco Silva went to mass at the Church of Our Lady of the Conception. The Capuchos were there in the front row. No one from Pardais – not even Sr. Morais – attended.

Once I went to a large bullfight in the Vila, and the equestrian bullfighter Zé Maria Capucho was one of the attractions. The band was playing beautifully and a lottery-ticket vendor was sarcastically proclaiming: 'Now you'll have marble for your graves! And later in the evening that'll be some dinner party in Pardais!' He was of course referring to the fact that the band was so good because one of the bullfighters could afford to hire it. Zé Maria owns *herdades* and quarries and his own marble company. Thanks to the profits, he can finance the very expensive activity of equestrian bullfighting. The symbolic universe of bullfighting, bulls and horses will be further examined in Chapter 4, since it is particularly salient for definitions of masculinity. There Zé Maria Capucho will have an important role to play. For now it is with the 'money' trope that I wish to conclude.

The Other Value of Money

Money, for Giddens (1992a) is one of the mechanisms of disembbedment associated with modernity. Simmel (1978) said that money shortened distances, allowing the proprietor and his goods to be far apart, thus marking a great difference in comparison to situations where property owners and goods were in direct relation – a situation in which economic commitments were also personal commitments. In Pardais, to use money ostensibly is to show that one has full autonomous agency.

Money, above all else, is the symbol of the product of work. The description of intense and arduous working hours in the quarries goes hand-in-hand with the notion that a man 'does not need to look at another man's hands' (meaning he does not have to feel envy and does not have to beg). Money gives independence: to the domestic group and to the individual man. Money is also used, of course, as a rhetorical device. Beto, before the annual festivities endlessly repeated that he had spent three hundred and fifty *contos* (a large sum: £1,500) on clothes for himself, his wife and children in order to attend two weddings. Ruivo (a *cabouqueiro* worker whose father is an invalid and who lives with his mother and three young brothers) is often found with thirty *contos* (30,000 escudos) or more in his pocket: he shows the money, describes how and on what he is going to spend it – usually sumptuary goods – and explains the local philosophy on the importance of a man not being a 'slave'.

It is important to stress that none of this should simply be interpreted as a 'nouveau-riche' attitude. Money is visible and it circulates in collective contexts, in all-male contexts where it is required to buy drinks for others, to invite others; it is given a moral significance that reverses the dichotomy freedom – slavery. If money is what 'makes imagination move in the brain' (as Estorninho said, referring to Saddam Hussein's evil character), that same imagination (the temptation for negative things) can and should be controlled by a sense of morality. And morality is checked by other people's opinions. In a scene on the Brazilian soap opera *Tieta* that was a hit during fieldwork, there was a conflict situation between the minister of a sect called Assembly of Christ the King (the 'bad guy') and a converted ex-alcoholic (the 'good guy'). In the café, while watching the episode, a man commented: 'This soap is a riot, but what that man is saying is right – you can't buy heaven'. The character in the soap opera was saying that the greatest goods are God, Love and Charity and that money should be spent on food, clothes and in giving to the needy.

Upon returning home from an evening out, in my car, Zé Ganhão and Leonel were elaborating on the theory that 'all that women want is money'. On one hand they meant prostitutes, but on the other hand, other women do too, either they want men to buy things for them or they want to make convenient marriages. Zé Ganhão said that 'if you want to find a woman, you have to look for one among those who work in agriculture, since they are poorer, and so easier to pick up. Things are difficult around here. Since this is the centre of money, they prefer for several of them to go out with just one guy rather than to distribute themselves among more men with less money'.

It is quite obvious that many aspects of the 'money culture' are really aspects of the culture of capitalism, related to the village's insertion in the world economy as well as in global culture, inherently capitalist. Local production of a relatively scarce raw material – and a sumptuary one for that matter – places people from Pardais in direct dependence on world market fluctuations which can depend on political and armed conflict as far away as the Persian Gulf. On the other hand, the village is undergoing a full-fledged process of 'mediatisation': one can watch more television channels in Pardais than in Lisbon thanks to the proximity of Spain, bringing an influx of images and sounds of alternative values and lifestyles.

One cannot, however, see the world system as necessarily homogenising (which is the commonly held view). Hannerz states that cultural differences within the world system are not simply remains of the past. The expanding world system may create ideological disturbances on the peripheries in the shape of community revitalisation or ideological revolutions among the elites, for instance (Hannerz 1989:205). The more appropriate rendering of the situation would probably be that of tension: between diverging projects of values, moralities, consumption. It is a tension that goes hand-in-hand with processes of creolisation:

> ...the people of the periphery encounter the meanings and the symbolic forms of the centre with perspectives which are both formed and capable of being reformed, and the very fact that they are shaped by the experience of being at the periphery will contribute to making them different from those of the centre. (Hannerz 1989:213)[8]

Forms of consumption and consumer culture in Pardais reflect this state of affairs. 'Money' is the general equivalent in a symbolic negotiation between the values of savings and commensality, personal strategies of prestige and the influence of global culture by such means as fashion, music, behaviours, publicity etc. In direct relation to masculinity, this is a process that allows for the experimentation of alternatives to hegemonic masculinity – television and film, for instance, provide specific men with alternative models for being male. In sum, noisy, confusing, exciting and also depressing times are taking place in Pardais.

NOTES

1. The usefulness of the concept of Honour and Shame has been widely contested. The literature on Mediterranean societies (e.g., Campbell 1964, Peristiany 1965), while stressing the moral code of male honour guaranteed by the control of female sexuality and fertility, did not fully explore the gender dimension in these values. There were of course exceptions, such as Schneider (1971). The main problem however, seems to lie on the very definition of a culture area that is more diverse than unified, as one goes from the historic-geographical overview of Braudel (1983) to the several ethnographic minutiae, and in the creation of a backyard exoticism by northern European anthropologists (see, on this, Pina-Cabral 1989, Herzfeld 1980). Class divisions in the 'Mediterranean' did not rely on codes of prestige solely, but on the very historically particular forms of land ownership, relations of production, and state ideologies. My use of 'honour' has solely to do with the local use in Pardais of 'respect'.

2. See also Boissevain (1974) and Riegelhaupt (1967).
3. Although physical strength is not the founding principle of masculinity, as it is in, for instance, Mexican *machismo*, sexuality is. On these differences regarding cultural principles of masculinity, see Gilmore (1990) and Lancaster (1988).
4. Alentejo is the Portuguese region with the highest rate of suicide. It affects mostly old men, and women in general. It has been speculated that it is related to the small influence of Catholicism and to the atomised nature of social organisation. However, in Pardais, there were three cases of suicide by women during my fieldwork. Causes were explained as relating to terminal illnesses and depression. There were no male attempts, except for the narrative of Altino Valente's father's suicide by hanging in Vila Viçosa's public water fountain. He had been the victim of a con man and became indebted. Male suicides are often described as caused by issues of honour, whereas female ones are seen as 'natural' consequence of female 'emotional instability'.
5. Unfortunately I was not able to follow Laura Nader's (Nader 1969) call for 'studying up', the study of the rich and powerful instead of only the 'underdogs'. As a matter of fact the patience that people from Pardais had towards me and my questioning was in great part due to my social precedence in a country where social hierarchies still have an unfortunate *ancien régime* flavour. Powerful people made direct access difficult and constantly cut off any chance of approaching them.
6. After fieldwork, in the local elections of 1993, Rui Capucho had obtained an unmatchable triumph by politically supporting the Mayor of Vila Viçosa. The latter, formerly elected as a Socialist, this time ran for the Social Democrats, and won. The local-national connection is now stronger, and Sr. Morais, who did not change party, fears the possible negative consequences for Pardais.
7. Electoral results in 1991 Legislative elections, in Pardais: Socialists 159, Social Democrats 101, Communists 67.
8. On the cultural aspects of globalisation (thus expanding and also criticising Wallerstein's approach on the world-system) and the fetishism of commodities and mass consumption, some important contributions are made by Taussig (1980) and Appadurai (1990), although they are somewhat marginal to the scope of this essay. The same could be said about Jameson (1984), regarding the culture of capitalism. In Perspectives II (Conclusion) I will expand further on the relevance of the theme of modernity and globalism as one of the avenues for the development of gender studies.

4. IN THE COMPANY OF MEN
Masculine Sociabilities

*T*his chapter will focus on how discourses and practices of masculinity are constructed and reproduced in sociability outside of work. This is a sociability between men: a case-study of the café as the 'men's house' will be of central importance, and it will be complemented with 'going out' to *bailes*, festivals and, mostly, to nightclubs – *boîtes*. Finally, the symbolic universe of bullfighting will be dealt with as a metaphoric text on ideas of gender and masculinity.

The House of Men: The Café as a Masculine Space

For someone coming from an urban culture, the *taberna* is usually regarded as something typical of villages and the poorer urban neighbourhoods; it is connected with vague ideas of tradition, of something that is being lost with modernity. The café, on the contrary, conjures notions of urbanity, cosmopolitanism and bourgeois culture.

It is true that the taverns are disappearing, but this process is occurring both in the cities and in the countryside. It does not necessarily mean that 'tradition' is being 'lost', as long as one understands tradition as a set of practices and meanings that are managed and reformulated by those individuals and groups that sustain them – not as simple testimonies of times gone by or as patrimonial remains. In Pardais the tavern has disappeared, and has been replaced with a different physical space and locale for consumption: the café. In the café, nevertheless, the interactions and functions connected with the traditional tavern persist.

Only a decade ago there was one tavern in the village, and its owner was Sr. Morais' father. Since then, two cafés have opened. One is owned by Estorninho, the other by Fazendas. The former is located in the upper part of the village (*o café de cima*), the latter in the lower part (*o café de baixo*), and neither is a direct continuation of a *taberna* business. Estorninho left his venture as a small quarry owner and opened his café with the money resulting from the sale of his business; Fazenda's father co-owns the café with his son, but also has a coal business in Vila Viçosa.

Sr. Morais' father's old tavern (like so many in rural Portugal) was located in an old house with thick walls, no windows, dark and cool inside, and with a long bench along the outside wall, where old men sat for long periods of time. He sold mainly wine, tobacco and some staples. At its peak it even had a refrigerator, an uncommon utility at the time; this relic was kindly loaned to me during my stay in the village.

The modern cafés, on the other hand, are located in newer houses, made of brick and concrete, with aluminium framed windows. They are furnished with plastic and formica tables and chairs, modern refrigerated bars, *expresso* coffee machines, radio and television, telephone, and bathrooms. They sell mainly coffee and beer, but also multinational brand ice creams, sweets and appetisers made in Spain, and so on. Like the tavern, however, they are patronised mainly by men.

The fundamental differences between the old tavern and the present-day cafés are threefold. The first has to do with the physical aspect of the place: the café is understood as more comfortable, modern and well equipped; secondly, the type of consumption is an important element, in a nutshell, the move from wine to beer; thirdly, the type of customers, from exclusively masculine to (ideally) masculine and feminine.

The first point is related to two other issues. First, the café owner's life story: he typically accumulated capital through the sale of small plots of land to the marble industry or the sale of a previous business. The rise in standards of living triggered by the 'white gold' economy has raised the expectations for consumption and comfort. This is the second point. Both aspects are reflected in local identity, since part of the village's prestige is indicated by the quantity, modernity and quality of the local cafés.

The second difference is directly related to the relationship between prestige and patterns of mass consumption. The culture of wine has a strong symbolic association with rural life and poverty, for wine was home-made. Beer, on the other hand, as a bottled product commercialised through advertisements, appeals to the values of consumerism and goes against the production for use that wine symbolised.

As for the third difference, it is what one could call the 'frustrated project'. Local comparisons between villages which focus on their cafés are always centred on whether they have a modern enough atmosphere so as to make women feel welcomed and comfortable. In the case of Pardais, they allow this in a limited way: women go to the café during men's 'dead hours', that is, in the middle afternoon (after men have taken their after-lunch coffee), mid-morning (when men are away working and women are on their shopping rounds), or yet on Sundays.[1] It is not in the café that women socialise. In this sense, cafés still fulfil the same function as the tavern: they are places for the interaction of a specific social category, that of working-class men, which is today's equivalent of the rural journeymen of the past.

Urban café culture only started in Lisbon after the great earthquake of 1755, and it did so thanks to the support and incentive of the Enlightened prime minister, the Marquis of Pombal. He publicly supported the fact that cafés could be places for debate and the making of a public opinion. In the nineteenth century cafés had already become true centres for political and literary opinion making, through the institution of the *tertúlia* (informal debate groups of literati). They were exclusively male preserves. The first woman in Lisbon to have penetrated a café was a foreigner and she had to disguise herself as a man in order to do so (Dias 1987). This regime was continued until the post Second World War period. The female writer Ilse Losa, who came to Portugal as a war refugee in the 1940s, recalls how she felt diminished by not being allowed to walk alone in the streets of Oporto or go into a café. Only recently have two developments occurred: the end of *tertúlias* and the opening of cafés to both sexes.

The larger provincial towns, such as Vila Viçosa, went through a similar process, although cafés remained until later as masculine preserves. They are also divided along the lines of local political clienteles, and mostly along class lines. In Vila Viçosa there is a diversified range of cafés and similar places: from the 'Framar', which used to be the landowners' café and today is the quarry owners' café, to the 'Pastelaria', a predominately female and petit-bourgeois place (thus specialising in pastries), to the café 'Cortiço', which is frequented by the village men when they come to the weekly market or to attend fairs; there are also a number of taverns that serve traditional dishes and appetisers, night-time *pubs* (these are not the same as British pubs, they are more like private clubs) divided along class lines among young people. Two categories of public places were added in the last decade: the *discoteca*, where you can dance and fraternise in groups; and the *boîte* which, in the local sense, means a place of semi-prostitution, and is strongly supported by villagers. Both are usually located in towns or in isolated *montes* in the countryside. In the villages the range of options is very limited: the most one can find is an 'emigrant's café' (as in São Romão, an agrarian parish with strong emigration to Switzerland). These cafés have imported features that allow families to patronise them: they resemble restaurants more than cafés. Villages sometimes have a café in the *Casa do Povo* or Recreational Society, which is usually patronised by older people.

What goes on at the village cafés that makes them so important for an understanding of masculinity? At an impressionistic level, one drinks at the café, especially alcoholic drinks; one eats appetisers and small entrées, one plays dominoes, billiards, cards, table football; and one watches television. Also noticeable is that the customers are mostly males, they know each other, they gather in groups, drinks are paid for in turns according to rules of commensality, and the most perceptible action is talking.

In eighteenth- and nineteenth-century Europe workers considered drinking as an inseparable and even compulsory part of work. The same was true for agrarian landless journeymen until quite recently. Drinking was repressed at work only by the demands of the new systems of production, thus finding a new locus – both physical and temporal – in public institutions of commerce and leisure. This was a response to the growing work discipline, to the alienation of control over the labour force, shorter working days and the rise in the standards of living of the working classes. This process occurred quite early in northern European contexts, but it is a recent one in Pardais. This explains in part the rise of the café as an alternative to the tavern.

In Mediterranean societies, the bar or café is a focal institution in public life. It is the main stage of masculine sociability; it is the male gender that is associated with public life. It is in the café that one can find the telephone, an utility that is absent from the majority of the village homes; the official ordinances, and the posters announcing festivals in the region, can also be found there. The café owner, furthermore, acts as an informer and guide for any newcomer. For any man, the café is acceptable and compulsory as the place to be when outside work. It is the 'men's house' (the Melanesian analogy is more than simple irony), in the sense that domesticity and loneliness are seen as non-prestigious – as symptoms of anti-sociality and diminished virility – by the men; and because even women themselves seem to push men away from the domestic space which is feminised to the point where male presence is undesirable. However it is not enough to be among other men. What one does with them – drink, smoke, share, talk, compete and play – are culturally coercive activities. Without practising them one does not practice masculinity and sociability. These activities, furthermore, are not to be undertaken with just any men, but rather with social equals: the rich tend to be more domestic or go to other types of public places. These activities are also not supposed to be undertaken in just any way: the café is not – contrary to a first ethnocentric appraisal – a chaotic place for the liberation of impulses, but rather a space for interaction within boundaries of formality and etiquette.

The café marks off a specific social time, that of leisure. Other alternatives – such as hunting, going out in the evenings to feasts, *bailes* and *boîtes*, etc. – are done in smaller groups of friends who are either bachelors or, if they are married, manifest in those moments a nostalgia of bachelorhood.[2] In the café one is also exposed to one's 'enemies': sometimes it is café x, where one never goes because there is some conflict with the owner or his family. Enemies or not, men are always potential rivals in the competition for the symbolic capital of masculinity, at the same time that they support the ideal fraternal equality of the members of the same sex (a notion that is often juxtaposed with class equality).

Rituals of masculinity in the cafés act in the sense of masking the dependence that the landless worker used to have towards the female members of his household and the domestic group in general, as well as his economically and politically fragile position in society (Driessen 1983: 131). Most striking in café culture is ritualised exchange. The most commonly exchanged objects in everyday café life are cigarettes and alcoholic beverages; these must be consumed together; the notion of the solitary drinker is a negative one, a fact that helps to prove that the motivation for drinking is not necessarily or fundamentally an alcoholic one. The drunkard runs the risk of having his wife show up at the café to fetch him, thus losing face with his peers. Furthermore, if his behaviour is recurrent he can build himself a reputation as a drunkard – a negative identity. The altered state of consciousness must be occasional, festive and shared. Offering drinks also replaces the male social incapacity for offering cooked foods, something women can do, or expressing affection through domestic hospitality, an exclusive of the close family.

Singer (1988) says that social scientists, when referring to drinkers who were raised in educated environments, seem to look for 'problems' that could result from alcohol consumption. On the other hand, though, when they refer to drinkers of uneducated backgrounds, they are usually inclined to look for the 'problems' resulting from alcoholism. As if drinking were the cause of trouble for some (the dominant) and an 'escape valve' for others (the dominated). What happens in the real world is that drinking and becoming drunk involve two social fields of possibilities: talking and acting in a non-responsible, non-accountable way (see Menéndez 1993). In sum: one drinks in order to state the truth (the truth that is hidden by community, or the truth in the sense of personal unorthodox opinion) without being punished afterwards for having done it.

Regarding the type of exchange that commensality involves, Gilmore says (he is referring to Andaluzia):

> Commodity exchange among Andaluzian males is more than mere bar courtesy, more also than a trivial prelude to networking and material calculation. In aggregate, the ritualised exchanges in the bars are the basic moral order of society, their trajectory demarcating the structural contours of kith and kin, vitalising a complex system of opposing values such as equality and hierarchy, competition and deference. [...] In this sense the flow of minor comestibles like cigarettes and drinks transcends both the principle of reciprocity and of individual calculation, and represents, as Mauss (1974) put it, the 'movement of the whole society'. (Gilmore 1991:28)

Together with drinking comes talking, in the sense of conversation, which in and of itself is an act of exchange. Talk around drinking is directed by the rhetoric of overstated stories, predominantly hunting, fishing and sexual stories; loud vocal commentaries on work, sex, women, and football are the rule; politics and comments on the rich are left for the *sotto voce* of more restricted groups. Groups gather around a table, usually with the purpose of sharing a game or a snack; but it is most common to stand up, circulate, showing that one is receptive to whoever might drop in, and ready to leave if an invitation occurs.

Drinks are seldom paid for by the drinker and seldom a man drinks alone. Paying for others and drinking with them goes beyond individual calculation and reciprocity. Commensality is similar to the above-mentioned 'whole movement of society', something that is quite visible in the fact that the reciprocity of drink buying is never immediate and sequential but rather deferred in time. It also expresses a political ideal, that of the fundamental equality of men: as a community, as a social group (the workers), as a gender. It constitutes an alternative to the absence of reciprocity in the wage relation between employer and employee. However, the notion of equality implies both communion and competition, friendship and rivalry. This is what happens with the constant demonstrations of friendship, which are repeated endlessly with the rhetoric of question and reiteration, at the same time that one is always challenging the patience of others with provocation, or gossip about those who are not present. Masculinity, because it is fragile and constantly (re)constructed, and menaced, unites and opposes men. Thus, the game of drinking continuously, of buying and being bought for, creates superiority and inferiority in never-ending rotation among relative equal partners.

The structure of masculine norms has a limitation, however: that of family organisation. The two are not compatible. That is why one never sees father and son drinking together. Sometimes they even avoid entering the café if the other happens to be there. Son-father deference is incompatible with competition among men. The only exception seems to be the sporadic presence of a father with an infant son, still classified as belonging to the domestic feminine world. He is thus metaphorically 'kidnapped' from that world and starts his apprenticeship of café culture by imitating the body postures of adult males, or undergoes the joking ritual of drinking his first beer. On the other hand, brothers, but mostly matrilineal cousins and brothers-in-law, or even those born in the same year, make up cohesive groups.

The café does not only define a masculine place. It also shows clear borders that demarcate interior from exterior space. It has a strong potential for visual communication between outside and inside. It is like a home, the home of men, their domestic world, of men who think of themselves as representatives of the community. It is also there that it becomes evident how global the village becomes, mainly through television. This allows for the germination of a new tradition – the soap opera – a commonly shared narrative, an on-going story that stops conversations, is watched and listened to, and then used as motif for new conversations. The story is interpreted by means of making analogies between characters and sequences in fiction and characters and sequences in village life.[3]

Café etiquette and formality exist in spite of the antagonistic character of many of the café activities, and counterbalance them. This is a characteristic trait of café culture, not a contradiction. One is supposed to greet all who are present when entering the café; one is supposed to accept the offer of a drink after politely and rhetorically declining once; one is supposed to drink it next to the person who paid for it or at least make a mental note of the debt, in case the offer came from the other end of the room through a gesture emitted to the bartender. It is equally important not to let a foreigner offer whatsoever. That is why I only felt that I had been accepted in the community when I was able to start paying for drinks.

Etiquette is more elaborate around the theme of masculinity. Masculinity is portrayed more by means of sexuality than by violence or physical strength (which is probably more characteristic of Anglo-Saxon and Germanic bar brawls, or of Latin-American *machismo*). The most evident traits are a series of gestures: touching another man's testicles (seen as the symbol of masculinity's corporeal residence), reclining against the bar in a pose, showing the potential for violence by loudly banging coins on the bar zinc, or domino pieces or cards on the table, strong claps on each other's backs, or by not crossing one's legs while sitting.

Men see themselves as naturally charged with sexual drive. They claim that it is the wife's duty to control them, but also that women are dangerously insatiable. The dichotomy between the pure, maternal woman, and the impure, easy-going and home-wrecking woman is thus established. The model of masculinity is both competitive and hierarchical, and that is why it includes the spectre of femininity in disputes for masculinity. Competition is about feminising other men: by means of gestures that jokingly invite the other for sex, turning the 'victim' into a symbolic woman; by joking behaviour that involves fondling a man's behind; or even by monetary competition, since economic capacity is associated with rank in the social hierarchy, which makes metaphorical use of the masculine-feminine and active-passive dichotomies. Mostly, the use of the homosexual trope is widespread. Homosexuality is understood not as a lifestyle or personal option or even 'sexual orientation', but rather as a possible sexual outlet; hierarchically, it is seen as the display of a passive role, that of the person who is penetrated. The person who penetrates does not lose his masculinity at all.

The practice of the 'men's house' is largely conveyed by means of words and rhetoric. Verbal wit, the ability to reply, the narrative of prowess, the prevalence of narrative emphasis over explicit content, are all arts that are practised and performed in the café. One can aggravate and provoke others, challenging their masculinity (and analogous categories of identity: capacity to work, cunning, economic success, physical strength, independence from patrons etc.) by testing the other's capacity to reply even better – with a sort of superior coolness that is intended to put the provocateur 'in his place'.

The formality and the cultivation of expertise with words counterbalances sexual and physical aggressiveness through the ideal of self-control, the contention of exacerbated emotions and also the praise of the funny man. That is, he who has the gift to provoke laughter, provided that it is not simple foolishness (which is non-prestigious, something visible in the way that old men, the very poor and the handicapped are treated)[4] but rather through the ability to manipulate metaphors, to play with words, to use proverbs in the right context, to tell jokes and – the most prestigious – to recite poems.

New types of café are also in the making. A man from Pardais, currently living in Lisbon (he is Filomena's brother), wants to move back to the village one day and open a café where 'one is not allowed to walk in wearing work clothes and where women may feel at ease'.[5] Thanks to young people who are mobile owing to their motorbikes and who have mass consumption habits, new traditions are being invented or imported, in pubs and discos, places where a different masculinity is being constructed *in praesentia* of the girls, who have obtained higher levels of education and enjoy greater mobility and freedom in the larger urban centres.

The re-contextualisation of the café may open up the way for the challenge to commonly held notions on gender. However, the simple opening of masculine space to women may not mean equality in gender ideology. A similar process, that of the Greek *kafeteria* in Greek villages, was studied by Jane Cowan who calls our attention to other dividing lines:

> Though a site where the traditional restrictions of a local gender ideology are being contested, the *kafeteria* is hardly a revolutionary institution (...) The *kafeteria* offers a new model of human 'being' stressing leisure and luxury and celebrates a capitalist culture that, although it encourages males and females alike to show who they are by spending and consuming, also entails other forms of gender inequality. (Cowan 1991:201)

In Pardais this process is visible in the fact that the growing mobility of women is not due to any economic and social independence, but rather to their attempts to adopt bourgeois standards, made possible by their husbands' salaries – a convoluted way of circumventing the high incidence of female unemployment.

As long as what goes on at the café is the reiterated praxis of masculinity, the café will pursue the tradition of the tavern as a place where representation and realignment of social inequality and the ideal of equality take place via the idiom of gender.[6] Brandes (1991 [1980]) says that the men of the village he studied in Andaluzia worried mostly about issues of identity, related to their place in the social hierarchy, and to their relations with women. By analysing metaphors of masculinity present in folklore, he says that this allows an escape outlet which is culturally acceptable for frustrations and feelings (see next chapter).

In folklore (whether jokes, songs, poems, and so on), concern with power, domination and control are central. These can be expressed at a spatial level (with analogies of the 'height = power', 'kneeling = women' type), or at the verbal level (differential treatments of *tu* and *você*, that is, informal 'you' and formal 'you' in Portuguese, *tu* and *usted* in Spanish), or yet at physical level (Brandes [1991]:238). Ritual, narrative and playful acts are, as Bauman (1986) has said, performances. In Chapter 5 I shall analyse oral poetry from that point of view. Next I will analyse the performative aspects of men's evening leisure activities, as well as those that revolve around the culture of bulls and bullfighting.

'Sun Rising': Night Time as Masculine Time

During outings to other villages, for attending *bailes*, festivals and *boîtes*, the importance of friendship in the constitution of social and emotional ties that tend to be exclusively masculine is obvious. Cutileiro referred to friendship in the following way:

> ...friendship is not (...) a generous and affectionate sharing of sentiments or a pleasant communion of affinity and interest. It is rather a system of exchange of favours, in which each person keeps a record of his credits and debts [but] there is also an emotional element (...) If friendships do not seem to be (...) lasting, their manifestations are usually very exuberant (1977:309), (...) and the proverb 'friends are friends, but keep business apart' reflects the basic ambivalence of friendship relations. (1977:310) (my translation)

As a matter of fact, during the first baile that I attended, one of the aspects that struck me the most was the exuberance of emotional expression among friends, in face of the public audience. It was also common to hear all sorts of moral statements about friendships, such as 'He who gives me more is my best friend' or 'You treat me well, I'll treat you well; you fuck me, then I'll fuck you'. While talking about friendship as an exchange of favours foreseeing future need, Beto would say 'don't harm anyone, so that they treat you well; treat them well, so that they don't harm you'. He liked to mention the example of the parents of a child that was in the hospital in Évora at the same time as Beto's daughter. He would say that he would do anything for those people, since they had been kind to him, had taken him to the train station, the mothers had exchanged photos of their children and so on. In this narrative, he would list all the favours he had already done for me. In another situation, a man was philosophising on why it was that men like to be with other men more than with their own wives without their being 'other intentions'; yet another man was amazed at the number of women with whom he had friendly relations 'without any evil', thanks to relationships of camaraderie at the work place – an important shift in gender separation that arose for the few men who work in white-collar jobs. A boy, when telling me who the people were he usually went fishing, hunting or collecting mushrooms with, realised only then that it was always with one of his cousins, one of his brothers-in-law and a brother-in-law's brother-in-law: that is, the group of friends seemed to have some sort of permanence that sounded strange and new to him, thanks to kinship: not too close (brothers do not often develop friendships like this), but not too distant either (people with whom kinship ties can not be traced).

Papataxiarchis (1991), describing the birth of a new anthropology of masculinity (Whitehead 1981, Brandes 1981, Herdt 1981, Herzfeld 1985) centred on the way men see themselves as men, says that the phenomenon of masculine friendship can not be seen only in terms of economics or politics. For him, instead of being an appendix of the androcentric structure, friendship is an aspect of anti-structure, connected with leisure, with commensality in alcohol and gambling, and it is characterised by the absence of economic functions:

> (...) relations of friendship in Mouria are regarded as the crowning expression of an ideology that stresses normative equality among all men (...) [against the] inequality that arises from age, family background, social class, wealth, professional occupation or marital status. Status differences are thought to divide men, while friendship is considered as the bond that resists all division. (1991:159)

Things are not very different in Pardais. That is why friendships occur between men of the same age, mainly bachelors. Contrary to Mouria, however, the universes of kinship and friendship are not kept apart; similarly to Mouria, men uphold the notion that masculine friendship is more emotional than instrumental. Papataxiarchis says that the sentiment

of friendship does not belong to the same constellation of cultural meaning as the sentiment of kinship. Both are demarcated as aspects of different ideologies of gender and juxtaposed as essential components of
different programmes for prestige-oriented action. Thus, the sentiment
of kinship constitutes the domestic domain around feminine and uter-
ine ties, fragmenting the world of women along kinship lines and limit-
ing their reach of relationships outside kinship.[7] Basically the author
argues in favour of a perspective based on gender and the person, rather
than on one based on exchange.

David Gilmore (1980), who tends toward the latter approach, provides us with some useful indications for the understanding of friendship, with his account of the Andaluzian distinction between *amistad,*
compromiso, and *amistad de confianza.* The first is friendship resulting
from interaction in the neutral ground of the café or bar, culminating
with *juerga* (in Portuguese *borga,* the equivalent of Pardais' notion of
saída, 'going out'). The second moves from the bar to the home, with
mutual expectations of support and mutual help in case of need and a
tacit invitation for all ritual occasions; the third would involve the con-
fiding of personal secrets. Gilmore says that it is supposed to be based on
affect and ostensibly deprived of self-interest.

Neither the exchange perspective nor Papataxiarchis' alternative
should be unique or mutually exclusive. Interest and emotion imply each
other whether in kinship relations or in friendship relations (see Medick
and Sabean 1989). If one pays attention to the genealogical chart at the
end of this book, one can verify that the kinship relation between the
families of Zé Ganhão and Leonel extends a long way back in time: Zé
Ganhão's father's mother's mother's mother's father (FMMMF) was
Leonel's mother's father's father's father's mother's brother (MFFFMB).
Leonel's mother's mother was Zé Ganhão's mother's mother's sister, thus
being quite probable that, when children, they spent long periods
together, given the close relationship of mutual help in child raising
characteristic between mothers and daughters, as well as between sisters.
Between Beto and Zé Ganhão and/or Leonel there is, however, no kinship relation.

With regard to schooling, Beto attended elementary school between
1973 and 1980; he repeated first grade three times, the first phase twice
(first and second grades) and the second phase twice (third and fourth
grades). Only the first year of Beto's schooling coincided with a year of
Leonel's schooling: his last. Leonel attended school for six years, having
repeated third and fourth grades. Zé Ganhão attended school for eight

years, and repeated the first grade twice, the third and fourth grades once; he was Leonel's contemporary throughout the entire period. Through parental and schooling data one can say up to a certain point that the friendship between Leonel and Zé Ganhão goes way back: they grew up together. The friendship between Leonel and Beto though, existed in the absence of any parental, kith or schooling coexistence. Probably because the masculine sociability of the café and 'going out' fulfils the function of creating ties that are independent from family and work.

A sociological analysis of friendship is not of concern here,[8] but rather the understanding of what happens when friends are together. We have seen what type of sociability occurs at the café; we can now take a look at what goes on during the outings of groups of friends away from the village, as a context for a discourse on masculinity. The best way to present this is by recalling a night out with some of my village friends. What follows is a direct quotation from my field journal:

> The *saída* was decided during a café conversation with Beto, Leonel and Ruivo.[9] We took my car – I seem to have become a sort of chauffeur – and started the evening with dinner in a restaurant in Borba. Ruivo was very excited, and he talked endlessly of his prowess and frustrations with his motorbike; sometimes he would shift the conversation to his relationships with several women in bars and *boîtes* that he goes to. He has a very detailed memory of events, people, hours, places – the evening outing seems like an epic narrative whose events are well registered... After dinner they took me to the first *boîte*, right there in Borba. I had never noticed it, there were no signs outside the garage door. But it was closed, so we (I...) drove to Elvas, where they led me immediately to the *boîte* called 'Poni'. I was nervous, wondering how one could possibly afford 9,500 escudos for a bottle of whisky at the previous *boîte* that was closed. The 'Poni' is a place that can only be defined with the word 'kitsch', with regard to decoration, with several young and not so young women sitting alongside an immense bar waiting for invitations for the customers' tables.
>
> Two of them introduced themselves instantly: Fernanda, around forty years old, a false blonde, her parents and son living in Lisbon, whom she visits now and then, and Iva. We sat down at a table with the two women, plus two others that were called by Ruivo in order to match the number of guests. The situation was quite embarrassing for me, so I found myself telling Iva that I was there on 'work'. She was obviously the most 'educated' of them. I dared to tell her that I found our professions to have some similarities, since we both had to be with people independent of our feeling for them; she complained a lot

about the amount of alcohol that she had to drink and how only very seldom did she meet men that she liked. We even exchanged tips on professional trickery: she told me how she managed to pour whisky into the plant vases, and I told her how I had once pretended to go to the toilet in order to take some notes.

My companions had great expectations about my performance. They seemed to have accepted the fact that I was only talking with the women, instead of touching them or letting myself be touched by them. They are what is known as *alterno* women, that is, they earn a monthly salary, but make most money out of percentages from the drinks sold to clients. They only sleep with clients on a (supposedly) strictly personal basis, after giving them their phone numbers and waiting for an invitation for dinner and a night out.

The next place was called 'Zig Zag', on the outskirts of Elvas. The sinister aspect of the place was quite intimidating: it was a huge shack in the middle of an empty area. The inside was painted dark blue. It was freezing cold, humid, and there was nothing on the walls. Immense sadness. Outside were parked some expensive cars that belonged to the owner (a woman) and her son. They tell me that right there, at the entrance, a man had recently been killed. He owed huge debts to the owner. The owner's son is the main suspect, but my companions regarded as perfectly natural that he had not yet been arrested: 'that's what money and contacts are for'. Inside, at the table, I was joined by a black woman, named Marisa, but not for long: Ruivo sent her away with rude manners; he says he doesn't like her and that as a matter of principle he does not like coloured women. She was replaced by an ill looking creature, a blond girl from Alentejo who could have been thirteen or thirty years old. Symptoms of drug abuse were quite evident. The others were a woman in her thirties, a young mulatto (who says she lives with her mother), and a girl from Lisbon, very congenial and spirited, who joined Leonel.

Ruivo had already arranged to pick up two of them the following Saturday, so as to take them to a *baile* in Alandroal. According to him – and he was very happy saying this – it would end in a big mess, since he knew that some other guys from Pardais had also invited them. So he arranged with the women to pick them up in a certain spot on the road one hour before the time they had arranged with the other guys.

Slowly, Beto began to touch the woman next to him. He was very gentle. Leonel was behaving in his usual cool and distant manner, and he pretended to be courting. Ruivo, on the other hand, was literally grovelling on the floor under the table: he was taking off the women's shoes, sticking his hands up their skirts, up until he could fondle their breasts. He was euphoric. He was cussing a lot. The others kept apologising to me all evening for Ruivo's behaviour. But they did not hold any grudges against him, for they felt it was his passionate nature that led him to behave like that. In the end it was he who paid for the bottles of whisky. In my terms, a small fortune.

The most salient aspects in this type of activity have both similarities and differences when compared to café sociability: the group of men is smaller, and it has friendship as a basis for its constitution; the space is outside the village; the consumption of alcohol is complemented with the access to women whose social identity is of the type that men talk about in the café. The activity is half-clandestine, wives and mothers suspect and even know that men frequent these places, but they are never the subject of conversation outside groups of men. It is this which confers upon this activity the characteristic of being a form of the reproduction of masculinity. The game of seduction is an unfair one due to the social exclusion of *boîte* women; it is rather the imagery of seduction that is at stake here and its projection in the evaluation that other men make of each other's masculinity, here understood as efficacy in sexual predation. In this sense it is analogous to bullfighting, where the bull really does not stand a chance of winning. So the women of the *alterno* do not have a chance of saying no.

Another field of masculine sociability outside the village is the visiting of *bailes* and festivities in other villages or small towns. The group that takes these evening outings is less cohesive: it can be the same as the small group that visits the *boîtes*, but it can be any number of men who, while at the café, decide to share an available car. The dynamic is not as charged because one expects to find most men and some women from the village at the *baile* – there is no great moral judgement upon this activity. Old people talk of old times' *bailes* as apparently more ritualised: *bailes* fulfilled the function of providing the meeting ground for marriage partners. Today *bailes* are mostly for 'entertainment'. They are the context for a rhetoric of seduction (to go to the *baile* 'to see the women', 'to see if one strikes lucky'); but what goes on most of the time is the conviviality among men who, more than dancing and courting, stay together, drink, look for exciting situations of conflict or – still – court women, although already in the new sense of looking 'for an adventure', not for a prospective partner in a relationship.

The friendship between Beto and Leonel was already cooling off and that between Leonel and Zé Ganhão was warming up when the three of us went to a baile in São Romão. Nights out were also a privileged occasions for obtaining information on day-to-day life, since some embarrassment and shame on the part of my friends was forgotten for a few hours. I will transcribe a part of my field journal:

On the way to São Romão I am told that Fernando Capucho, the equestrian bullfighter's father, owns – he is 'the old man' – the properties where Zé Ganhão is presently working as a tractor driver. Leonel breaks into the conversation to say that he does not like the 'old man', since he is known to prefer those men who 'lick his boots'. Zé Ganhão says he wants to be 'clean' and that is why he – and not his boss – will pay for his truck driving licence; he wants it badly and it costs 98,000 escudos. He wants to pay for it himself because he does not want to 'owe' anything to his boss; he knows, and he accepts the fact that employers can 'buy off' the 'engineers' (driving-school examiners). Leonel, a bit more cynical, says that he should let his boss go ahead and pay for 'they [the bosses] don't deserve anything'.

When we arrived in São Romão, Zé says that we should not go to the 'faggot's café'. He means the owner of a café who is renowned being a homosexual; Leonel immediately says that he doesn't like homosexuals either; however, in a sarcastic tone, he adds: 'well, as long as they pay it's all right'. So we went to the 'Tropical' instead, before the *baile*. There we talked about the money difficulties that Leonel is having. It seems that Romeu (a young man who is protected by the bullfighter and who has lately been showing off a fantastic motorbike) asked him in front of everybody at the café if he needed any money; Zé thought this was 'indecent', and accused Romeu of being a 'boot-licker'; the only person worse than him, apparently, is another man who is competing with him for the job of driving the boss's horse wagon.

Several men from São Romão say hello to our small group: they hug each other, showing hospitality, and then proceed to fool around with some ritualised mock-fighting around the issue of who is supposed to pay for the drinks; then they have their arms around each other's shoulders again.

Tonight seems to specialise in less prestigious stories about the respective families. Zé Ganhão tells us that his uncle – Estorninho's son-in-law's father – was a 'son of a bitch': he loaned some money to Zé's father to help buy his house and then showed up and asked for it. When Zé was in Lisbon in the military service, he waited outside for his uncle to come out of work, he then insulted him, tore the bank notes and threw them in his face. Zé was not afraid, since an uncle is not supposed to hit a nephew, especially if it is the uncle who is to blame for his nephew losing respect for him. However, his uncle did want to hit him. In sum: this uncle did not abide by the rules of honour and etiquette, he was outside them, and so he now carried the epithet of 'son of a bitch'.

Leonel takes the lead and mentions his uncle who let his two children starve to death. He was the father of the Conceições' step-daughter – today the heiress. This uncle was Leonel's mother's brother-in-law and landowner of the land that Leonel's family rented; at fifty-six he became suddenly rich, since he had found stone somewhere. He started to demand a very high rent, conflict arose and Leonel's insults to his uncle were such that the National Guard was called in.

Many drinks followed. Zé Ganhão, showing that he is Leonel's friend, criticises with great ease Leonel's past as a 'junkie'. His argument was based on the premise that all the money spent on hashish would have been better spent on 'whores'. I believe that in rural Pardais (as opposed to urban and suburban areas) the former use of money does not increase the capital of masculinity.

We did not go to the baile until much later. The *baile* always seems to be a nice excuse to leave the village. Only those who go as couples, or single men who go to meet their steady girlfriends, seem to go immediately to the *baile*. Tickets were of two kinds: those for married people (one-hundred escudos) and those for bachelors (two-hundred escudos) – the matrimonial status as a categorisation of two types of people, punishing the single. Leonel tricked the ticket vendor by saying that he was married, and this really scared Zé. Inside – it was an enclosed pavilion – it was very hot and crowded, and a band was playing while a few couples danced: mostly lovers and couples who were engaged, married couples, and women. The fact that women can dance with each other is quite important, since it shows how there is no symmetry in gender. It is unthinkable for two men to dance together (except in Carnival transvestism). The spectre of homosexuality does not hover over feminine relationships, which are seen as totally imbedded in kinship. It is the homosociality of men, together with the predatory notion of masculine sexuality, that invokes the danger of homosexuality, thus revealing the fragility of masculinity and the latency of homosexual desire in a culture of gender that discourses endlessly on the superiority of men.

We left the baile and went to the same café that they had initially said they would never go to. We sat and five minutes later a fight started. Chairs went flying. The café owner, previously classified as 'the faggot', had seen a client stealing a box of toothpicks from the counter. He had told him to put them back. The other had started to protest against the price of the mini bottles of beer. The brawl that followed was very ritualistic, as they almost always are: they take place in public and there is always someone there to restrain the contenders just in time. Everybody thought the owner was right, but Zé Ganhão commented that the contenders belonged to 'the sect'. And he added, laughing almost anxiously, that for himself he 'liked cunt, not ass'. We went once more to the *baile*, since Zé wanted to stay longer, 'to see those who had no partner'; to this Leonel replied that next time Zé had to 'round them up' (an expression also used in tauromachy), to 'twist them around'. Zé, however, picked a girl from the crowd as the object of his projected affections. He never even spoke to her, but he held her image in his memory. When we drove back to Pardais, Zé kept on talking abut the desire he was feeling for sex and how, since he did not have a woman, he would have 'to dig a hole in his pillow'. I asked him if he ever takes any precautions when he sleeps with someone, and he replied that he doesn't use 'the little shirt' [condom], but that 'I stick this one thing [incomprehensible] in the woman's thing and they don't get pregnant'.[10] Leonel comments: 'It's big trouble when they do get pregnant!'. Zé had a ready answer: 'In that case it's thirty *contos* [30,000 escudos] for the *desmancho* [idiom for *aborto*, abortion]'. Zé kept on unwinding the rosary of that evening's frustration: 'She was so eager! She almost placed herself under me!', when in reality this was a tremendous overstatement. I think she hardly noticed him. He had definitely noticed her, though, and that was why he said that he was tired of 'fucking with his eyes'.

We arrived in Pardais when the sun was rising. This is probably why the activity of going out in the evening to *bailes*, festivals and *boîtes* has the code-name 'watching the sunrise'. Night time is men's territory.

Taking the Bull by the Horns: Bullfighting as a Theatre of Masculinity

Between Easter and the end of summer, an ever-present element in many of the region's festivities are bullfights and *garraiadas*, or 'tauromachic entertainment' as the publicity posters announce. Bullfighting is a nation-wide spectacle, and only occurs in larger towns and cities, since a bull ring is necessary and it is a complex and expensive business. *Garraiadas*, on the contrary, can be held in the most tiny and remote village, for all you need is a *touril* (a circular closed-in ring) or an open space that can be barricaded with wooden boards or even horse carts. And all you need are local men and a bull, as well as spectators. Pardais has a *touril*, which is walled in with a few breeches. The Capuchos built it, and throughout the summer a series of *garraiadas* are held there.

Bullfighting is characteristically a southern tradition, from southern Portugal to southern France, including the Castilian and Catalan speaking countries and, as a consequence of Iberian expansion, also of Latin America. It involves many elements of a gender ideology, based on an interpretation of nature and culture, manhood and womanhood, life and death, individual and society. The gendered elements go from the symbolism of the bull itself to the acting and performance of the bullfight and the *garraiada*: energy, wilderness, horns, blood, penetration of the sword, the game of seduction and deceit, death, and so on. The *garraiada* is simply the freeing of one or more animals in an improvised arena. The animals are almost always calves or very young bulls. Solitary men or men in small groups play with the animal, until they can perform a *pega de caras* (literally, a head-on catch). The *pega de caras* consists of one man jumping up between the animal's horns while wrapping his arms around its neck. The other men then help him by holding the horns, body and tail in an imitation of one aspect of Portuguese bullfighting. It should be noted that in Portuguese bullfighting killing the bull in the ring is forbidden. It has thus developed into a form of spectacle: it involves bullfighting on horseback, which is as much bullfighting as a demonstration of equestrian expertise; *toreador* performance without killing the bull; and *forcados*, who do what people at *garraiadas* emulate – catch the bull bare-handed. During the *garraiadas* it is normal for a local patron to be among the audience: he will wave a bank note on the end of a stick – the prize for the group who manages to catch the bull.

Bullfighting and *garraiadas* raise the question of how a certain ritualised show with local people's participation can be seen as a text that makes sense in a certain cultural milieu and how it both calls for and illuminates gender categories. Pitt-Rivers' contribution is still probably the most interesting one, even though his material is Spanish. The Portuguese writer Ruben A. summed up in a poetic expression what bullfighting is all about: 'seduction and command' – but unfortunately as anthropologists we can not be satisfied with such a synthetic observation. Clifford Geertz, on the other hand, provides us with the terms for ethnographic comparison and the basis for a scheme of analysis while referring to a structurally similar event – Balinese cockfighting:

> Like any art form (...) the cockfight renders ordinary, everyday experience comprehensible by presenting it in terms of acts and objects which have had their practical consequences removed [...] What it does is what, for other peoples with other temperaments and other conventions, *Lear* and *Crime and Punishment* do; it catches up these

themes – death, masculinity, rage, pride, loss, beneficence, chance – and, ordering them into an encompassing structure, presents them in such a way as to throw into relief a particular view of their essential nature (…) An image, fiction, a model, a metaphor, the cockfight is a means of expression; its function is neither to assuage social passions nor to heighten them (though, in its playing-with-fire way it does a bit of both), but, in a medium of feathers, blood, crowds, and money, to display them. (Geertz 1973:443–444)

The quote suggests that the metaphors of Balinese cockfights are similar to those of bullfights and garraiadas.

For Pitt-Rivers (personal conversation) the *corrida* is a rite, a sacrifice, less pagan than one might think, much more connected with Catholic religion. It is the claim of *hombría* (Spanish for manhood, in the moral sense) through the sacrifice of a virile animal. The sacrificed bull (an actuality in Spanish bullfighting, symbolically in the Portuguese version) gives humans, by means of its immolation, the male qualities of the animal. Bullfighting is not simply a fight, since the bull cannot win; unless it is forgiven for its nobility, for incorporating the values that are promoted by the cult of the bull. That is probably why bulls (with names, pedigrees, family histories and life stories) are as important in the folk tradition of the *aficionados* (bullfighting fans) as the bullfighters themselves. Although in the *garraiada* there are elements of play, and less of a ritualised sacrificial element, Pitt-Rivers' idea is that it is not a show, since it does not just represent reality. It is reality.

Bullfights and *garraiadas* follow the religious cycle. At all patron saint's festivals one is held after mass: 'After the purification of the sacrifice of the Lamb the sacrifice of the bull restores to grace the mores of everyday life, releasing the faithful from an excess of sanctity' (Pitt-Rivers 1993:12). This does not mean, however, that there is an intention to erase the purifying message of the mass, but rather an aim to integrate it into daily life. It is a ritual means of ensuring society's stability: so that men can be men and social order be maintained. The bull, invested with positive masculine characteristics, is there to be sacrificed.

It is thus that the bull – which demonstrates its ability to personify the values for whose representation it was created, such as aggression, courage, straightforwardness, nobility and other masculine virtues – is treated with great respect. In the bullfighting milieu one knows the bulls individually and in Pardais it was not uncommon to overhear someone mentioning a bull's name, weight, provenance and curriculum. Elements of the bull's qualities rub off on the men who compete with it in a more

serious *garraiada*. The *garraiada* allows the lower-class males to incorporate the nobility that is normally granted only to professional bullfighters; although there is a clear consciousness that the bulls are not as large
and fierce in the *garraiadas* – a confirmation of inequality in access to
masculine capital as consequence of class.

In the *garraiada* specifically, the audience is the community. Those
who come from neighbouring villages come to criticise, to say that the
local festival is not as good as their own. Groups of men organised to
compete with the bull are village-based groups. By gambling with their
masculinity they are also gambling with their village's reputation, whose
public side the masculine gender is supposed to represent.

Pitt-Rivers' symbolic analysis of the Spanish bullfight shows that the
matador symbolises a feminine role in the first *tercio*, whereas in the third
tercio (that of death) he attains a hyper-masculine embodiment, by appropriating the phallic values of the bull, which he then transfers on to the
audience (this is symbolised with the cutting of the ears). This is related to
the fact that the sexes, in the religious context, can be either mutually exclusive – as in daily life – or cumulative. As the *corrida* goes on, the *matador*
throws away his feminine symbols. His sexual ambiguity is related to the
role of performing a sacrifice: first he is a priest, with his cape, then a beautiful woman in the first *sorte*, and finally he is a male, a man transformed
into a bull when, through blood, he feminises the bull. So men sacrifice the
bull and receive in exchange its sexual capacity. It is an exchange between
nature and humankind. This can be semantically extended, in Pardais, to
the relationship that men have with what they see as wild nature: hunting
is a passionate activity for men, one of appropriation of nature.

In hunting, the appropriation of 'savagery' is carried out in the act of
eating the hunted animals, in a group of men, at the café. In the *garraiada*, this appropriation is achieved in the triumphal moment of the
pega, of holding the bull by its horns. The proverb 'to hold (or to take)
the bull by the horns' means to be straightforward, unhesitating, coura-
geous and honourable. In some villages in the region, the animal is actually eaten during a public barbecue in the village; and it is men who are
the cooks. Pitt-Rivers also writes about the consubstantiality that underlies food ingestion. Sacrifice is an act of 'grace', a notion Benveniste said
originated in 'what gives pleasure'. Grace is attained through consub-
stantiation, which is achieved by commensality, a form of establishing a
brotherhood of blood (Pitt-Rivers 1988:6).

While describing a bull festival in Tordesillas, Spain, Pitt-Rivers sums
up the symbolic importance of the bull:

(…) he is the symbol of sexual sin, of wild nature, of virility, of noble manliness, of fertility, he has phallic horns (…) He is sacrificed to the Holy Virgin (…) He is both bad and good. As an animal he is sub-human yet he is the means of communicating with divinity. He is food, he is sex and his Passion echoes (…) that of the Saviour: entry in triumph into the town, judgement, mocking, expulsion into a rural setting where he is immolated and where his physical essence, a kind of reproductive grace or *baraka* is born back to assure the future (…). (Pitt-Rivers 1988:27)[11]

Events that involve the competition between animals and humans (and, in these cases, specifically males) reveal a good deal about the relations between nature and culture and, most of all, about the similarities and differences between humans and animals and between different categories of human beings (especially gender differences). Bullfights and *garraiadas* are texts and performances of this relationship. They are like the Balinese cockfight or even the Andaluzian cockfight described by Marvin (1984):

Certain characteristics of cocks are observed by men (they are noticed in the first place because they relate to characteristics valued in men); this image of the bird's behaviour is incorporated into men's self imagery, the imagery is read back onto the bird's behaviour as an evaluation of it and then, through the cockfight (a cultural construct built around the cock's natural characteristics), the imagery is read back once more by men. (Marvin 1984:68)

I have mentioned previously how the bull's horns are phallic symbols, caught by the men in the *garraiada*. Horns are a cultural symbol that is constantly used by men in Pardais, similar to other Mediterranean societies.

Let me reintroduce here the stories of various people regarding the 'horns' complex. Guedes (see Chapter 2) is a man from Caldas da Raínha, not far from Lisbon, but he lives in Alandroal and he is a frequent client of the *bailes* in the region and hangs out a lot in the cafés of Pardais. He is very much admired for his physical strength and he is feared because he has a reputation for liking to fight, a suspicious characteristic since it demonstrates lack of self-control – aggressiveness should be verbal or ritualised as provocation, not the actual physical violence. Guedes' story is told as an example of moral codes on affections, faithfulness and infidelity. He was married, he owned a very successful fruit farm in Caldas da Raínha, he was well-off, had a daughter and a steady family life. One day he met a woman 'who charmed him', he disappeared with her, leaving his family and everything behind. Eventually, he 'landed' (as if a shipwreck victim) in the Pardais area. He had two sons by his mistress. The daughter from the first marriage looked for him for years, until one day a friend of Guedes' met him in Estremoz and told him that he had seen Guedes' daughter looking for him. Guedes asked him not to tell his daughter that he knew where he was. Later, his new wife, the mistress, *armou-o* (decorated him), *pôs-lhe os cornos* (put the horns on him) – i.e., she slept with another man. Guedes began to be negligent, decadent. He lost jobs, ended up as a cattle shepherd, slept alone in a shack up in the hills. These two situations (to be a shepherd and to be alone) are highly negative for masculine prestige. One day his daughter showed up. The man who told me the story said: 'They fell into each other's arms and wept'.

In another episode – one that is almost equally a myth – I was told the story of the ancient owner of the Santo Aleixo puppets (a famous folk puppeteering tradition from Alentejo), from Santiago de Rio de Moínhos in the Borba municipality. The puppets belonged to Baubau, for whom worked Talhinhas (this man became nationally known as the master puppeteer). One day Talhinhas 'became friends' with Baubau's wife (friendship between men and women is seen as impossible; it always means a sexual relationship). Because he was very honest he confessed to Baubau. The latter did not lose his temper, and said: 'Listen, you have always been my servant and I your master. Now you'll be master and I will be servant'. And, as a matter of fact, he passed on to Talhinhas the whole administration of the puppet company. When he had lost sexually, he had also lost in professional status, in hierarchy, even though for him it was very important to guarantee the continuation of the puppet tradition. The story, however, was told by Zé Seco, for whom art is a supreme good. Caralinda, who overheard the story, made a comment: 'I couldn't do that! I couldn't stand having someone chewing my game [*caça*, literally, the product of hunting] in my face'.

A third story: a man from Pardais, who lives with his parents and his daughter, was introduced to me by Raposo with a discrete hand sign meaning 'horns'. The man's wife, Estorninho's son-in-law's sister, one day disappeared with a man from the north, who was supposedly the owner of several *boîtes*. The story goes that she had already traded that man for another, after having secretly sold his Mercedes for a large amount of money. No one knows where she is. As with Zé Ganhão's case, the 'horns' did not destroy the masculinity of the victims, since the women in question proved to be 'vicious' (or a *cabra* – goat – a loose woman) and, most of all, because she left the village. As a matter of fact, one day a man told me that he just could not understand why men 'on whom horns have been placed' always want to shoot their wife's lover instead of shooting the wife: 'The other man only eats if she lets him!'

Anton Blok (1981) argued that the symbolism of horns for the betrayed husband – the *cornudo* (the one with horns) – must be understood as an integral part of an archaic pastoral honour code that is built upon virility and physical strength. The opposition between rams and billy-goats is fundamental here. In the Portuguese case, he says that *cabrão* is a synonym for *cornudo*, with the double meaning of billy-goat and betrayed husband. Blok says that billy-goats tolerate the sexual access of other males to the females in their territory. In ancient Greece and Rome, the billy-goat was considered as a somewhat anomalous and lascivious animal, a representative of unbounded nature. In contrast, the ram does not tolerate any rivals, and a single ram can impregnate a whole flock of sheep. Zé Ganhão was particularly graphic in describing this very fact whenever he spoke about his flock. The ram represents virility and strength. The ram is thus a symbol of power, the billy-goat one of shame. Among the Sarakatsani described by Campbell (1964), rams and men are opposed to goats and women. We also know the common juxtaposition between goats and the devil, sheep and the faithful. These are homologies, not only external analogies between social groups and animal species – they are internal homologies between two systems of difference: between animal species (nature) and groups of people (culture) (see Lévi-Strauss 1962).

So the horns – when 'one puts the horns on someone else' – are not the bull's horns. Even so, in daily practice and discourse, all horns tend to be generalised into one category, and so people use the bull's horns to talk about the same issues. Still, and in order to return to the world of bulls, there is yet another case that has to do with sexual symbolism, social precedence and masculinity. It is the case of Zé Maria Capucho, the equestrian bullfighter. I will again use a quote from the field journal:

> I went to Zé Maria Capuchos' estate today, since Zé Ganhão who now works there invited me to come along. He asked his boss for permission, and although we have not yet been formally introduced, he granted it. The *herdade* is considered to be small (175 hectares), but it has a swimming pool, tennis courts, huge stables and horse training rings, and a bull ring with a balcony. We went to the horse-training pavilion first; it was decorated with enormous golden-framed mirrors on the walls, and a balcony with sofas. There was a woman sitting there: she was young, she had an urban appearance, and only later was

I to discover her relationship with the bullfighter: she is a singer (apparently well known in the world of bullfighting), and has a record dedicated to Zé Maria, with songs that praise his dignity and courage and manliness. The *cavaleiro* Zé Maria came in and out several times but never said hello to me [he never would in the entire year]. I guess I was just a guest of one of his employees. Although he is short and very thin, his demeanour follows the *marialva* code: chin up, chest out, firm and decisive steps, an imitation of a horse's grace and nobility.

The event of the day was a mare's covering. She had given birth nine days before, which meant that she was on the 'labour moon' (*lua do parto*), i.e., quite fertile. 'Just like the women', said one of the servants. Another servant, who was right behind another mare cutting her tail hair in an elaborate design, was the victim of some crude jokes. He remembered the story of a man who copulated with a mare because the horses were taking too long to make up their minds. There was a strange sort of sexual tension in the air, as obscenity grew rampant and the crude analogy between women and the mares was established as the source of humour.

At that point, they brought in a horse to cover the mare. But the horse was hesitant, he kept running away from the mare. The *cavaleiro* immediately said in a very spiteful manner: 'This one is a *maricón*' [he used the Spanish word for sissy, not the Portuguese *maricas*. Not just because the bullfighting world is very Hispanophile, but also because Spanish is seen as a more macho language – the imperial idiom – and Portuguese as too soft, poetic and feminine]. So the men brought in a second horse. In a jiffy it got excited, climbed on top of the mare and copulated, all in less than a minute. The men watched with satisfaction, while making comments on the animal's dexterity and the size of his sexual organ.

Afterwards we went to the bullfighting ring. Zé Ganhão was driving a tractor for watering the sand in the ring. The *cavaleiro* was shouting commands from the outside. He became very angry, jumped in to the ring, shoved Zé Ganhão away from the driver's seat and took a hold of the wheel. He started to drive the tractor in high speed, with harsh gestures. His skinny body was in apparent contradiction with his gestures and that made me think how the actual physical shape is not central to *machismo* – it's rather a matter of body language.

The cows that were in the back stables were selected. They were cows because this was just a training session. It is only in the real thing that the contender has to be a strong male. The *cavaleiro* left for a while and returned riding a horse, and so did his *espadinha*, the helper who decoys the animal with a cape. Several other men came in, holding *bandarilhas* (the short iron picks that are stabbed in the bull) for the *cavaleiro*. The first cow was quite wild and the *cavaleiro* did not like this, he kept on yelling that she was *mexida* (that she had been 'touched'), meaning that she had been in a fight already. I would discover later in the day that it had been Zé Ganhão himself that had forgotten to cut the cow's ear – a sign of being *mexida*.

While fighting the next cow, the *cavaleiro* kept on yelling all sorts of obscenities to the cow, all of a sexual nature. In the balcony, once again there was the female singer, wearing riding boots and a Spanish *señorito* hat. On the opposite side of the circular wooden boards, myself and the servants from Pardais. They were all commenting – feeling safe with the distance – on all that the *cavaleiro* did and said; they were very scornful, sometimes jealous and even vindictive. When they commented on the singer's breasts in a *sotto voce* I could almost feel the greed and the envy towards their master. The *cavaleiro* proceeded with his show, the servants watched.

Yet again annoyed with the cow, he decided to stop. Zé Ganhão told him that he and I were leaving since we had made arrangements for lunch with some friends. But the boss decided to have Zé Ganhão water the arena once more, when he could easily have asked some other man to do it. Zé Ganhão obeyed.

My informants never like a *cavaleiro* in a bullfight; they prefer the *toreadores* and even more so the *pegadores*. It is the reverse for the upper-class people, who admire the equestrian art more. This is related to the homology that exists between the different skills in the bullfight, and work. That of the *toreador* or *pegador* is more physical, risky; that of the *cavaleiro* is more distant, mediated by the horse and more aesthetically elaborate. Besides, in order to be a *cavaleiro* one needs large amounts of capital, since horses, their maintenance and the production of the show are expensive. Bullfights are also theatres of social precedence and hierarchy. The *cavaleiro* appropriates and dominates the macho attributes of the horse in its fight against the bull: his masculinity is almost beyond comparison because it is grounded on social privilege. Whereas the men who fight on foot cannot appropriate the attributes of the horse.

In Geertz's interpretation there is perhaps an excessive weight in the idea that the cockfight is a 'text' that 'says something', and less attention is paid to what the rite 'does'. He is right, though, when he says that treating the cockfight as a text means to stress one important aspect: the use of emotion for cognitive ends. What the cockfight says, it says in a vocabulary of sentiment – the emotion of risk, the despair of losing, the pleasure of triumph. The same is valid for the men from Pardais when they watch a bullfight, and even more so when they take part in a *garraiada*. These are the emotions that social life consists of and which place individuals in social interaction. It is a sort of sentimental education: 'What he learns there is what his culture's ethos and his private sensibility (or, anyway, certain aspects of them) look like when spelled out externally in a collective text' (Geertz 1973:449).[12]

Sentiments and emotions – mainly masculine ones – will be the subject of the next chapter.

NOTES

1. Time is also gendered: Sundays are practically the only days when one can see husband and wife together in public, as a family, since their children are also with them. The morning hours, when men are already at work, are a period when the village is 'feminised'. The only men around are the unemployed elderly – and this reinforces local notions of juxtaposition between work and masculinity, domesticity and femininity. Some annual dates are also inter-sexual: local fairs, religious festivals, the village feast; and, of course, those rites in the life cycle that have a ceremonial aspect to them, such as christenings and weddings. The only public space in the village that is exclusively feminine is the washing basin – but what women do there is not classified as leisure, but rather as work.

2. In another context that I have studied (Trás-os-Montes, north-eastern Portugal), the status of male celibacy constitutes the axis of organisation for a specific group (*os rapazes*, the boys) which ritually performs its specificity during the *Festa dos Rapazes*, a period during which the group creates a society apart, with its own laws, symbols, rules, recruiting and space. Although in Pardais the bachelor condition (as we have seen with Sr. Altino Valente) has social salience, such groups are not formally organised. I think this is due to the fact that strategies of marriage and land inheritance in the north-east have a determining effect on the constitution of this socially and economically liminal groups. See, on this, Vale de Almeida (1983).

3. During my stay I was fortunate to be able to follow the broadcasting of the Brazilian soap *Tieta*, based on Jorge Amado's book. It is a narrative that takes place in a rural context, portraying emotional and sexual topics of a joking kind, that pleased the people of Pardais enormously. Characters and conflicts in the soap were appropriated as a mirror of local Pardais reality, thus 'mediating' it.

4. The main targets of joking are: Ruivo's father, 'Xula', 'Tareco', and 'Funil' (all humorous nicknames). The first is a paraplegic, as a consequence of wounds from the Colonial War and a subsequent motorcycle accident; he has a strong speech impediment. The second is an elderly bachelor, and has a strong curvature of the spine. The third is also a bachelor; the fourth is an elderly man who is divorced. 'Xula' likes to make practical jokes, 'Tareco' is very irritable and

refuses to drink beer – he only drinks wine; 'Funil' gets drunk very easily and always laughs when people make jokes about him.

5. When visiting the village one year after fieldwork, a third café had opened. It was in the garage that had initially been a possible residence for me. The café provides more elaborate snacks, typical of an urban category called *cervejaria* (beer house); it is decorated like a pub and is attended by people of both sexes and families.

6. On the topics dealt with in this section, important contributions can be found in the following works: Cordeiro (1991), Brandes (1979), Cowan (1991), Douglas (1987), Driessen (1983), Gefou-Madianou (1992), Gilmore (1990), Herzfeld (1985), and Papataxiarchis (1991), among others.

7. However, on feminine friendships in Mediterranean contexts, see the alternative views of Handman (1991) and Uhl (1991).

8. The literature on friendship is now vast in anthropology: Pitt-Rivers (1973) and (1977), Foster (1953) and (1960), Wolf (1966), Brandes (1973) and (1981), Gilmore (1975), Murphy (1983), Fortes (1969). It is Giddens however who is most explicit when he refers to friendship and intimacy as modern substitutes for kinship and community relations. Among the young men of Pardais there is a latent existential conflict between these two forms of affiliation: the morality of 'opening oneself up to another' typical of modern friendship often clashes against the moral obligations of kinship.

9. Ruivo is an adolescent *cabouqueiro* who together with his two brothers provides for his mother and sisters. This is due to his father being handicapped as a consequence of war and motorcycle accident injuries. He did not have a close friendship relation with the other two, and it was I who invited him to come along with us. Still, in the confined time and space of one 'outing', everything happens as if friendships were deep. There is no direct consequence for the way people relate to each other the following day.

10. The Portuguese word for pregnant is *grávida*, the verb *engravidar*. This only applies to women. For animals you say *prenha*, and *emprenhar*. This last word is closer to English. It is the word they used to refer to women. One must be careful in concluding that there is a debasement of women here: the human-animal distinction in language for pregnancy is very bourgeois and urban.

11. Pitt-Rivers' itinerary is interesting because we can glimpse how the issue of gender can elucidate the ritual and symbolic logic in an innovative way. Like Lévi-Strauss said about myth, Pitt-Rivers claims that rites do not 'say' things, but rather they 'do' things: they establish the who, how, when, what and where of social relations and they solve contradictions. However the order of gender cannot be guaranteed through external social control; it needs the consent as well as the embodied lived consensus of the social agents. In this sense, rites are also performances and moments of symbolic dispute.

12. See also, on more recent theories of ritual, theatre and performance: Turner (1974 [1969]), Turner and Bruner (1986), and Schechner and Appel (1990).

5. HEARTS OF STONE?
The Gendered Poetics of Emotions

*T*he original title of the Portuguese manuscript of this volume was *Hearts of Stone*, a Portuguese idiomatic expression meaning 'lack of feeling' that is stereotypically associated with men. This chapter is subdivided into three parts that will address the issue of the social reproduction of emotions and sentiments that are culturally perceived as gendered. First, through an analysis of oral poetry as a masculine preserve for the expression of dysphoric sentiments. Second, focusing on women's lives, an analysis of women's roles, of family and domesticity in the creation and reproduction of masculinity. Lastly, I will address the socialisation of sentiments and gender in children.

Masculine Sentiments: Oral Poetry and the Performance of Emotions

Television is to blame
for so many unhappy women
so many disgraced girls
yet daughters of good roots.

They see important things
while walking in the street
women don't go naked
but don't dress as before
the more elegant ones
who have certain crises

it's like that in all countries
it's a world thing
they only blame Portugal
for so many unhappy women.

Women let themselves be fooled
watching so many soaps
the men kissing the women
they like to see and hear
they even stop sleeping
they lose many a night
if we analyse this well
it's all a low-life thing
I hear the old folks say
that television is to blame.

Many folks are fooled
watching so much television
even those [women] who aren't
like to watch the disgraceful life
they're daughters of their beloved mother
by father and mother cherished
with love and charity
when they reach a certain age
so many disgraced girls.

Many are students
they need to learn
others, with great wisdom
that no one has taught them
that's the wondrous thing
that they are masters and pupils
they go to the main churches
those who are religious
but part of them are sly
though daughters of good roots.[1]

After a few weeks in the field I listened to this poem, the author of which was José Seco. It was late in the evening. In the almost empty café, Zé Seco (Jr.), the poet's son, was reading this poem to three or four of his friends. I was immediately interested in the poem's content of social criticism, and with the fact that it was being read among men. The listeners' attitude, however, was not one of scorn – contrary to what one might wrongly expect, taking into consideration that women are usually targets of male criticism. Many of the images and expressions used in this poem are not currently used on everyday conversation. The listeners were paying attention, they were serious, and seemed to be reflecting on what was being said. Another poem followed, its tone very different:

I leave it all written
never get confused
close tightly the boards,
the wood of my coffin.

One day when I die
take me to the cemetery
to that serious place
for those who stop living
so everyone knows
where I remain buried
the holy ground is respected
that is a large sentiment
if I still have time
I'll leave it all written.

Take me with charity
to my sepulchre's grave
to that dark house
where there is never light
nobody goes willingly
to that sad darkness
those who are there
none of them are happy
when that day arrives
never get confused

I live with this sorrow
in this world I suffer
if I die they will take me
to a house that moans water
my body rots there
under the closed-in ground
even dressed and with shoes
no one can help me
but before I go there
close tightly the boards.

Have a mass said for me
for my soul when I die
the earth eating me
not even my bones are spared

> the earth is greedy for everything
> according to the symptoms I'm told
> I die full of passion
> not even God can save me
> don't forget to close tight
> the wood of my coffin.

The listeners paid extra attention to this poem's reading. It was followed by grave nodding of the heads, sullen facial expressions and the uttering of sentences like 'such is life'. In normal everyday circumstances the fear of death is not expressed; even at funerals, the bodily and verbal expressions of grief and mourning are a feminine speciality. That is why the way that the sentiments of this group of men were being expressed, and made acceptable through the rhetoric of poetry, placed this field of expression in sharp contrast with the moral ethos of emotional expression by men. Men are almost never supposed to freely express sentiments and emotions that can jeopardise their self-image of strength and self-sufficiency. The episode opened up for me the possibility to explore the locus of the expression of 'non-masculine' sentiments by men. Before starting the analysis, however, one more piece of narrative.

The poems quoted in this and other chapters were made by Sr. José Seco. I collected dozens of his poems, as well as some by anonymous authors. These poems are called *décimas*. The *décima* (literally, the 'tenth') follows a rule: it is made up of an initial refrain or *mote* (a thematic motif) of four verses, followed by four strophes of ten verses each. Each strophe ends with the same verse as that in the *mote*, sequentially. José Seco creates his poems without the help of writing. Like the vast majority of 'popular poets', as they are locally known, he is illiterate. This means that there is some actual sense in talking about writing and speaking as two differentiated modes of expression, allowing for two different ways of experiencing the world. It would however be wrong to share the premise that these differences are based on a kind of 'mind' or form of 'thought' based on dichotomies such as primitive / civilised, traditional / modern or any other. The technique – and the constraint – of oral modes, are specific inasmuch as the 'texts' produced have to be memorised. And the best way to do it is by giving them a fixed form or structure, by making them circulate collectively, and by the fact that the meanings expressed have resonance in local ethics and morality.

An interesting anthropological question would be that of the relation between individual creation (to which folklore studies normally do not pay attention) and the cultural symbols and meanings utilised by the poet and which have the social group as a source. More important to this essay, though, is the fact that this kind of poetry is a vehicle for the expression of emotions and sentiments, and the fact that these are gendered; the idiom of emotions reports to the masculine and feminine categories and these are, in turn, largely constructed on the basis of emotional metaphors. If we add to this the fact that the creators are almost always men and that it is among men that the *décimas* are normally divulged, then we have defined the field for a socio-cultural complex.

The field of 'popular poetry' or 'oral poetry' somehow helps one not to see society and culture as mere normative collective structures; in the forms of symbolic production we see people engaged in the practices of social life; these people tell stories, thus giving cognitive and emotional coherence to a much more confusing personal and collective experience; in doing so, they also negotiate the social identity of both creator and group. Narrative – whether in prose or verse – does not, then, passively reflect social institutions and culture, but is rather a constitutive part of them in the very act of telling. The production and reproduction of society occur in practice.[2] The same holds true for poetry.

Décimas narrate local or national events that were either witnessed, or told and reported in the media; extreme situations such as death, accidents, illness or imprisonment have substantial weight in the range of themes. The narration normally contains some sort of moral judgement or a demonstration of the ambiguity and contradictions of the narrated facts: social hierarchy and inequality, the ideal equality of all human beings, filial love, ingratitude, loyalty, the contradiction between stealing as a necessity and the sinful aspect of that action – to mention but a few of the poems collected. Some poems, although just a few, are merely descriptive, narrating the local geography, comparing villages, enumerating the calendars of feasts and saints.

The author of the texts is a specialist in memorising them, in a context where they cannot (or could not) be registered in writing; but they are also the texts of an author who reflects upon and criticises the patterns according to which the group is supposed to behave. The social change of global modernity has also been felt, as in the case of poems on the Gulf War (the pretext for a poem on the fear of war) or the criticism of changes in feminine mores triggered by soap operas, as in the above-quoted *décima*. The act of reciting the *décima* (or of singing it, since *décimas'* authors can also sing in competition with other author-singers until one of them runs out of repertoire, resistance, or improvisational skill) complements and contrasts with other forms of narrative: those of everyday life, in conversations in small or larger groups, normally in the space par excellence for masculine sociability – the café.

The *dezedor* (literally 'he who says', that is – the poet) works with signs and symbols that are part of a semiotic system that up to a certain point lies beyond him. However, since the poem is recited in public, conjuring all the power of recited words, the *décima* poetry is morally ambiguous: it is not sacred enough to justify the power it has (contrary to, say, a prayer) and yet it is not sufficiently secular for that power to be the same as ordinary eloquence (Geertz 1983). For Geertz (using the example of the Islamic equivalent of a *dezedor*), 'the man who takes up the poet's role in Islam traffics, and not wholly legitimately, in the moral substance of his culture' (1983: 109). For him, certain activities seem to be adequate to demonstrate that ideas are visible, audible, that they can be presented in ways that allow the senses (and through them the emotions) to confront them (Geertz 1983:119–30). Such would be the case of poetry.

The poet selects from an oral archive, recalling that which has meaning. In that archive events, verbal or otherwise, have a hierarchy of meaning. However, what gives true coherence to events and the understanding of them is narrative itself. One can not see the narrated events as the raw materials of *décimas*. *Décimas* become things-in-themselves, similar to works of art. And narrative takes place, it is made, in the act of performance.

To have the gift of the word, to know how to reply, to play and fool around with language, are all key attributes of personhood and masculinity in this context. The distinction between everyday discourse and narrative is blurred by a poetic that is as much part of verbal discourse as of social action. What does change is what one talks about. Café conversation follows certain guidelines, recitation follows different ones. If during café conversation, for instance, women are ostensibly treated like objects, in poetry, on the other hand, there is space for the sentiment of love – for sentiments of loss and abandonment, emotions that are seen as typically feminine, but that men can appropriate through the rhetorical resource of poetry. It is even possible, through fiction, to assume a feminine voice. Here is one example:

> My name sounded
> I was already dead
> you thought I was not alive
> so you had a new husband
>
> (him) We are both right
> I will explain why

you thought I wasn't alive
but I was in prison
I had no communication
so as to write to you, adored one
you are married with another
while being my beloved wife
I have suffered much in life
my name sounded loud.

When I left this place
I left behind children and trouble
father, mother, wife and children
and went to suffer what I did
the day I came back
I was very upset
I walked around my meaning [I thought and worried]
in sad life thinking
I thought I could forgive you
You thought I was not alive.

(her) Since you said good-bye
my soul has had no rest
if we're both put on a scale
which of us was sadder?
the only sorrow I have
is not being yet buried
if I am forgiven by you
my destiny is to cry
I can not accept
That you knew upon arriving.

I can not live like this
with so much heartbreak and sorrow
my eyes are full of water
for not being in your possession
punish me if I deserve
if it's for me you've suffered
you are the same you were
you've always been my sorrow
for thinking you were dead
that's why I have a new husband.

The event is a mythical one but is locally referred to as having really occurred in a nearby village. It is a paradigmatic story of a misunderstanding, and it intertwines the complexity of emotions and the norms of social relations, what is and what should be. Any text is a construction. Once it narrates an event, then the event itself is (re)constructed.

A process of individual creation, the expression of poetry is also a public recitation. It is a praxis, a performance. For local people it is not the same if a *décima* is read from a piece of paper or if someone other than the author recites it. The capacity to convey an emotion is one of the *dezedor's* gifts, it lies as much in textual content as in performance. Texts are situated in particular contexts, with individual performers. Performance brings to the surface both the oral literary text and its meaning, as well as the structure of social roles, relations and interactions. As Benjamin said, 'the storyteller takes what he tells from experience – his own and that reported by others. And he in turn makes it the experience of those who are listening to his tale' (Benjamin 1969:87 in Bauman 1986).

As far back as Goffman (1951), stories of personal experience have been examined as important instruments in interaction, including the presentation of self and the construction and communication of a sense of situated reality. In the village, and in the masculine space-time of the café, all men invest in the strategy of personal statement with the help of narratives of experience. The *dezedor* has a further asset and skill, that of knowing how to 'give meaning to things' and of doing so through poetic language, a kind that can use as a resource those sentiments which, in daily life, are catalogued as 'feminine'.

The approach to emotions that I share stresses social discourse and the analysis of specific social situations. Maybe the best definition of discourse is still that of Foucault: 'discourses ... [are] practices that, in a systematic way, shape the objects they talk about' (1972:49). Emotions can be approached from the point of view of discourse on emotions, as well as from the point of view of emotional discourses. A good theoretical support is, of course, Lutz and Abu-Lughod's (1990) work, in which emotion is seen as a discursive practice: emotions as phenomena that can be observed in social interaction, granted that part of it is verbal. For those authors, 'rather than seeing them as expressive vehicles, we must understand emotional discourses as pragmatic acts and communicative performances' (1990:11).

Emotional discourse, then, is a form of action that affects the social world. Recalling Wittgenstein, conversation on emotions can be interpreted as being about social life and as taking place in social life. It is not about inner states of soul. However, emotions are also formed as experiences that engage the person as a whole – the body included. The same happens with the *dezedor*, who knows how to use his body adequately:

looks, pauses, intonations of the voice, body postures. Bourdieu defines the body *hexis* as a set of techniques and postures that are learned habits which reflect and reproduce the social relations that surround them and constitute them (1977:90). Or: 'L'hexis corporelle est la mythologie politique réalisée, incorporée, devenue disposition permanente, manière durable de se tenir, de porter le corps' (1980:117).[3] The *dezedor*, while reciting, exaggerates both the verbal and the bodily rhetoric of masculinity. He acts even more seriously – more manly – when he utters 'feminine words'. Part of his magic lies right there.

For Lutz and Abu-Lughod, sociability and power relations are two fundamental aspects of social relations connected with the discourse on emotions. In another article, Lutz (1990) notes that in the North American context discourses on emotions are related to gender ideology. She says that this discourse only appears to be about inner states. It is, in fact, about social life and, particularly, about power relations. The *décima* quoted at the beginning of the chapter illustrates just that, as does the *décima* about the widow who was not a widow after all: only death could free her from the constraints of matrimonial obligation. It is in personal life that the ideals of the moral system must engender forms of behaviour and of talking related to sentiments. Poetry occupies a privileged place in this: how is it used, how do people react to it?

In the context of Egyptian Bedouins studied by Abu-Lughod (1986), one can find some striking similarities with Pardais. There is among the Bedouins a particular kind of sensitivity to playing games with linguistic forms, and the evocative power of the elements of oral texts: sound, alliteration, intonation, rhythm, are all stressed in recitation. Poems acquire meaning by drawing upon images and experiences of the shared world, using little metaphorical invention; poetical elements are seen as tools for the articulation, transmission and evocation of sentiments. Most poems have little abstract impact, and that is why content is crucial for meaning. They are formulaic and traditional, appropriating themes, metaphors, sentences, structures that have been already in use but that are recombined in order to express new meanings.

For Abu-Lughod the sentiments in poetry tend to be negative or dysphoric. Through poetry the weakness that could threaten the code of honour is expressed, and that happens thanks to the social context of its performance – among equals, lovers or friends. One does not sing or recite in the presence of social superiors, people of the other sex or older people. In my context, José Seco's son was to reveal himself to be an excellent poet. However, he assured me that his father did not know it, even though he (Zé Seco Jr.) was already fifty years old. The public avoidance between father and son is a social rule that is verbally expressed as an emotion of 'uneasiness' or something that 'doesn't feel right'. Social distance also makes the town bourgeoisie unaware of the existence of village poets, except when the bourgeois liberal political ideas or the neo-romantic attraction towards rural exoticism exerts its power, thus reifying the category of the 'popular poet'.

The use of an idiom of childhood suggests that the poems may be amoral (not immoral) (Abu-Lughod 1986: 244). It is common to use the character of the son, the mother-son relation, and infantile helplessness. Owing to the contingency of being masculine, it is really a poetic of lack of power and autonomy. Comparisons with women are always a central theme or preoccupation, as well as those with people higher in the hierarchy. Loss of prestige is seen as a form of infantilisation. In the extreme, nostalgia for dependence on the mother (a time in a man's life when one does not have to 'be a man') acquires the meaning of paradise lost. Here is an example, in which is also obvious the guilt that a son feels for having cut the ties with his mother – a necessary move in adolescence for acquiring culturally recognised masculinity:

> The son is not capable
> Of cherishing his mother's love
> he knows how much he misses it
> only after she is gone.

> The mother lives passionately
> ever since she bore that son
> after birth she raised him
> in all helped by God
> she was very content
> of bearing the child in peace
> as soon as you can you'll go
> walking away on your own two feet
> the mother loves him tenderly
> the son is not capable.

> My dear adored son
> child of my entrails
> never in life will you find
> anyone who'll love you more
> I don't know if you recall
> seeing your mother toiling
> feeding you her share

a certain percentage
the son has no courage
of cherishing his mother's love.

Note that this too was composed by a man, José Seco. Basically Abu-Lughod says that poetry allows the expression of that which the social code does not allow. It legitimates certain sentiments, and if recited or sung in the right context, it ultimately says that he who recites lives according to social patterns; that his adhesion to moral codes is simultaneously voluntary and hard. Emotions and their expression are seen as belonging to the feminine world. A world of emotions that are at the same time a sign of weakness and potential danger. Men are left with bravado and the maintenance of honour and prestige, which lie, before all, on the capacity to be (to become) men – a moral category. This folk vision, however, is curiously similar to western scholarly visions on emotions as the antithesis of reason. The pre-enlightenment West has, furthermore, equalled masculinity and reason, femininity and emotionality.[4]

Emotions are not things opposed to thought, but rather 'embodied thoughts, thoughts seeped with the apprehension that 'I am involved" (Rosaldo 1984: 143). The analytical frames that make the self an equivalent of spontaneity, genuine sentiment, privacy, unity, constancy, inner life, and so on, and oppose these to 'persons' or *personae*, mask, role, rule or context, are a reflection of the dichotomies that constitute the modern Western self (Rosaldo 1984: 146). In order to overcome this limited framework, social sciences have either tried to relativise, historicise or contextualise the discourse of emotions (Lutz and Abu-Lughod 1990).

One of the main sexual divisions in local theory lies in the attribution of rationality to men and emotionality to women. Or, rather, of emotivity as something feminine, and rationalisation as something masculine. Emotions are supposed to weaken people, but they are also forces that push one to action. So the notion that emotions should be controlled is crucial, as well as the definition of who has the capacity to do so. Men are supposed to control their emotions because it would be culturally inadequate to express them. Women, however, are supposed to control them because they would be dangerous.

Perhaps ever since Foucault, one could say that the cultural construction of feminine emotions can be seen not so much as repression or suppression of emotions in men, but rather as creation, stimulation of emotions in women (Lutz 1990: 87). In any case, it is in the closed circle of female friends and relatives that women most often verbalise their emotivity. They are the specialists of romantic love, of pain and sorrow, of nostalgia, of religiosity. Of the sentiments expressed in the *décimas*. In public, and with the exception of certain ritual moments (such as funerals), the control of emotions is blatant in their attitudes of modesty, embodied in the very way of walking, in postures, and in the control of sight. Regarding men, they have two basic outlets: the excuse of altered states of mind (as in heavy drinking or, for the younger generations, in hashish smoking), or poetry.

However, is this interpretation not one that again places emotions at the 'inner' level, an almost psycho-biological one, one that culture would cover like the lid of a pot covers steam? If we pay attention to the contents of the *décimas* here transcribed, we can see how they 'talk' about what men should not 'talk' about in everyday life. Nevertheless, there is a whole field of emotions that can and must be expressed in everyday life. The question seems to be, then, the gendered character of emotions and sentiments: its differential attribution to men and women. Thus, the poetry of the *décimas* somehow brings masculinity closer to femininity, within the limits of a socially defined rhetorical formula.

When Beto used to tell me his disturbing dreams, mostly related to death in the quarries, saying that he would stay awake at night 'trying to get my brain away from that meaning' (literal translation), I could not decode his dreams since I am not an analyst. Now I think: maybe I should have composed a poem.

Women: Resignation, Resistance, Rebellion

For women, 'Küche, Kirche, Kinder'. This famous German phrase was pronounced, of course, by Adolph Hitler. It probably represents the highest degree to which the social oppression of women was taken, in a patriarchal political project led by a State. Many totalitarian political projects simply put in the writing of the law the same lines of inequality and cleavage that pre-existed in social practice. 'Kitchen, Church, and Children' is what, at the limit, women in Pardais are supposed to be dedicated to: the domesticity of family life, the guaranteeing of tasks that are conducive to the physical reproduction of the domestic group. To marry is, for women, the achievement of adult status and of some power, a power that is directed to the home and projected on to the children.

Cutileiro said that in Vila Velha marriages were dictated mostly by sentiment. Although this is mostly an ideal form, it is true that the lower strata do not possess property, that inheritance only occurs after the death of the owners (not at the time of the children's marriage), and that dowry is practically non-existent. The process of courting itself is seen as a romantic moment that will eventually lead to the constitution of a new family unit, not as an alliance between two kin groups. There are many cases of couples coming from families that do not get along, and the institution of *juntar* allows for the beginning of conjugal sexual life without the previous meeting of the material conditions necessary for the constitution of a new domestic group. The local ideal is in fact the autonomous nuclear family.

As I have mentioned earlier, the qualities that are sought for in the spouse are twofold. For the man, it is mainly the capacity to earn a living; for the woman it is mostly sexual modesty. These two principles are contained in their negative opposites in the idea of *vício* (vice): it is libidinal in the woman and economic (gambling and drinking excessively) in men. The constitution of the couple is part of a life project that completes the notion of person and its gendered aspects of female and male. That is why adults who are single are victims of scorn: women because they display excessive virtue (religious piety), although they are never suspected of homosexuality. Single men for lack of masculinity and suspicion of homosexuality.[5]

Being married is seen, among men, in an analogous way to their vision of work: it grants honour, it is a constitutive part of public prestige, but it represents a sacrifice of adolescent, pre-nuptial freedom, and a contract that involves the risk of dishonour due to the potential adultery of women. Doubts persist due to the ambivalent notion of women's nature.

The expression of sentiments of love has its time and place in the life cycle. It happens mostly during the period of courting and terminates – publicly – after marriage. The same type of sentiments continue to be expressed by women, mostly in a phantasmagoric way, through the mediation of soap operas, romantic novels and the exchange of information regarding the love life of the rest of the village. For men, the issue is too feminine to be touched upon, and so it is cornered in poetry. Romantic love, Western passionate love, is the model in action and it is felt to be in contradiction with the status of being married. That is why it is so common to hear joking, sarcastic, or regretful remarks on marriage and, at the opposite end, lyrical, sentimental compositions on how love is supposed to be at the root of a lifetime's engagement. In general, the sentiment that is expressed is one if instability and illusion:

I swore to love you eternally
I still remember that day
You too swore eternal love
What wonderful times those were
However when you told me
Our love will end today
You saw me laughing but
inside my sad soul was crying
When, however, I was told
That you were caught in another's arms
I started singing, for my sorrows
Live occult among joys.

(Anonymous author)

For women, marriage has so far been the way in which the complete status of 'person' is achieved. Due to the division between public world as masculine and domestic world as feminine,[6] marriage means for women the possibility of managing a home. This means not only the physical space, but also the sustenance of the home, ideally guaranteed in monetary terms by husband and sons. These two aspects (control over the domestic space, and raising children) have a major influence in the constitution of gender in children. The mother-daughter tie will last beyond the daughter's marriage, in a relationship of mutual support. But the mother-son tie is more complex and plays an important role in the definition of the unstable character of masculinity.

I have mentioned several times the ambivalent nature of men's attitudes towards women. From a Freudian perspective, one can see this ambivalence as the result of unresolved Oedipal desires that can be attributed to too long an intimacy between mother and son. If one does not want to emphasise Oedipal conflicts, there can always be found strong pre-Oedipal ties with the mother, centred on oral gratification. An aggressive style of motherhood would push the boy toward an ambivalent attitude: in order to separate himself from the mother and become an individual he would split the image of the feeding nurturing mother from that of the devouring mother, thus resulting in the split between the image of the Virgin and that of the Seductress.

However, Stoller and Herdt (1993) write about a force pulling in the opposite direction. They write about the regressive nostalgia felt by men in relation to the warm relationship with their mother and passive dependence on her. Gilmore (1986) provides some examples drawn from Andaluzian oral poetry, in which the anxiety about maternal constancy includes fantasies of abandonment. For him, 'The songs represent magical efforts at restoration of the absent love object specifically through identification and incorporation – a theme first enunciated by Freud in his anatomy of mourning and melancholia' (1986: 229). Similar examples exist in Pardais, as in the *décima* above transcribed about the son 'who does not know how to cherish his mother's love'. Generally, these poems show the opposite of hegemonic masculine sentiments: desperate men, feeling dependent on women, feeling inadequate, infantile, and women portrayed as powerful, generous and self-assured (Gilmore 1986: 230).

These aspects are connected with what could be called a feminine compensation for the lack of public and political power. In a context where domestic life is completely vested on women and seen as non-prestigious for masculine hegemonic ideology, it is turned around by women, since it is at home that future men are raised. That is: the constraining of women in the home has its obverse in matrifocality.

Machismo, understood as a 'pattern of masculine behaviour that involves culturally sanctioned demonstrations of hyper-masculinity' (Gilmore and Gilmore 1978: 149) can be seen in psycho-dynamic terms as

> (…) having a compensational purpose for resolving the inner psychic conflict between masculine and feminine identities. We locate this conflict (…) on a blocking of lower class [*jornaleros*] masculine development caused by conditions of economic failure on the part of the man, on a matriarchal pattern of the domestic unit, and on the lack of participation in the local political process. (Gilmore and Gilmore 1978:150. My translation.)

Thus we return to the issue of the so-called *machismo* of *cabouqueiros* (the equivalents in Pardais of *jornaleros*) as a post-Oedipal mechanism of de-identification with the powerful mother figure. Social class division must play an important role here, since among the upper classes the father is more often present at home, does not frequent the cafés and the street as much, and his prestige is largely guaranteed by economic status. In the lower-class family – although supposedly patriarchal – practices are markedly matriarchal (or, more accurately, matrifocal). As a matter of fact, the other striking element in Pardais is the weakness of the interaction ties between father and son. The father's absence from the home increments the difficulties that the son has when he starts de-identifying himself from his mother.

The woman and mother is often called and seen as the *patroa* (literally the 'female boss'), in a mixed attitude of fear and irony by men. She administrates the husband's salary that he gives to her in full, she takes decisions about consumption and expenditures, and she establishes the networks of mutual help. In a study on the menstrual taboo regarding pig slaughter ceremonies (*matança*), Lawrence (1982) shows how women manipulate their knowledge of their bodily cycles in order to make decisions on who to invite for help in the *matança*, thus being able to control the cycle of reciprocity:

> At the matança the greatest threat to a household's economic well-being is posed by the purported destructive effects of menstruation on processing pork (...) They liken this natural, regularly occurring event to a disease, albeit a temporary one, which affects a woman's entire body (...) Furthermore they are thought to have special powers over which they have little or no control (...) Cross-sexual pollution is feared during a woman's menstrual period. (Lawrence 1982: 88)

It is striking that 'feminine power' be based on aspects that take us back to biology: their capacity to conceive and give birth, to suckle, to take care, plus the menstrual cycle. These are the same elements that are used by the hegemonic masculine ideology in order to make the association of women with nature and thus bar their access to the (public, political) domain of culture. These are, then, the same elements that women themselves use in order to guarantee their control over their domestic groups and to establish village networks.

Lawrence also says that in societies where nuclear families predominate, women are not compelled to overcome or bypass the masculine hierarchy inside the home in order to achieve their domestic objectives. This is because the woman's relationship with her husband is conditioned by the degree to which his position of authority at home is based, or not, on forces outside the home; that is why a weak masculine power in the home is related to his lack of power in the community (Lamphere 1974: 111 and Reiter 1975: 272). In Pardais, women organise themselves in social networks autonomous from those of men, establishing relations with other homes, but not in large, public groups equivalent to masculine ones.

The commonly-held idea about friendship in Mediterranean contexts is that women do not form friendship relations owing to their social restriction to the domestic space. Uhl (1991) demonstrates, with a Spanish example, that women overcome the necessity for friendship relations by 'masking' them as domestic relations. What happens in Pardais is that this veil not only covers feminine friendships, but women's public discourse reinforces the androcentric vision that friendship is 'men's business'. One should not, however, confuse strategic discourse with concrete practices.

For instance, Handman (1991) tries to demonstrate that feminine friendships in the Greek village she studied constitute one of the most solid armours of society. True female friends are recruited from among germane cousins beyond the third degree of kin relation, from among childhood friends and from among wives of brothers-in-law (in a context that is patri-virilocal). With regard to values, the women of Arnaia enumerate trust and fidelity (the capacity to withhold a secret), help in case of need, compassion in difficult moments, and the capacity to share joys (1991:17). It is not – and the same holds true for Pardais – mere courtesy in social relations. Among neighbours, women make an effort to keep good relationships, often called 'friendships', but talked about in intimate conversation as not 'true' friendships. In Pardais, women make a clear distinction between 'neighbours', 'relatives' and 'friends'. Although one single person may fulfil all three descriptions at once, the distinction is made because a 'relative' is someone with whom the relationship is usually distant. It should be noted that the term for female relative (*parenta*) means just this; if the kin relation is a close, friendly one, then it is not called *parenta* but rather the actual specific relation (sister, sister-in-law, and so on).

In meetings and reunions of women, whether they be neighbours, relatives or friends, their subordinate social condition is often self-represented in an ironical fashion. In fact, women seem to have three behavioural alternatives regarding their situation, which have been outlined in three words in an article by Herzfeld (1991): silence, submission and subversion. Although women have ways of expressing their resentment towards masculine control and men's pretensions to superiority, they do it by ostensibly subscribing to that which they subvert. Through irony, they can play with the tension between an ideology of consensus and the lived experience of social division:

> Although women often use verbal irony, especially when mocking their men folk's pretensions of bravery, their silence can be especially effective (...) women often do indulge in bawdy badinage when they are among friends (...) I had nevertheless taken the most difficult route. This is because I worked at understanding the silences that I encountered rather than the talk that I did not (...) They voiced social criticism, a critique of men that was often of great severity, exposure of all their problems including even sexual ones, with great ease. (Herzfeld 1991: 95)

Let us take Manuela's case, for instance. She is more or less twenty years old, and she is Caralinda's daughter; she managed to graduate from high school, and she was living together (*junta*) with Francisco, whom she subsequently married. She was a Census (population statistics) agent in 1991, the year of my fieldwork. I accompanied her many times on her data-collecting visits. I had offered to drive her to the most remote corners of the *freguesia*, which was profitable for me, since then I was able to visit practically all the families. Our conversations were very pleasant and surprised me by the easiness (and knowledge) with which she spoke about her intimate life, her feelings, her body even, and all in a way that I could never find in any young men in the village.

However, my outings with her triggered a lot of gossip. One day I was casually complaining about a back pain to Zé Ganhão and he replied that the best thing for the pain to go would be to go to the *campo* (the countryside, any place outside the village) with a blanket and Manuela, for she 'would not say no'. I was upset with this, but let it somehow go on, for the sake of information. Zé admitted that she was nice but warned me that she was 'ruined' (*estragada*). Supposedly Francisco knew that she 'betrayed' him frequently but did not mind for he liked her very much. Zé Ganhão's opinion was that she did not 'understand that to be *junta* or to be married is the same; but she always tells people she is single'.

However, in my conversations with Manuela what surprised me the most was how easily she spoke about her infertility problem. She had tried to become pregnant several times and had not been able to do so. She had consulted with several doctors and described in detail the therapeutics, and the workings of her body in relation to fertility. She had a thorough knowledge of her body. One day she finally broke the news that she was pregnant. When I attended her wedding one year later, after the child was born, I had the clear certitude that Zé Ganhão's opinion on Manuela's purported immodesty had no real basis whatsoever. Zé and the others had jumped to their own conclusions due to the cultural gap between her and themselves and because of the fact that she had not been afraid of publicly announcing her independence and the rules of freedom and mutual respect that she had imposed on Francisco when they started living together.

The local ideology of the domestic model derives from religion, woman's destiny being the bearing of children and their raising. That is why marriage, the constitution of a home, and procreation are seen as 'obvious' options for women's life careers. For Loizos and Papataxiarchis

(1991), kinship plays a central role in the definition of masculine and feminine identities; the sexes are represented as being on a relationship of complementary, mutual dependence and ideal equality. Women are supposed to keep their expressive potential restrained among modest and controlled demonstrations of emotion and silence, thus resulting in what Herzfeld (1982) calls 'dyssemia' between externalised conformity and internalised protest in relation to the androcentric norm. Thus also the great importance of ritual and symbolic forms of women's expression, mainly through religion and its rituals. These occur in public spaces, but they are managed by women and use domestic symbolism as a resource: 'The more prominent women are within domestic kinship, the more womanhood is represented exclusively in kinship terms and their religious poetics merely confirm them in the prestigious role of mother and mistress of the house' (Loizos and Papataxiarchis 1991: 15). Gender and kinship can be viewed as mutually constructed, as Collier and Yanagisako (1987) state. Up to a certain point, gender and kinship go together as idioms of domesticity and the person, but in certain contexts external to marriage (such as the café), they are constructed in mutual exclusion and opposition (Loizos and Papataxiarchis 1991: 25). Thus, in the domestic sphere, kinship implies gender, but in the café, gender turns against domestic kinship at a symbolic level.

In the area of Vila Viçosa the cult of Our Lady of the Conception is a predominant one. The cult is connected with the dedication of Portugal as a country to this Marianic avatar. From this arises the importance of the cult in the area and the obvious association between Marianic cult, ideology of maternal, virginal and familial femininity, and also nationalism. In a local newspaper, *O Arauto da Padroeira* (property of the Roman Catholic Church) one could read at the time of the celebration of the Restoration of Independence (1 December, national holiday) and of Immaculate Conception (8 December, also a national holiday):

> On the eve of the turn of the millennium, a vast sensitising of the Christian people of Portugal towards renovation of the dedication to the Patron Saint and Queen of Portugal, will certainly constitute a new and powerful factor of re-christianisation and re-evangelisation in which the Church is engaged (...) Another 8 December is approaching, a day in which the Church will celebrate the mystery of the Immaculate Conception. We want to reaffirm that Mary of Nazareth, the Mother of Jesus Christ, was not tainted by the original sin. We say that Mary was conceived without original sin.

In Pardais, the church is frequented almost solely by women. They are the ones who take care of the religious aspects of the feast for the patron saint; they fabricate the ornaments, they decorate the processional platforms, they carry them in the procession. Younger women, with some high-school education, lead Sunday School classes for children. A large majority of houses have a portrait, usually in painted tile, of Our Lady of the Conception over the entrance door. She is a doubly meaningful invocation: not only did she conceive without sin, she herself was conceived without sin.

The emphasis on the Marianic cult and also in the figure of the Infant Jesus (and not Christ as an adult, the Saints, or the Holy Ghost), together with the effacing of the character of St Joseph, create the local paradigm of the domestic structure of the family and its matrifocality. The church is a symbolic 'house of women': they attend it, they take care of it. It is an overarching house, containing all of the houses in the village – and not so much a representation of the village as some corporate entity. This is clear when one realises the indifference men feel towards the church and religious activities. The cult itself is seen by most men as something feminine in and of itself: silent, obedient, knee-bending, introspective.

The Virgin (as Our Lady of the Conception), the Infant Jesus, and the patron saint Catherine of Alexandria are the central figures of feminine devotion. At the time of the procession, during the village annual feast, the platforms with the statues of saints are carried on the women's shoulders. They make a complete circuit of the village, stopping at each of the four corners. Through the mediation of the holy characters, it is women who are presenting themselves by means of presenting their religious virtues in opposition to political virtues (or virtualities). They are the specialists of a secret world, that of the relationship with what is sacred. It is presented once a year as having insurmountable power.

If Our Lady of the Conception stresses the idea of the honourable woman, and the Infant Jesus that of the male child dependent on the mother and shaped by her to be a great man, then Saint Catherine of Alexandria is the subject of a happy coincidence: she was a scholarly woman who challenged the pagan authority of a patriarchal potentate and was killed for it. I could never avoid connecting her with the young women of Pardais who carry St Catherine's platform and are precisely the few people in the village who have pursued an education and might have better skills and tools to understand the workings of local social relations.

Whatever the validity of my interpretations, Pardais deserves a whole different and new research, made in dialogue with my essay. It would ideally have to be one done by a female anthropologist among the young women of Pardais.

Innocence Lost: Boys Learn Masculinity

Throughout fieldwork I had a privileged relationship with the children in the village, mainly with boys who attended the local elementary school.[7] On the one hand, they visited my house frequently – practically everyday, because they knew they would have plenty of paper and pencils to draw with. On the other hand, I helped edit the school's newspaper, made a video with the children and managed to establish a relationship of trust with the two female teachers.

The school and the streets are two spaces where children are not ascribed to the home. Still, they are controlled in the streets by the feminine networks, and the family's relation with the school is created mostly by the mothers. In Chapter 2 I mentioned the constitution of gender identities through games and play. Now I would like to address how boys and girls are prepared for adult professional life, for citizenship in the nation-state, and how their slow separation from the family takes place.

School teaches children how to read, write and count. The model of life that is proposed by the teachers is based on the premise that it would be good to continue education beyond the (now) legally compulsory ninth grade, so as to have access to 'a better life', meaning white-collar instead of blue-collar jobs. However, I did an exercise with the children in which they were asked to draw on the theme of their parents' professions and the professions they wished to have when grown up. In this, 'realism' seems to have the lead: boys wish to work in the quarries or in professions of public spectacular success (football and bullfighting mainly), and girls wish to be teachers or mothers. These two aspects – the mental-manual division of labour and the sexual division of labour (and of sexual labour too), were analysed for the English case by Paul Willis:

> The mental/manual distinction alone presents a fertile field for the construction of naturalised divisions in human capacities. What is surprising is that a portion ... of those who make up the social whole are content to voluntarily take upon themselves the definition and consequent material outcomes of being manual labourers. (Willis 1977: 147)

This does seem to be surprising since in the dominant ideology of modern society it is intellectual labour that brings most benefits. What happens is that manual labour seems to be associated with the social precedence of masculinity and mental labour with the social inferiority of femininity. It is a strange inversion of the rational/emotional dichotomy as corresponding to masculine/feminine (unless what we mean by 'rational' is the 'power' to decide). Sexual division of labour and gender seem to come together in a mutually justifying way. Willis analyses the process in the following manner:

> If a form of patriarchy buttresses the mental/manual division of labour, this division, in turn, strengthens and helps to reproduce modern forms of sexual division and oppression. It is precisely because there are divisions at school and work which operate objectively to their disfavour but which can be understood and inverted in patriarchal terms that those gender terms must themselves be continuously reproduced and legitimated. If the currency of femininity were revalued then that of mental work would have to be too. A member of the counter-school culture can only believe in the effeminacy of white collar and office work so long as wives, girlfriends and mothers are regarded as restricted, inferior and incapable of certain things. (Willis 1977: 149)

The author is referring to 'counter-school culture' adolescents in an English industrial region, and one knows how Anglo-Saxon masculinity models stress physical strength more than sexual assertiveness. But in Pardais, too, things are somewhat similar. This becomes evident if we consider the issue of 'school failure', since the boys who repeat grades, those who are in elementary school at thirteen when they should have finished it at nine, manifest the desire to work in the quarries. They say they do not feel that they are 'children' anymore, for they 'have a man's body'; girls in a similar situation are accused of only 'wanting to court'. Boys who demonstrate a greater intellectual capability for studying and who will probably continue their formal education, embody modes of behaviour that set them apart from virile masculinity: they do not play violent games, they do not run away from school, they have an elaborate discourse on how dangerous the quarries are.

'School failure' has, in the last decade, been a hot political issue in Portugal, due to the high rates of failing at all levels of the educational system. Anthropologist Raul Iturra comments:

> While the ideas conveyed by school are abstractions of reality, the practice of peasant work materialises ideas by means of hands, feet, the entire body that is used in all its strength to mould nature. Although there is the mediation of the working instrument, this is

also shaped by the way the body learns how to move. The practice of peasant work is a systematic application of physiology as developed through work (…) There is a distinction between listening in scholarly life and watching-and-doing in working life; to it corresponds another distinction: that between thinking and memorising, or between abstraction for understanding and abstraction for reiteration. (Iturra 1990: 96–7)

In Pardais and at the school a difficulty is perceived in passing from the logic of action and experience to that of scholarly abstraction. When it comes to notions of the Person, it is hard for the children to foresee satisfaction and prestige in a profession that requires studying. Particularly so when, as in the case of boys, the central element for the constitution of their sense of personhood is masculinity. And masculinity is seen everyday, at home, in the street, as being the same as their fathers do and are. In the drawings I have referred to, even the 'working instrument' Iturra mentions is easily replaced by the caterpillar machine.

Only among girls does the profession of teacher appear, even though children of both sexes are equally exposed to the teachers. However, the teachers are women, and their profession is seen by girls as the best possible destiny. In fact, girls are the ones who carry on studying until much later; and the teachers also fulfil a maternal role that girls can identify with. In a previous work (Vale de Almeida 1991) I analysed the third grade school reader that was used for many years during the dictatorial regime that was in power until 1974. I analysed it as a text and iconography that strengthened in children's minds a connection between Nationalism, Family, and Sexual Division. At the time my intention was not to denounce some 'conspiracy', but rather to show how many of the ideological elements conveyed in that book were actually no more than the ideological tenets of peasant life as systematised in religious theory and in the dictatorial law. There was a reciprocal construction of the categories, both *ancien régime* statements. School readers have changed since then, as has the political system. They now promote notions of the person based on the concept of citizenship, and individual capacities, rather than hierarchy, subjection and meritocracy.

Nevertheless, when analysing texts that had been written by the children and the teachers for the school newspaper, I realised that they too, contained 'deep' elements – with a strong emotional base – on the family and genders that are structurally the same. Let us see first, what had changed. In a text on Woman's Day, including an interview with a local woman who works in a nearby factory (and who is classified as 'active woman'), the following is said:

> WOMAN'S DAY We intend to call everyone's attention to the role and dignity of women, and lead to consciousness raising on the value of the person; to understand her role in society, to challenge and review prejudices and limitations that have been imposed on women.

If compared with quotes from children's statements in two articles – one on 'mothers', the other on 'fathers' – we can see how, once opinions come straight from children, the father comes out as a figure identified with work, the mother with affects:

> FATHER'S DAY: 'My father is fat, a good worker and I like him a lot' (J. M., boy); 'Father goes to work everyday and he is my little buddy' (L., girl); 'My father works at the café and is very nice to me' (E., girl); 'I like my father a lot. He goes to work everyday' (E., boy); 'My father works in the quarry and is very good to me'. (H., boy)
>
> MOTHER'S DAY. 'Mother, you are so pretty!' (A.C., girl, and A., boy); 'I love you, mummy!' (N., girl, B., C., and H., boys). 'On mother's day I made a gift for her' (P., boy); 'Mother, I like you so much and I what to kiss you a lot' (M.J. and L., girls); 'Mother is happy' (M., boy). 'Mother, you are my very good friend' (A., girl); 'Mother, I like you a lot, dear friend' (S., boy). 'Mother is pretty, and hurrah!' (V., boy)

Nuno Porto, also in an analysis of the dictatorial school reader (Porto 1991) writes about the construction of gender as a structuring principle of a discourse on society. A person's conduct is then defined as an outcome of the family nucleus, structuring values and practices according to gender: children feel recognition and respect for the father, who in exchange gives them knowledge, work and sacrifice. Mother receives the due love, and in exchange she gives love to others.

In the drawings regarding the parents' professions, the dichotomy quarry work / domestic work is graphically expressed by means of the representation of open space in the case of the father's profession. On the other hand, father figures are rather small in scale and are closely connected with heavy machinery, whereas mother figures are more prominent. In the drawings on what children expect to be as grown-ups, many boys have elaborately drawn the caterpillars: powerful machines driven by the boy-as-a-man. In one of the drawings the activity of hunting is even depicted as a possible profession and in some others the world of bullfighting exerts its fascination. In one of them a thirteen-year-old boy demonstrates a sophisticated knowledge of all the horse's apparel, the animal anatomy, bodily posture of the horse rider, and the sexual organs of horse and bull. Another boy depicts a soccer match, shown in a vertical perspective, including the whole field and all the players, showing an understanding of team work and rules of the game as represented in the correct boundaries of the field.

There are still two exceptions. In one of them, the son of a shopkeeper draws a hospital scene: technical competence and the authority of the medical profession are well represented, including the extra character of a female nurse depicted in smaller scale. Gabriel, whom I have mentioned in Chapter Two, shows how he wants to be a 'scientist', in what is a clear statement in favour of 'mental work'. Finally, practically all the drawings made by girls represent female teachers.

In 1985 I conducted a short research based on children's drawings (Vale de Almeida 1985). The context was the small town of Binghamton, N.Y., in the United States. An important section of IBM's offices were situated there. In a local school, I asked a group of children to draw answers to these same questions that I asked in Pardais. I realised that the logo IBM, or the drawing of a computer occurred in most cases. Sometimes the computer depiction itself worked as an icon of the general idea of 'work'. It was of course due to the environment and the fact that most children's parents worked at IBM. In this sense, what happens in Pardais may also be related to this process of 'imitation'. However, at the level of gender, none of the American boys mentioned marriage and procreation, whereas all the girls did, as a complement to their professional choice.

The learning process is at all levels – and not only at that of gender – a process that involves much mimesis, un-reflected practice and training, an accumulation of repeated gestures and automatic forms of thought. Much of social reproduction happens in this unconscious manner. A short description of a Greek context is elucidating:

> It is therefore not surprising that two of the personality traits that the young Pourianos boy quickly develops are defiance and aggressiveness (...) he knows that he must obey a parental command given in a harsh tone of voice without arguing (...) he learns also very quickly the costs of being insolent with his father. Lastly, he becomes quickly aware of the value that all Pourianis bestow on work. (Handman 1983: 136–7, my translation)

The process of learning and the process of socialisation have, then, three contexts: school, family, and the group of children. In modernity we should of course add the virtual world of the media, particularly television. Regarding gender, it is in the family that the practices of imitation train the body to be culturally masculine; as they train thoughts and words to think and say certain things, and not others, on what men and women are. In the group of children, that knowledge is tested socially, evaluated by others, and detours are censored. At school, children receive a written doctrine on aspects of history and life in society that are always marked with the symbolic stamp of gender.

There is however, a moment when these children start moving away from their original families. It happens after they have finished the State's compulsory education and the Church's Sunday School that trains them on the ethical principles of family relations and work as divinely legitimised. The passage to the status of adult men is a decisive step and process for masculinity's success.

We are used to understanding those moments of passage in the life cycle as being ritualised. We even see them as examples for the understanding of 'Ritual' as a rubric in anthropology. So there has been little attention paid to non-ritualised passages to adulthood and manhood. One exception is Murphy's (1983) work on the passage to adult manhood in Seville. There the transition is seen by the actors themselves as a socially conflicting process, characterised by manipulation, confrontation, and negotiation in a power relation between father and son.

As in Murphy's context, there is no rite of passage in Pardais in which the status of child gives way to the status of adult man. In the past something close to a ritual form happened during the *sortes*, after boys had gone for military inspection to see if they were fit for the army. Today it still occurs as a renovated folklore practice and a pretext for a *baile*, especially considering the shortening of military service and its increasingly voluntary nature. Only through marriage and the establishment of a separate household is the son free from the father's supervision. Murphy sets several phases in the relationship between father and son: first, from birth up until six or seven years old, when the youngest child is the focus of emotional attention in the house, the father playing the role of defender of the youngest; secondly: the distance between father and son increases when the latter enters neighbourhood play groups.

It is during adolescence that the boy feels the strongest pressure from the group of friends for distancing himself from home, from motherly care, and from fatherly authority: 'In order for the teenager to lay the groundwork for a plausible claim to manhood, he must begin to act like a man. This requires at least two resources his father controls: freedom

to participate in the life of the street and money to support that participation' (1983:383). Finally, and this is the third phase, son and father
relate in a 'man to man' fashion.

Murphy's context is an urban neighbourhood. One of the main differences is the harsher, more direct control by the father of his son's
activities. In Pardais it does not happen so. In urban contexts age has
become an important factor for the affirmation of exaggerated masculinity. However, in the village, class distinctions lead to a heavier affirmation o exaggerated masculinity among the lower classes. Even so, both
levels of identity (age and class) act together in a period of the life cycle
when exaggerated demonstrations of autonomy, excess, adventure and
masculinity occur. In Pardais they are characterised mainly by the masculine sociabilities outlined in Chapters 2 and 4.

Murphy does not deal with the relationship of avoidance between
father and son in public situations. I believe this avoidance – quite obvious in Pardais – happens because what goes on in public masculine
milieus is not kinship, but rather homosocial masculinity. It is competitive, on the one hand, and reinforces solidarity on the basis of friendship
and/or commensality. It is though, incompatible with 'home'. Thus the
so-called separation from the mother and the world of feminine emotionality is not replaced by an alliance and friendship with a masculine
father, but rather with men at large. It does seem like a world and an
existence devoid of feelings. It is still a mystery how men who follow the
hegemonic model can cope with this.

Also still mysterious are the processes that have recently been dealt
with by the anthropological and sociological approaches to the body
and embodiment. What learning does the body undergo, what gestures
and attitudes are learned in an un-reflected way, but that still (or
because of this) inform others and the self of his belonging to a gender
construct and his consonance with hegemony? It is a crucial question
for further research.

One day I overheard a boy who as mad at another boy yell: 'You're
not a man, you're not a boy, you're nothing!' I would like to think that
this essay might one day help him understand that things do not necessarily have to be so.

NOTES

1. I have opted for the most literal translation possible, since it seemed impossible to translate in a similarly poetic way. This results, of course, in some awkwardness and in absence of rhyme.
2. See Giddens (1979) on this. Language, according to Wittgenstein's semantic theory, is inseparable from the constitution of forms of social life as continuous, ongoing, practices. For Giddens, structure is both the means and the outcome of the reproduction of practices.
3. Free translation: 'The body hexis is the actualisation of the political mythology, thus embodied, turned into a permanent disposition, a durable way of behaving, of using the body'.
4. See, on this, Seidler (1987). As for the use of 'emotion' and 'sentiment', Portuguese dictionaries define *emoção* (emotion) as 'psycho-organic state of a brief and intense affective tonality, characterised by a sudden rupture of mental and physiological functions', and *sentimento* (sentiment) as an 'affective state that is preceded by a mental representation (…).'
5. In modern urban societies too, lesbianism has remained taboo longer than male homosexuality. I believe this is due to the gender hierarchy and the refusal to admit that women may not feel sexual desire for men. For instance, the emphasis on lesbian sex in pornography for heterosexual males is an appeal for the spectator to 'fill in' the absence of a phallus.
6. The public/domestic dichotomy has been often used in approaches of the inferior status of women. Rosaldo (1974) focused on the distinction between the institutional and activity foci of men and women, in which the feminine identification with domestic activities would derive from their primary role as reproducers. Later the author tried to overcome these dichotomies, and tried rather to understand relationships between men and women as aspects of a wider social context (Rosaldo 1980).
7. The elementary school was attended by forty-three children: sixteen boys in the first phase (first and second grades), four of whom were repeating grades; twelve girls in the first phase, one of whom is repeating; and eight boys and seven girls in the second phase (third and fourth grades). As for the parents: twenty-seven fathers worked in the quarries and one in another profession; twenty-eight mothers were housewives and five worked in other professions.

6. Excursio
For an Anthropological Approach of Masculinity

Sex, Gender and Feminism

When I left for fieldwork I took along with me a question for which I was seeking an answer. It had to do both with anthropological knowledge and with my own identity: what does it mean to 'be a man' from a social point of view? The question is as complex as it is apparently naive. For the large majority of people, and on that level which in the social sciences is known as common sense, to be a man fundamentally means two things: not to be a woman, and to have a body that shows male genitals. Complexity lies after all in the naive attitude of remitting to the body's physical traits a question of personal and social identity. Being a man, in everyday life, in social interaction, in ideological constructs, is never reducible to sexual characteristics, but rather expandable to a whole set of attributes of moral behaviour; these are socially sanctioned and constantly re-evaluated, negotiated, and remembered. In sum, they are in a constant process of construction.

The distinction between sex and gender is still the fundamental starting point for research on masculinity. It was based on the distinction between biology and culture that anthropology has promoted for quite some time. It was elaborated from the 1960s onwards by feminist critical theory. The conceptual separation between sex and gender meant to show that the latter is the cultural elaboration of the former. (This is not without its own problems, as I shall explain later). Cultural variation in male and female social roles, as well as the personality types taken to be normal for each sex in each culture – as presented by Margaret Mead in *Sex and Temperament* – was cultural determinism's entry into the field of sexuality and gender. In 1981, with the feminist movement in full maturation in anthropology, Ortner and Whitehead open the *Sexual Meanings* collection stating that:

> (…) natural features of gender, and natural processes of sex and reproduction, furnish only a suggestive and ambiguous backdrop to the cultural organisation of gender and sexuality. What gender is, what men and women are, what sorts of relations do or should obtain between them – all of these notions do not simply reflect or elaborate upon biological 'givens', but are largely products of social and cultural processes. (1981:1)

In this sense, the search for an answer to the initial question means the need to analyse the cultural requisites that, in Pardais, are necessary for an individual of the male sex to be considered a man. These requisites are not strictly corporeal, although interpretations of the body are strongly mobilised for the discourse on gender. The requisites can be found at all levels of social life, from family to work, from prestige and status to social class and age, and include verbal and body language. The list would be as vast as the totality of the social. That is why I have not chosen a privileged locus for the construction of masculinity (even though my data focuses on everyday sociability), a characteristic of this study that makes it difficult to fit on one of the classical thematic shelves in the discipline. Marilyn Strathern, while making explicit her notion of gender, helps me make this point clearer:

> By gender I mean those categorisations of persons, artefacts, events, sequences, and so on which draw upon sexual imagery – upon the ways in which distinctiveness of male and female characteristics make concrete people's ideas about the nature of social relationships. (Strathern 1988: ix)

As for the specificity of studying masculinity, David Gilmore (1990), for instance, states that the explosion of feminist works on sex and gender in the last decade has left practically untouched the cults and codes of masculinity. I think, on the contrary, that it is precisely in some of the feminist literature that one can find the theoretical basis for the interpretation of masculinity. However, the androcentrism that feminists have pinpointed on anthropology has not only silenced feminine voices; it has also silenced the diversity of masculine voices, particularly those that defect from the homology between masculine, public orientation and political power – in short, hegemonic masculinity. By making the masculine an implicit equivalent of the social, anthropology has taken away autonomy and possibilities for critical deconstruction. This process is analogous to the non-questionability of heterosexuality in everyday life, even on the part of those liberal spirits that try to bring into the light the 'question' of homosexuality.

Being a man in Pardais is not the same as being a man among the urban intellectuals in whose milieu I live. It is not the same as being a man for those who follow the social norm of heterosexuality, and for those who have bisexual or homosexual identities. The same could be said of other comparisons, if one replaces sexual orientation with social-class affiliation, ethnic identities or religious beliefs or for that matter any other level of social identity that may cut across gender or be cut across by it.

This is probably why it is hard to study masculinity with one exclusive paradigm, although one should acknowledge that such is the difficulty of social-science research in the present period of paradigm transition. In some sense, all perspectives can contribute somehow. The question is that gender is an area of study (and an arena of social life) which introduces a significant epistemological novelty. Contrary to class and social institutions such as the family, gender cuts across them in a transverse way. It is not only a cut in vertical metaphors of structure, hierarchy or 'levels'; it is a recent theme and a difficult one to introduce in the social sciences, because it is difficult to introduce in social and political life itself. This becomes evident when one realises that with regard to race hardly anyone today thinks that skin colour is really the ultimate cause of racial inequality; however, when it comes to gender, it is culturally difficult not to be tempted to see in sex and in the body the root of gender.[1] That is why gender is the 'last frontier' in social scientific critical reflexivity. It constitutes personal and social identities although it does not create in and of itself social groups, but rather categories.

Without the surge of women's studies and feminist theory in anthropology (and, one should add, gay critical theory), it would never have been possible to even pose masculinity as an issue of research. In the last fifteen to twenty years a series of books and articles focusing on women as social actors have appeared. The main starting point was the notion that anthropology was largely androcentric. This position is of course a strongly political one, since androcentrism in anthropology is probably no more than a reflex of androcentrism in all structures, including knowledge structures, in the society that produces it.

Feminism germinated mostly in developed countries, particularly in the Anglo-American world – both social and academic – thus being a phenomenon of late modernity. That is at least the way it has been received in most peripheral and semi-peripheral academic milieus. However, feminism's theoretical and anthropological scope cannot be underestimated for those reasons: Marx, Weber and Durkheim were also products and agents of the developmental peaks in their time and place, and yet are useful and irreplaceable for the understanding of any society.

The collection edited in 1975 by Raina Reiter, *Towards an Anthropology of Women*, was in some way the founding work of feminism as a critical theory in anthropology. It included many articles close to the biological and physical sub-areas of anthropology since it was necessary to refute evolutionary theories that stated that sexual roles were directly related to anatomy and had been established definitely thousands of years ago.

However, the collection included one seminal (or 'ovarian', as some would say) article, whose importance for feminism (and for masculinity studies) in anthropology cannot be forgotten. It was Gayle Rubin's 'The Traffic in Women: Notes on The "Political Economy" of Sex'. Rubin set out to understand the system of relations of women's oppression by means of juxtaposing Freudian and Lévi-Straussian theories, in a similar move to that of Marx in relation to classical political economy. She tried to localise women's oppression within the capitalist dynamics, by means of analysing the relation between domestic labour and the reproduction of labour. This is a point of agreement with Marx; but she states that it is one thing to explain women's usefulness for capitalism and quite another to say that such usefulness explains the genesis of women's oppression (1975:163). In other words, there is a historical and moral element – as Marx himself had said – in the determination of the value of labour that is different from other commodities (1972:171 in Rubin 1975:164). For Rubin it was therefore necessary to deal with this historical and moral element which makes of a woman a spouse as one of the worker's needs. Resorting to Engels' distinction between relations of production and relations of sexuality (Engels 1976 [1884]:71–72 in Rubin 1975:164), she explains what she calls the 'sex/gender system' (acknowledging that other possible names could be 'mode of reproduction' or 'patriarchy'):

> A sex/gender system is not simply the reproductive moment of a 'mode of production'. The formation of gender identity is an example of production in the realm of the sexual system. And a sex/gender system involves more than the 'relations of procreation', reproduction in the biological sense. (Rubin 1975:167)

Thus Rubin looks for the locus of reproduction of the sex/gender system in the area of kinship, saying that kinship systems can be many things, but are always made of and reproduce concrete forms of organised sexuality (1975:169): 'kinship systems are observable and empirical forms of sex/gender systems' (1975:169). From there, she analyses the issue of exchange of women, acknowledging that it is not the same as commodification – since objects have a *hau* in primitive systems – but still implying a distinction between who gives and who takes, thus making men the beneficiaries of the product of exchange, social organisation (1975:174).

According to her there is an 'economy' of sex and gender. The sexual division of labour would be a taboo against the similarity between men and women. This taboo, by means of underlining biological differences between the sexes, created gender. It is also a taboo against anything that is not the pairing of man and woman: 'At the most general level, the social organisation of sex rests upon gender, obligatory heterosexuality, and the constraint of female sexuality' (1975:179). Individuals, then, are engendered in order to guarantee marriage. Heterosexuality can be seen as an instituted process, and the incest taboo thus presupposes a previous taboo against homosexuality. However, Rubin is not wholly satisfied with anthropology, since the discipline does not explain how children are marked with the conventions of sex and gender, at least in current descriptions of kinship systems. That is why she calls for the help of psychoanalysis, which she regards as a theory on the reproduction of kinship. She then describes the Freudian theory of pre-Oedipal bisexuality and calls upon Lacan as a way of rescuing Freud from biology and to promote his theory as a theory of language and cultural meanings: thus in the Trobriand Islands, for instance, a man...

> ...calls the women of clans into which he can marry by a term indicating their marriageability. When the young Trobriand male learns these terms he learns which women he can safely desire. (1975:189)

In Rubin's interpretation of Lacan's work, the Oedipal crisis occurs when the child learns the sexual rules imbedded in kinship and family terminology. His/her libido and gender identity are then organised according to cultural rules. Drawing from E. P. Thompson's (1963) work regarding the transformations in the structure of personality of the English working class during the Industrial Revolution, Rubin draws the parallel by saying that just as social forms of work require certain types of personality, so too social forms of sex and gender require certain types of people

145

(1975:189). This juxtaposition of Freud and Lévi-Strauss via Lacan is harmoniously outlined in process terms by Rubin:

> Kinship terms require a division of the sexes. The Oedipal phase divides the sexes. Kinship systems include sets of rules governing sexuality. The Oedipal crisis is the assimilation of these rules and taboos. Compulsory heterosexuality is the product of kinship. The Oedipal phase constitutes heterosexual desire. Kinship rests on a radical difference between the rights of men and women. The Oedipal complex confers male rights upon the boy, and forces the girl to accommodate herself to her lesser rights. (1975:198)

Rubin proceeds by saying that the next step to be taken would be a Marxist analysis of sex/gender systems, since these are products of human activity in history. She calls for the need to write a new version of *Origins of the Family*, one that would acknowledge the mutual dependence of sexuality, economics and politics. This feminist project that seeks its foundations and tools in psychoanalysis, in structuralism and in Marxism, symbolises nicely the state of the art in the 1970s and the thrust of epistemological innovation that was brought forth in anthropology by feminism.

Only five years prior to Rubin's article, the Portuguese ethnologist Jorge Dias published a paper called 'An Ethnologist Looks at Intersex'. Throughout this short article, he refers to classical cases of ritual transvestism, *berdaches*, and so on, and stays close to Mead's theory in *Sex and Temperament*. The last paragraph states:

> In the markedly patriarchal western society, activities and behaviours adequate to men and women were clearly defined. Today, however, we see women wearing trousers, driving taxis, smoking, drinking whisky, cutting their hair short, and we see men with long hairdos and – particularly in America – we see them doing house chores, sometimes even wearing plastic aprons, and still this does not mean that they are transvestites. French fashion will promote this year the 'unisex' fashion, fit for either men or women.... (1970:11–12, my translation)

I could have chosen a passage expressing a more violent reaction from some other author. It is, however, precisely the non-reactionary character of this passage that is curious: despite the ethnologist's relativism and effort of understanding, the passage reveals, through his awe, the archaic situation of Portuguese society of the time, if one is to compare it with societies where a discourse like Rubin's could be produced. The author's awe in face of the exotic curiosities he mentions clearly identifies the fields of work and uses of the body as terrains of sexual control, and is in and of itself a sign of the cultural difficulty in accepting changes in gender relations. Changes that, in the 1970s, were happening not only in anthropological theory but also in modern societies at large.

In the aftermath of the 'cultural revolution' of the 1960s and the changes in post-war global economic and social relations (as well as in the level of 'transformations of intimacy' and reproduction, as Giddens [1992b] suggests), feminism comes out as a full blown social movement. The post-war period also sees the end of colonialism and the emancipation of many Developing World nations and states. Anthropology finds itself in a deep crisis in terms of two of its foundations: the exotic Other, before whom anthropology sees itself as an accomplice in an uneven power relation; and family and kinship, whose structures had now to be rethought in the light of non-essentialistic sexual identities.

Feminist critical theory enters anthropology via the criticism of women's absence in the ethnography. The issue, however, is extended to the subject of 'power': informers are men because men are closer to power and representation. The 1960s had questioned power by means of challenging the established notions of individual and society – thanks to the importance of psychoanalysis and Marxism, which had been rediscovered as both interpretations of the world and analytical instruments, more than therapeutic and social change projects. Both areas of thought concurred with the idea that there is no determining biological nature as such and that both societies and individuals exist in a history of inequality and contradiction. Inequality in power can reach, in the last instance, the individual bodies and persons, their use of pleasure and their reproductive capacities. Feminism then invents the slogan 'the private is political'.

Most feminist studies in anthropology shared, nevertheless, a taken for granted notion of natural heterosexuality – and Rubin is an outstanding exception. If patriarchy was attacked and scrutinised, if the mechanics of reproduction and its origins were sought, particularly with the explication of women's oppression, the specific analysis of masculinity was also left untouched. That is, if one accepts the notion, as I do, that masculinity and patriarchy are not synonyms.

Ortner and Whitehead's 1981 collection was probably the most influential book in the second wave of feminism, already more integrated in anthropological practice under the heading 'gender studies' as opposed to previous 'women's studies'. For the editors of *Sexual Meanings*, gender, sexuality and repression should be treated as symbols, invested with meaning by the society under analysis. Their project was the analysis and interpretation of those, relating them with other cultural symbols and meanings, on the one hand, and, on the other, with specific forms of social life. The essays in the book were largely focused on cultural aspects, but do not exclude social, political and economic contexts for the symbolic constructions at stake, even though the editors do state that both traditional Marxism and Durkheimianism have an inadequate concept of culture. Ortner and Whitehead's approach is centred on social actors and their mediation, a perspective that draws much inspiration from the whole interpretative genealogy from Weber to Geertz.

In most of the ethnographic cases in the book metaphorical binary oppositions can be identified. These include oppositions such as nature versus culture, or self-interest versus social good. In practically all cases one can verify that 1) men are defined by status categories or social roles, whereas 2) women are defined in relation to men and kinsmen; 3) the same lines that divide women from men, cut across gender categories internally, and 4) in all cases there is a conceptual separation between a 'world of men' and a 'world of heterosexual relations'.

Kinship and marriage are seen throughout as privileged means for the production and reproduction of gender ideologies. However, in all societies it is the sphere of prestige that mediates between the organisation of kinship and marriage, on the one hand, and the ideology of gender on the other. That is why Ortner and Whitehead infer that what is universal in gender ideologies is so because it is also universal in prestige systems. The authors also mention Rubin's 1975 paper. Prestige is structured by kinship and marriage, the distribution of the means of violence, the relations of production. Prestige structures are like a screen between the various material, family and political structures which impinge upon cultural conceptions of gender and masculinity. Prestige structures (of the 'social honour' or 'social worth' type) have not been fully analysed, even though social actors are well aware of them. As an example, Brandes' study of gender folklore included in the collection does not unveil some hidden erotic world but rather people that have some anxiety about status.

Marilyn Strathern's paper in the collection states that the anthropology of male-female relationships has always separated two aspects: first, stereotypes or symbolic representations of the sexes; secondly, how women adapt to their position, and how they manipulate or acquire informal power. Strathern warns the reader of the danger of placing women as central actors in the systems, if proper attention is not paid to the local concepts of the Person. In her New Guinea case, she says that antagonism between men and women is of metaphorical value. Through the imagery of sexually based differences a vast array of values are ordered; what is at stake as a central element is the dichotomy between 'self-interest' and 'group action', the types of behaviour being themselves sexed. Thus, gender is not only about men and women. That is why women have to dissociate themselves from the 'handicap' of being females, just as men have to prove that they can use there male potential. A person of either sex can behave in either a feminine or a masculine way.

Is the 'Weberian' project in Ortner and Whitehead's collection incompatible with a basically, although not vulgar or orthodox, Marxist one? Godelier's (1982) New Guinea case study would be a good negative answer. For Godelier, when the Baruya say that men play the main role in the fabrication of a child this means a reality that exists in thought, although being as real socially as the other elements of male domination (such as the control over the means of production, of violence and so on). It is specific because it is made of a series of gestures, rites and symbolic practices. The latter are devices for conveying the ideas of the world of thought to the world of the body, nature and, simultaneously, ways for transforming them into social relations. Although I would be hesitant in subscribing this apparent separation from thought and body (as I shall explain later), Godelier says that it is the belief in the concrete efficacy of symbolic practices that triggers the fact that for the Baruya to show symbolically means to demonstrate, since it is a form of acting and producing results that are verifiable in the multiple visible signs of men's superiority over women in everyday life (Godelier 1982). For Godelier it is necessary to analyse the ideas that a society creates about the body and the discourses it sustains about male and female bodies, and also – with the help of their bodies – a discourse on sexuality and a discourse of sexuality. That is how the body language creates a living consensus and accomplishes one of thought's functions – not only to explain but also to persuade.

> In any given culture it is the differences that sexuality introduces into each sex ... that becomes the terms, the lexicon, of the discourse that sexuality is constantly asked to have about society and the cosmos (...) Everything would be simple if thought did nothing but reflect, represent society; but all the difficulties of scientific analysis of the ideal part of the real arise from the fact that thought does not simply represent society, but is also in and of itself a producer of society. (Godelier 1982:352, my translation from the French)

149

In 1975 Rubin had written that sex and gender were intertwined; ten years later, however, she was discarding this notion: 'I am now arguing that it is essential to separate gender and sexuality analytically to more accurately reflect their separate social existence' (1984:308). Ortner and Whitehead agreed: '...to be reminded of the power of social considerations to override libidinal ones, both in fantasy and in practice' (1981:24). Caplan (1987) wonders whether we can face the possibility of a discipline of sexuality that would combine feminism, anthropology and history. Ross and Rapp (1984) had previously distinguished three areas in the field: that of kinship and family as represented by Goody, Macfarlane, Flandrin and Stone, among others, and which they consider to be 'gender blind'; community studies, especially those on peer groups; and analysis of 'world-systems': religion or law, with the outstanding contribution of Foucault. Ever since 1975, according to Vance (1991), social constructionism has triggered a series of research initiatives on the issue of sexuality. Presently, the AIDS epidemic has led to further research on the socio-cultural processes of sexuality and gender.

The issue of the relation between sexuality and gender leads us directly to issues of identity. For instance, gay men in the West or the *xanith* (transsexuals) of Oman (Wikan 1977) collide un-harmoniously in the three aspects of sex, gender and sexuality.[2] In this sense, the Mediterranean, Asia and the Middle East are like an interstitial area between two other areas (Africa, and the West) with regard to sexual attitudes. Fertility is valued but only with partners of the right status. Rank is more important than biological sex or gender identity. For Lancaster (1988), *machismo* is, in Wittgensteinian terms, a 'different game', ruled by different norms; or, in Marxist terms, it represents a different sexual economy; or, still, in Foucaultian terms, Latin sexuality represents a different discursive practice from that of the Anglo-Saxon world. He thus makes a distinction between bourgeois or Anglo-American sexuality, on the one hand, and peasant, or circum-Mediterranean, or Latin-American sexuality, on the other.

In my opinion a turning point was Yanagisako's 1988 work. According to her, the separation of biological facts of sex from cultural facts of gender opened the way for the type of project outlined by Ortner and Whitehead: the interpretation of gender as a system of symbols and meanings that influence and are influenced by cultural practices and experiences. Everywhere gender is seen as an elaboration of a biological difference, leading to dichotomies such as that between the public and the domestic (Rosaldo 1974), nature and culture (Ortner 1974), production and reproduction (Harris and Young 1981). For these authors, heterosexual intercourse creates kinship and gender together with children. Yanagisako, however, says that when we analyse race we do not believe that physical difference is really relevant. This suggests three issues in her thought: 1) how are people constituted as gendered subjects in specific cultural systems?; 2) how are gender categories defined? (since they do not result everywhere from the same differences); 3) when and if sex is the basis of gender, one should ask how this self-referential system is constructed (Yanagisako 1988:4).

Yanagisako suggests that we have to explain, rather than to presume, the practices through which a system of differences between people is made to appear invariable. She says that now that we have questioned our past model of the natural basis of sex and have started to explore cultural practices through which people are sexually constituted as sexual subjects, we have to keep in mind the gendered character of these practices. Yanagisako concludes by saying that we cannot leave sex aside in our analysis of gender since it is the discursive space from which we initiate comparative studies of gender. One should not forget, however, that while sex is seen in the United States as the central nucleus of gender – it does not have to be like that in other contexts or forever.

For Strathern, society is not constructed independently of gender, and that is why society can not be an explanatory context for gender. Relations of gender are neither more nor less autonomous than all other social relations. She thus proposes to put an end to two myths: first, the myth that feminism invented anthropological interest for women and gender. Secondly, the idea that feminist interest supports anthropological tradition. Academic feminism, she says, has a post-modern structure; anthropological dichotomous perspectives, of the we/them type, are simply modern. What is specific to anthropological feminism is the fact that it pays attention to the specifics of social and historical circumstances under the rubric of the sex-gender system (Rubin 1975) or social relations of gender (Young et al. 1981). In pre-feminism, and for the purpose I recall Herdt's 1981 New Guinea example, the assumption is that the creation of masculinity is first and foremost conceptualised by actors as a matter of acquisition of a sexual role. The question is: neither from an anthropological point of view nor from a feminist one should we be satisfied with the notion that men's cults are cults 'for making men'.

Individual sexual identity is a Western cultural issue. The concern with hetero- or homosexual performance – and, I would add, the need to 'choose' either – make erotic behaviour an important source of self-definition. It is we who make a role out of sex, since we can not take for granted that Melanesians, even though they use greatly the gender imagery, are really concerned with individual identity. Some authors consider sexing as a previous state, and some localise it in discourse, and yet others pay attention to the ideological origin of the categories that are used for thinking the sexed self. But before one can reach a unitary theory of gender identity, one needs a unitary theory of identity. Thus, those who are concerned with the social and cultural construction of gender do not feel the need to decide on the previous or derived sexing of the body. Their concern is rather with the relation between the male and female categories. Strathern suggests that making clear the metaphorical basis of systems of classification should be their task (Strathern 1988:69).

The sexual-role strategy in the 1970s failed, according to Strathern, because male and female stood unchallenged as fixed reference points. In the West, domesticity is in fact associated with childishness and childishness with lack of autonomy, because it is outside the sphere of wage, work place, and cultural production. But it can be otherwise elsewhere. The ideas of 'the person' become central in Strathern's thought; she says that sex demarcates different types of agency. That is why she now criticises the notion of 'social construction', since the 'construction' terminology reminds her of the close conceptual relation in Western thought between consciousness and reason, with reason demonstrating itself in system and systematic (Strathern 1988; see also Seidler 1987). In Melanesia, the collective life of men should not be understood as an underlined sociability that is the source of hegemonic values that are at the same time masculine and social. One should not take for granted certain collective activities of men, nor describe the Melanesian forms of collective life using the Western model of 'society'. Collective actions should be seen as a type of 'sociality', coexisting with another – domestic relations – , the relation between them being alternative, not hierarchical. Strathern says that rites do not 'make men' nor 'make society'. Westerners believe too strongly that there is such a thing as a person, a culture, that culture serves to communicate with others, that it is the common property and that it has an author: men. Although her example is from Melanesia, its inversion confirms many of the statements already made about gender in the West.

This point of view could be complemented with LaFontaine (1981, who says that the procreative powers of women are not a universal external factor, shaping society, but rather one formulation among a series of cultural constructs that interpret that reality (biology being one of them). A lot has been said about how society constrains women to desire motherhood, but the relations between the definitions of men and their paternal roles have been widely ignored. LaFontaine says that the common association between women, bearing children and the domestic group has to be re-examined, since it is an incorrect conclusion drawn from two characteristics; women's exclusion from meetings where ritual and political issues are discussed, and the common symbolic association of women with the domestic group and men with society. The latter, I believe, also needs to be re-evaluated.

Discourse and Practice

The itinerary among recent authors on gender and sexuality has pointed me toward a theory of practice, and such parallel areas as embodiment and experience. It exerts a particular seduction in my case analysis, since it helps to solve some of the contradictions that are blatant in the mutual comparison of the contributions that I have reviewed. Collier and Yanagisako (1987) list some aspects of concern for a theory of practice: first, practice approaches focus on real people doing real things; second, this combines with a notion that the 'system' exerts a powerful effect on human action; third, this system is seen as a system of inequality, constraint and domination; fourth, it pays attention to the cultural construction of concepts of femininity and masculinity, this being why a system of domination should be understood as a cultural system (and for this they quote Ortner and Whitehead 1981). Furthermore, and this is point number five, theory of practice – like feminism – questions the partition of the system into base and superstructure (an aspect we have seen already with Godelier), society and culture, domestic and political, production and reproduction, as determinant and determined. Lastly, there is a political concern with seeing how practice reproduces the system, and how the system can be changed by practice (Ortner 1984:154).

As a matter of fact, at the present time, three tendencies seem to be penetrating gender studies with some advantage: the theory of practice, derived from criticism of orthodox Marxism; models of the relation between structure and practice developed mainly by Bourdieu (1972, 1980) and Giddens (1979); and the contextual analysis of self, personal action and inter-subjectivity. These approaches strike a balance, according to R. Connell (1987), between extrinsic and intrinsic narratives of the determinant aspects of social inequality: within the intrinsic ones, between those who focus on custom and those who focus on power; within approaches of power, between those that see the categories as previous to practice and those that see them as emerging from practice. However it may be, the trend is towards an account of the intertwining between personal life and social structure. For Connell, the outline of a solution may be in Bourdieu's and Giddens' work, in their proposal of interconnection between structure and practice, focusing on what people do via the constitution of the social relations they live in. A theory of practice points towards the historicity of gender at the level of personal life. The notion that forms of sexuality are socially constructed emerged from the work of radical historians and from the analysis of discourse and interactionist sociology. This opens up to the central fact of gender – the way its structures are lived, with multiple femininities and masculinities. The historicity of gender relations has not been understood because of the assumption that there is a trans-historical structure in gender: the sexual dichotomy of the bodies. This is a taken for granted notion that has poisoned theories of sexual roles, disregarding the need for a social theory. For Bourdieu, however, the idea of an active presence of structure in practice and of the active constitution of structure by practice was theoretically formalised, and it stands on the notion of social reproduction – the only point where it runs the risk of jeopardising the idea of an historical dynamic.[3]

As for Giddens' theory of structuration, in it human practice presupposes a social structure, in the sense that practice calls necessarily for social rules and resources. The balance that Giddens formulated as the 'duality of structure' is, in Connell's opinion, one of the theories that comes closer to the demands of a theory of gender. Connell outlines a theoretical programme for the study of gender within the parameters of a theory of practice. The division of labour, the structure of power and the structure of *cathexis* (emotions and sentiments) would be the main elements of any 'gender order' or 'gender regime'. Structural models and structural inventories would then be complementary modes of looking at the same kinds of facts (Connell 1987).

Now, Rubin's 1975 paper was extremely promising in this sense – and Connell recognises it too. But it lacked that intertwining of personal life and social structure. This has obviously been accomplished by literature, not by social science, if one is to discard the recent exceptions coming from reflexive anthropology. If a theory of practice for the field of gender were to be elaborated, the implications would be: that structure is not given, but rather historically created; that there is a possibility of structuring gender in different ways, reflecting the dominance of different social concerns; that structuration would be differently consistent and coherent; and that this would be the reflection of changing levels of contest and resistance. As for the received idea of the body's trans-historicity, a social theory of gender has to be autonomous with natural differences, biological reproduction, society's functional needs, and the imperatives of social reproduction.

With regard to the relation between modernity (which for Giddens includes what others would call post-modernity) and identity, Giddens (1991) states that today nothing is more clear than the fact that gender is a matter of learning and continuous 'work', not simply an extension of biological difference. He refers us back to Garfinkel's ethno-methodology and the case of Agnes, a transsexual, which shows that to be a 'man' or a 'woman' depends on close monitoring of the body and gestuality. In fact there is not one single bodily trait that separates all women from all men and there are few individuals who have the total experience of being members of both sexes: they are the only ones who can fully understand the details of body exhibition and the management through which gender is 'made'.

For Giddens the issue of the body in recent social theory is associated with Foucault. He analysed the body in relation to the mechanics of power, focusing on the emergence of the 'disciplining power' of modernity; the body becomes the focus of power and power, instead of trying to externally mark the body as in pre-modern times, subjects it to an internal discipline of self-control. Disciplinary mechanisms, according to Foucault, produce 'docile bodies', but Giddens still says that Merleau-Ponty (1962) and Goffman (1951) had better theories on body and agency. Curiously, Godelier (1993) also says that recent research on kinship and representations of the individual in several cultures have shown that sex acts as a 'ventriloquist's dummy': gender is forced to 'speak' about things that have nothing directly to do with sex. Bodies are used to testify in favour of or against the existing order (Godelier 1993:113).

Giddens outlines the state of affairs in the field of sexuality in the present period:

> 'Sexuality', in the modern sense, was invented when sexual behaviour 'went behind the scenes'. From this point onward, sexuality became a property of the individual, and more specifically the body, as eroticism conjoined to guilt was progressively replaced by an association of sexuality with self-identity and the propensity to shame (...) In sexual

behaviour, a distinction had always been made between pleasure and procreation. When the new connections between sexuality and intimacy were formed, however, sexuality became much more completely separated from procreation than before. Sexuality became doubly constituted as a medium of self-realisation and as a prime means, as well as an expression, of intimacy. (Giddens 1991:164)

At the onset there was a questioning of whether male domination was a universal given and why (Rosaldo and Lamphere 1974, Reiter 1975, Friedl 1975), followed by the questioning of the homogeneity of the 'masculine' and 'feminine' categories as possessing diverse social meanings (Ortner and Whitehead 1981, Strathern 1981). Lastly, authors like Collier and Yanagisako (1987) argued against the notion that cultural variations of gender and inequality are simply elaborations of a common natural fact. This positioning started by questioning the dichotomies at use (nature-culture, public-domestic, production-reproduction). The first dichotomy was criticised by Maccormack and Strathern (1980). Strathern demonstrates that the Hagen opposition between *mbo* and *romi* is not homologous with 'nature' and 'culture'; Bloch and Bloch (1980) have shown that there is a synchronic change in these categories and that symbolic systems are not isolated from social action. The second dichotomy stands on an *a-priori* definition of the domestic domain based on the mother-child relationship, and the third one was made explicit in Meillassoux 1975. He stated that the control over the labour of individuals is more important than the control over the means of production in agrarian contexts; for him, kinship is the institution that simultaneously regulates the reproductive function of the human beings and reproduction of the entire social formation.

Harris and Young (1981) tried to unravel the term 'reproduction', including social reproduction, the reproduction of the labour force and biological reproduction. A fourth dichotomy is that between 'feminine consciousness' and 'masculine consciousness', focusing on the different strategies of the members of the domestic groups, thus de-naturalising these. Bourdieu (1977), however, sought to counter the notion of the separation of the domestic and public spheres, by using the notion of 'incorporation' (or embodiment):

[for the child] … the awakening of consciousness of sexual identity and the incorporation of the dispositions associated with a determinate social definition of the social functions incumbent on men and women come hand in hand with the adoption of a socially defined vision of the sexual division of labour. (Bourdieu 1977 [1972]:93)

The same can be seen in Sahlin's (1985) analysis of the process of social change in Hawaii, in which the struggle for new meanings of hierarchy was simultaneously a struggle for chiefdom and gender relations.

For Collier and Yanagisako (1987), to overcome the dichotomies requires three types of postures: social systems are by definition systems of inequality; it is this that allows for the separation of equality and justice, and frees us from having to imagine a world devoid of socially created inequalities. The analytical programme would involve the cultural analysis of meaning, the use of systemic models of inequality, and historical analysis. Bourdieu (1972) said that one should analyse a social system not through the definition of an invisible, a-temporal structure, but rather by asking how common people, in the pursuit of their subjective ends, realise the structures of inequality. Thus it is necessary to understand commonly held ideas, i.e., how people evaluate each other. In sum, he seeks to understand how structure shapes people and how people, through their actions, accomplish the structures.

A model or a discourse of gender is a set of ideas that inform the activity of each sex in a given context. These discourses vary with context, and outlining them is more difficult when the context is less institutionalised (as in the case I deal with), as opposed to literary traditions, for instance. In a criticism of Collier and Yanagisako (1987), Loizos and Papataxiarchis (1991) said that, while in certain contexts gender and kinship are mutually implied as idioms of domesticity and the person, in other contexts – outside marriage – they are constituted in mutual exclusion and opposition, as in the case of friendship (1991:259). An instance of this is suggested in the case of the café discourse, which I describe in this book. In café discourse the sentiments of masculine solidarity focus on egalitarian relationships that are incompatible with kinship; the notions of home, conjugality and domestic interest are used as metaphors of materialism and calculation. In the Greek context, where relationships between people of the same sex are the rule, heterosexuality and procreation are excluded, in stark contrast with biological kinship.

When Gilmore (1991) asks himself if there is a deep structure of masculinity, he does not arrive at a conclusive answer, but rather defines three 'moral injunctions' that he says are present in all ethnographic contexts, and that seem to suggest that masculinity would be some sort of answer to specific psychological and structural deficits: a) a man must impregnate women; b) he must protect his dependants from danger; c) he must provide for his kin. This vision is too deterministic, since it states that the harsher the environment the more stressed is masculinity as an inspiration and objective. Ideology and environment would then be two strong factors in the equation of masculinity. The third would be psychological: the strongest danger for the performativity of human labour would be regression, the escape from reality. Thus masculinity could be seen as an incentive to replace the principle of pleasure with that of reality. Men would nurture their society by shedding blood, sweat and semen, whereas women would feed others directly – with their bodies, their milk, and their love.

Stoller and Herdt (1993) try to add sophistication to the contribution by psychology. They say that men create a protecting shield called 'symbiosis anxiety'. That is why masculine social behaviour shows so many defence manoeuvres: the fear of female autonomy, envy and subsequent spite toward women, the fear of entering their bodies, the fear of intimacy, the fear to demonstrate feminine attributes, and the fear of being desired by other men. We return to the notion that the first rule in the 'masculine profession' is 'not to be a woman' (1993:243). For women, on the other hand, it is 'to be a woman'. In his work on the Sambia, Herdt (1981) elaborates the four trends in the idioms of masculinity:

> 1) *perceptual correspondence:* the tacit and manifest responses to patterns of family resemblance (e.g., sympathetic or contagious 'magical identification') connecting different classes of phenomena (e.g., women and cassowaries), either in global or particular terms; 2) *genderising:* a form of anthropomorphisation in which men are prone, lexically, metaphorically, and subjectively, to polarise many natural phenomena and predicate their behaviour on the basis of human male or female gender traits, which are read back into cultural constructs (M. Strathern 1978); 3) *focal projection:* precise isomorphism pinpointing subjective links between human organs (or traits) and other phenomena (e.g., the pandanus flower is equated with the human penis); and 4) *perceptual splitting:* the categorisation of phenomena into manifest or tacit subtypes based on subjective premises or images (the perceptual filter) that affectively polarises (splits apart) the meanings attributed to members of the resulting gender classes (e.g., 'girl' versus 'boy', pandanus 'flower' versus 'nut pod'). (1981:299–300)

Sambia's masculine experience would then result in a subjective tension between the adult imperative of always behaving like a masculine warrior, and the infantile nuclear sense of having once been a small and impotent person intimately tied to one's mother.

I have shown previously how Bourdieu and Giddens were the main inspirations for Connell's ideas. His proposal for a new sociology of masculinity (Carrigan, Connell and Lee 1985) involves attention to three areas: firstly, sexual power, which should be dealt with within sexual categories, particularly the relation between hetero- and homosexual men, so as to understand the constitution of masculinity as a political order; secondly, the analysis of masculinity needs to be related to other current topics in feminism, such as the sexual division of labour, sexual politics in the work place and the interrelation between gender and class dynamics; thirdly, there should be a use of those developments in social theory that surpass structure versus individual and society versus person dichotomies.

Hegemonic Masculinity, Habitus, Embodiment

The notion of 'hegemonic masculinity' is central in my work. With this notion one avoids referring to the 'masculine role'. One is referring rather to a particular variety of social masculinity that subordinates other varieties.[4] If the fission between the categories 'man' and 'woman' is one of the central facts of patriarchal power structures and their dynamics, then, in the case of men, the crucial division is that between hegemonic masculinity and various subordinate masculinities. From here it follows that masculinities are constructed not only through relations of power but also through their interrelation with the division of labour, and patterns of emotional attachment. This suggests why the culturally praised form of masculinity (hegemonic masculinity) is in constant tension with the real lives of most men.

Connell does not disregard that one of the most important traits of hegemonic masculinity, together with its connection with domination, is heterosexuality. That is why we can say that the Foucaultian passage from the notion of 'lust' to the specificity of 'perversions' was fundamental for the historical constitution of current hegemonic masculinity.

As Paul Connerton (1993) says in *How Societies Remember*, so Bourdieu (1990) says that it is through socialised bodies – through the habitus, and ritual practices – that the past perpetuates itself in the lengthy period of collective mythology (1990:4). Masculine domination does not seem to need justification, the dominant outlook is expressed in discourses such as proverbs and poems. Bourdieu calls our attention to the fact that he is not referring to an ideology: if ritual practices and mythical discourses legitimate, their principle however is not the intention to legitimate. That is probably why the dominant vision is also expressed in objects and material life practices: in the structure of space, in the inner divisions of the house, in the organisation of time, in technical as well as ritual practices of the body, in postures, attitudes, manners and gestures. It is a system of categories of perception, of thought and action that, thanks to the concordance between objective and cognitive structures, generates the 'natural attitude' of doxa experience.

The division of objects and activities according to the masculine-feminine opposition is part of a system of homologous oppositions, such as high and low, above and below, making it seem that difference is already inscribed in the nature of things. This is also true for the body:

> La somatisation progressive des relations fondamentales qui sont constitutives de l'ordre social, aboutit à l'institution de deux 'natures' différentes, c'est-à-dire de deux systèmes de différences sociales naturalisées qui sont inscrites a la fois dans les hexis corporelles, sous la forme de deux classes opposées et complémentaires de postures, de démarches, de mantiens, de gestes, etc. (Bourdieu 1990:8)

The dominated person, in order to think, does not have anything other than the knowledge instruments that he/she has in common with the dominator – and those are nothing more than the embodied form of the relation of domination. That is why the relationship between dominating and dominated is not symmetrical. This is clear from the fact that the socially powerful men have greater sexual freedom whereas their wives have greater demands of 'virtue', in rural Mediterranean contexts at least.[5]

In the process of social construction of gender, the categories of perception are constructed around oppositions that refer back to the sexual division of sexual labour, thus structuring the perception of sexual organs and sexual activity. Bourdieu, however, does not say that resistance and cognitive struggle are impossible, and he points out the cases of parody and carnival.

The biological body – a socially constructed one – is also a political body. It is an embodied politic, something that becomes visible in the morality of honour, synthesised in a nutshell in one single Kabyle word: *qabel*, 'to look straight at', as well as in the body posture that it designates (1990:20). It is through the mediation of the sexual division of the legitimate uses of the body that the tie between the *phallus* and the *logos* is established.

It is quite common to hear people say that men (or rather many men) are also the victims of their domination. Bourdieu says that it is true, but that men are only dominated by their own domination, which is quite different from women's situation. The masculine habitus is constructed and accomplished in relation to the reserved space where the competition games are played between men, thus establishing an asymmetry between man and woman in symbolic exchanges, as well as an asymmetry between subject and object, agent and instrument. He explains this with the example of the matrimonial market as a paradigmatic actualisation of the relations of production and reproduction of symbolic capital:

> La question des fondements de la division entre les sexes et de la domination masculine trouve ainsi sa solution: c'est dans la logique de l'économie d'échanges symboliques et, plus précisement, dans la construction sociale des relations de parenté et du mariage qui assigne aux femmes, universellement, leur statut social d'objets d'échange définis conformement aux interêts masculins (c'est-à-dire primor-dialement comme filles ou soeurs) et vouées à contribuer ainsi à la reproduction du capital symbolique des hommes, que réside l'expli-cation du primat universellement accordé à la masculinité dans les taxonomies culturelles. (1990:27)

Bourdieu, by means of 'practice', and Merleau-Ponty, by means of 'per-ception', are the spokesmen of two of the most famous theories of embodiment. For the latter, the main duality in the domain of percep-tion is that between subject and object, while for the former – in the domain of practice – the main duality is that between structure and practice. The epistemological purpose of embodiment would be the col-lapsing of duality (Csordas 1990:7). For Bourdieu it would be a matter of outlining a third order of knowledge, beyond phenomenology and beyond a science of the objective conditions of the possibility of social life. Similarly to Merleau-Ponty, he tries to dislocate the focus of study from the perception of objects to the process of objectification, or from the analysis of social facts as *opus operatum* to the analysis of the *modus operandi* of social life. Such a strategy would lead to the collapse of dual-ities such as body and mind, sign and meaning, in the concept of habi-tus (originally introduced by Mauss 1980 [1936] in his famous essay on body techniques), a way of referring to the sum total of culturally pat-terned uses of the body.

Bourdieu takes the definition further. It is not the habitus as a collec-tion of practices, but rather as a system of lasting dispositions, the unconsciously and collectively inculcated principle for the generation and structuration of practices and representations (1977:72 in Csordas 1990:7). The 'socially informed body' is the unifying principle that pre-vents the habitus from generating practices in a random way.

This should be complemented with the theories of performance, closely tied to the study of ritual (see Turner 1974) and theatre anthropology, since these make excellent contributions to embodiment. Research around performances takes as its subject and method the experiencing body, situated in time, space and history, thus restoring the body as a locus of knowledge and ideological struggle, paying particular attention to face-to-face encounters rather than formal abstractions (Conquergood 1993).

One of the problems that gender studies raises is that of the scientist's political commitment. Bourdieu warns that the best of political movements is doomed to do the worst kind of science. Changes, however, are possible, even though within limits: bodies do not always understand the language of consciousness; that is why it is not easy to break a continuous chain of unconscious, 'body to body', learning (Bourdieu 1990:29). Changes may be helpful for understanding that which they have changed. In this case, late modernity is the ethnographically explicit context. Today, sexuality is something that each of us 'has', and is no longer a natural condition. It is a trait of the self, it is malleable, it is a juncture point between body, self-identity and social norms (Giddens 1992). When referring to the 'pure relationship', Giddens wonders:

> What do men want? In one sense the answer has been clear and understood by both sexes from the nineteenth century onwards. Men want status among other men, conferred by material rewards and conjoined to rituals of male solidarity. (1992:60)

Until recently, masculine sexuality was characterised by the following aspects: the domination of the public sphere by men; the double standard; the division of women between pure and impure; an understanding of sexual difference as given by God, Nature or Biology; the problematisation of women as opaque or irrational in their desires and actions; and the sexual division of labour. These are all social contextualisations. What about the lived and emotional experience of men?

Following the objects relations school of psychology (represented, in the aftermath of the Freudian schism, by Nancy Chodorow, in opposition to Kristeva's or Irigaray's Lacanian post-structuralism), Chodorow (1978) says that masculinity is like a detour in the separation from the mother. For both sexes, the phallus derives its meaning from the fantasy of female domination. It symbolises separation, but also rebellion and freedom. The Oedipal phase confirms the separation from the mother and the conquest of freedom: 'The masculine sense of self-identity is thus forged in circumstances in which a drive to self-sufficiency is coupled with a potential crippling emotional handicap' (Giddens 1992:116).

Sexuality and reproduction were mutually structured in the past. Today this is no longer so. The privatisation of sexuality occurred at the same time as the negation of feminine pleasure and the idea of masculine sexuality as non-problematic, and this after the remittance of homosexuality to the category of perversion. Following Holly Devor, Giddens outlines how things were 'before': 1) each individual was seen as male or female, with no intermediate categories; 2) physical characteristics and behavioural traits of individuals were interpreted as masculine or feminine following the dominant gender scheme; 3) clues on gender were routinely weighed and evaluated within the confines of accepted status behaviour patterns; 4) differences of gender thus constituted and reconstituted were applied back to form concrete sexual identities, filtering out and excluding all cross-gender elements; 5) social actors monitored their appearance and behaviour in accordance with a 'naturally given' sexual identity (Giddens 1992:198). As the author says, now that anatomy has ceased to be destiny, sexual identity becomes more a matter of lifestyle.

The concept of hegemony, as used originally by Gramsci, reports to organised, civil society, the hinge between the state and the economy, and it implies an enlarged notion of politics, one that is not confined to the state. Thus Gramsci widens the previous conception of hegemony in order to also include the cultural and intellectual fields: the modern Prince must create a national and popular will, must create a new common sense, socialising knowledge and the new world vision (Gramsci 1971). At the limit, hegemony is passive anti-revolution.

The concept of hegemony, then, is borrowed from Gramsci. He obviously did not use it to analyse gender, but rather class relations in his contemporary Italian society. It means social precedence attained beyond power dispute, in the organisation of private life and cultural processes (Connell 1987:184). Hegemony is not imposed on people by force, although the use of force is not excluded altogether. It is not through force that hegemony is achieved. It is a lived consensus. Nor does it mean the obliteration of alternatives. As Pina-Cabral said, in a personal communication, hegemony is a form of domination in which the dominated takes part in his or her domination. Hegemony is like a spotlight that, while illuminating a certain area, leaves other areas in a semi-darkness.[6]

In the field of gender, hegemony is a matter of the capacity to impose a specific definition over other types of masculinity. This means that the model that is praised corresponds, in real life, to but a few men – and this is quite visible in my ethnographic data. The concept allows for a more dynamic conception of masculinity. It is then understood as a structure of social relations in which several non-hegemonic masculinities subsist, although repressed and self-repressed by the hegemonic commonly held consensus.

NOTES

1. As previously mentioned, this is related to foundational views based on Divinity, Nature and Biology. One only has to look at the recent polemic around the 'hypothalamus' in the determination of homosexuality and the paradoxical way in which homosexuals engaged in social movements have reacted to this 'discovery'. Some acclaimed the biological legitimisation as a form of 'determination'; others fought it off with social constructionism and the notion of sexual orientation as 'personal choice'.
2. In the sense that 'biological sex', 'behaviour', and 'identity' are not all, and simultaneously, neither coinciding nor contrary to the norm. Many gay men in the West have a masculine self-identity, and a non-normative sexuality.
3. This is due mainly to the apparently repetitive cyclicity that underlies the notion of social reproduction. It is only apparent, however, since any system can change: in the case of masculinity this happens when heterogeneous masculinities find or force their space for social relevance.
4. My work does not deal with two areas of study: that of sex role theory and the field of 'men's studies'. The former belongs mostly to a specialised area, social psychology; the latter is just a generic designation, as was 'women's studies', one that has no theoretical relevance. Gender, as a structure of social relations, should be the sociologically embracing field.
5. Pitt-Rivers (1971 [1954]) had already noticed this in regard to the *señoritos'* wives as opposed to *jornaleros'* wives in Grazalema.
6. Paper presented at the Third Conference of the European Association of Social Anthropologists, Oslo, Norway, June 1994, in the opening of the workshop on 'Morals and the Margins'.

PERSPECTIVES II

❦

*T*he classical expression 'conclusion' conjures up the worst fears and perplexities, as if the process of arguing was as simple as one is led to believe. Instead, several years of research, including experiences as different as fieldwork, library and archival research, and the writing up of a text, constituted a much more fuzzy process, with many detours and crossroads. Sometimes I suspect that initial certitude and clarity have been replaced by doubts and uncertainties.

The simple fact of contacting and living with real people in the field, and the exasperating rationalism that writing pushes one into, make it difficult to 'conclude' – in the final, almost authoritarian, sense of the word. False modesty apart, I cannot find a better rhetorical device for replacing 'conclusion' than the phrase used many times before me: this is work in progress, the opening up of a path for others to improve and contest. So that others can build, and construct upon. Actually, 'construction' would be a better word than 'conclusion'.

Nevertheless, it is possible – and desirable – to answer some of the initial research questions by summarising the most striking points in this volume. It is as if they were the bricks in a construction that still lacks a roof.

The values that constitute hegemonic masculinity are those values expressed by men when they try to express a form of cultural consensus when verbalising opinions on themselves and others, when evaluating their and others' actions. These guidelines are 'laws' which, like the religious commandments, are known to everyone, are supposed to be enacted by everyone but, however, are not always followed or accepted by particular men. In *Dislocating Masculinities* (1994), the authors state:

Hegemonic masculinities define successful ways of 'being a man'; in so doing, they define other masculine styles as inadequate or inferior. These related masculinities we call 'subordinant variants'. (Cornwall and Lindisfarne 1994:3)

The main effect of this discourse – of these words that constitute that which they talk about – is social control. This is of course, a first analytical level, and a rather functionalistic one. This is control over action and expression, and the more it is exerted over particular men the more they stray from the hegemonic model. This implies a high level of self-control, of vigilance, of monitoring (to use Giddens' expression), that is applied in all domains of human experience to interaction: ways of talking, contents of what is said, ways of displaying the body, clothes, attitudes towards tense situations, conflict, emotions, and so on, as visible in the situations of sociability that I have outlined and described.

The ideas that direct the central hegemonic model, and which are called upon to legitimise or de-legitimise action – and which are expressed discursively and performatively – are a set of cultural meanings. These meanings have been inherited from the past, so that to some extent they are external to the will of particular men. These meanings rely on a symbolic classification that defines the division of the world into masculine and feminine as a main dichotomy, a classificatory principle. In this sense, ideas do structure social life.

However, this classification is neither neutral nor innocent. It is a matter of value and evaluation. The relationship between masculine and feminine can not be described with the metaphor of 'two sides of a coin' once we leave the world of symbolism and enter the world of social relations. It is a fundamentally unequal and hierarchical division. It legitimises a form of domination in which a person's gender grants social precedence or submission, in similar ways to what happens with other levels of social identity such as class, age or status. It is, though, a form of social precedence that depends on ideological tenets that are reproduced through a specific process of naturalisation: inequality between men and women as general social categories is not seen as a social process but as an ontological reality. Dominators do not have a 'guilt complex', and those dominated (women) apparently resign.

In this volume I have tried to show how hegemonic masculinity is constituted and reproduced through a series of different social relations and symbolic constructs. These include relations at the work place between different types of men; local notions of hierarchy, power and conflict that seem to transcend specific gender relations; forms of sociability and everyday interaction; the educational process; ritual and symbolic texts and performances; the notions of personhood, identity, and emotions. They all are part of a mutually constituting system in which gender is a master metaphor due to its purportedly essentialistic nature. The strength and resilience of gender constructs and metaphors lies greatly on this, thus creating the 'lived consensus' whose logic seems so hard to break.

This state of affairs is reproduced to a great extent through the body and processes of embodiment – an issue that I have not dealt with properly and am now including on my research agenda. Embodiment is to a great extent an a unreflected process, almost uncounscious. That is why gender politics have been the last issue of inequality in social relations to be tackled and confronted both in society and in the social sciences. Gender is so intimately connected with notions of personhood and the body that it is doubly difficult to see in it processes of social construction. In oral cultures this 'effect of resistance' may be even stronger since the body's mimetic learning corresponds to activities and capabilities that legitimate – make 'obvious' – masculine domination. The socially domesticated and trained body ultimately seems to 'confirm' 'strength', 'verticality', 'affirmation', 'activity' as innate masculine virtues.

In *Dislocating Masculinity* (1994) it is said that 'the contexts and criteria in terms of which men are differentiated from each other is an area which has been neglected in anthropology. It has also been neglected in much of the men's studies literature' (Cornwall and Lindisfarne 1994:19). This volume has stressed this aspect of 'different masculinities': the symbolic capital of masculinity is not evenly distributed and the 'sources of income' are multiple, that being why it also is possible to transcend hegemonic models by means of stressing some aspects instead of others or by stressing aspects of personhood that tend to be seen as gender-neutral.

As a matter of fact, men and women live in the midst of historical processes. The external conjunctures of their lives also change, as do the interests that individuals fight for which are not constant throughout their life cycle. Hegemonic masculinity does not remain the same eternally, it is not reproduced *ad aeternum*. There are conjunctures of contestation and negotiation, either on the part of men whose lives, thoughts and actions stray away from the central model, or on the part of women. This is what has been going on in modern western urban societies to such an extent that sexual politics have become one of the main social issues of the twentieth century. In a context such as Pardais, transformations in relations of production, the entry into global economy and culture, and the local dynamics allowed for by the inherent contradictions and ambiguities in any classificatory system, will certainly allow for change in gender relations, as I tried to indicate throughout this volume.

It is quite common to say that men are also victims of masculine domination. Many women may feel this statement to be dishonest. The truth however seems to be that the general category 'women' has 'nothing to lose but their chains', to gloss a famous Marxist sentence. They seem to be able to appropriate for themselves symbols and practices that are labelled as masculine, thanks precisely to the hierarchy that defines these as 'superior' and closer to the moral standards of personhood. Also, a process of relative 'feminisation' of social values has been occurring in the society at large, and women in Pardais are not unaware of the growing social salience of sentiments, introspection, self-reflexivity and so on. For men, however, it is rather more difficult to invent new identity forms since – following the dichotomous thought – the alternative is manifestly 'inferior'. They are like aristocrats who have 'lost everything' and no longer know who and what they are. Acknowledging that the hegemonic model probably is just a paper tiger might be the first step for the invention of new social relations and new identities relating to gender.

This work has followed a rather traditional perspective regarding the unit of analysis: a village. However, I believe that it was my concern throughout not to see it as an isolate and not to reify 'culture' or 'society' as a specific summary of people in a specific territory. This was achieved partly by constantly connecting local discourse with the notion of the nation-state and the global economy and culture; and, on the other hand, by paying attention to concrete men, rather than 'men' as an abstract category (although this is also important, since classification systems are always abstract and individual-blind). The main characters in this essay were actors in situations of male sociability, in situations of work, and in moments of expressiveness. Some theoretical, thematic and methodological aspects have, however, been neglected, and I believe that this work opened up – *hélas* only once it was finished – some new perspectives for the study of gender and masculinity in particular.

The search for meaning should consist of the 'mapping' of those semantic areas, as well as arenas for action, that are related to gender, as Marilyn Strathern suggested and not only on the masculine/feminine division as a men/women division:

> Strathern's argument focuses on how gender difference itself is constructed by considering local discourses of agency, causation, per-

sonhood and identity. From this perspective, 'idealised masculinity is not necessarily just about men; it is not necessarily just about relations between the sexes either'. (Strathern 1988:65) Rather it is a part of a system for producing difference. (Cornwall and Lindisfarne 1994:40–1)

This, I believe, has been an ever-present concern in this essay. Still, this task is rather more easy to carry out with regard to *strictu sensu* texts, and metaphoric texts such as ritual, performances and so on. It becomes more difficult to do so with the non-verbalised processes of embodiment. Some of the 'harder' aspects of human experience have been ignored by the social sciences, probably because they have been erroneously tagged as 'biological'. The study of the body, the socialised and the subjective body, as well as the processes of embodiment, is now only starting. Anthropology has a methodological difficulty in going forward in this subject, a difficulty that is greatly due to the 'empire of the word' in the discipline's manner of collecting data and of exposing results of research. This is being overcome slowly, either by the use of visual anthropology, or by the study of theatre, ritual and performance. Simultaneously, phenomenological approaches to the body and embodiment (such as Csordas's) or Bourdieu's approach to embodied 'habitus' are very promising for overcoming the still obsessive concern for not dealing with corporeal realities, seen as outside the concern of anthropology. These approaches still need, however, to be cross-fertilised with approaches to gender.

The social and cultural organisation of the uses of human bodies as vehicles for eroticism, sexuality, and reproduction is, therefore, on the agenda for anthropological research at the turn of the century, especially considering issues such as new reproductive technologies, the AIDS epidemic, demographic explosion, or the (re)constitution of male and female identities and unions. The growing 'personalisation' of sexuality in modern Western societies, together with the creation of social identities based on sexual discourses and practices, make it necessary to take into account not only late modernity's social and cultural processes, but also the processes of globalisation. The Western social constructs of gender and the analysis made by social scientists are transmitted to the general population and then return to ethnography under the guise of ever-renewed constructions. This fact generates, for instance, redefinitions at the local levels, creolisation, and global models. In multi-ethnic societies, for instance, the body, gender, and sexuality are mobilised for the definition and redefinition of ethnicity, class, consumption habits, and personal identity.

The field of studies on gender is part of the experimental moment in which anthropology is living. We need to overcome as much as possible the cleavages between the 'grammars' of Durkheim (as an emphasis on social structure and order), Marx (as an emphasis on history and political economy), and Weber (as emphasis on action and meaning). We should struggle for their convergence: the cultural meanings of certain social constructions of gender are, firstly, prior to the individuals and structure the framework for human and social reproduction; secondly, they take part in disputes for power, depending on different structurations throughout history and in a political economy of sex (today, a 'world economy' of sex); and, finally, they are manipulable by individuals in the dynamic and inventive constitution of their self-identities. It is also a thematic field that is particularly apt for the exercise of hermeneutic approaches, which are simultaneously reflexive and engaged in social and political transformation.

Culture should be understood more as a fluid field in constant (re)definition, somewhere between individual action and traditional heritage. If in so-called traditional societies the meaning of beliefs, practices and society is to a great extent pre-given, in modern society (which, after all, includes the so-called traditional ones) there is constant search for meaning, a challenge to pre-given meanings and interpretations.

I like to think that the de-construction of hegemonic masculinity is simultaneously at the core of the anthropological project, at the core of its experimental and reflexive moment, and at the core of one of the greatest social transformations witnessed in the late modern era – the changes in the social relations of gender. We need to analyse and compare how this strange and particular form of social precedence – masculinity – can be transformed in a more gratifying way for women and men's lives. Shakespeare had already addressed the mystery that I tried to address. And the end of his journey was yet an interrogation: 'What is your substance, whereof are you made, That millions of strange shadows on you tend? (Sonnet 53).

BIBLIOGRAPHY

Abu-Lughod, L., 1986, *Veiled Sentiments: Honor and Poetry in a Bedouin Society*. Berkeley: University of California Press.

Alcantud, J.A.G., 1990, *Canteros y caciques en la lucha por el mármol*. Macael: Instituto de Estudios Almerienses de la Diputación de Almería.

Arauto da Padroeira, O, no. 22, November 1990. Vila Viçosa: Fábrica da Igreja de Nossa Senhora.

Appadurai, A., 1990, ' Disjuncture and Difference in the Global Economy', in Featherstone, Mike, ed., *Global Culture - Nationalism, Globalization and Modernity*. London: Sage.

Assentos de Nascimentos, Conservatória do Registo Civil de Vila Viçosa.

Ariès, Ph. and Bèjin, A., eds, 1982, *Sexualités Occidentales*. Paris: Points.

Ariès, Ph., 1990, 'Para Uma História da Vida Privada', in Ariès, Ph. and Duby, G., eds, *História da Vida Privada*, vol. 3. Porto: Afrontamento.

Badinter, E., 1992, *XY de l'Identité Masculine*. Paris: Odile Jacob.

Bakhtin, M., 1968, *Rabelais and His World*. Cambridge, Mass.: Harvard University Press.

Baptista, F.O., 1980, 'Economia do Latifúndio - O Caso Português', in Barros, A., ed., 1980, *A Agricultura Latifundiária na Península Ibérica*. Oeiras: Instituto Gulbenkian de Ciência - Centro de Estudo de Economia Agrária.

Barros, A., ed., 1980, *A Agricultura Latifundiária na Península Ibérica*. Oeiras: Instituto Gulbenkian de Ciência - Centro de Estudos de Economia Agrária.

Bauman, R., 1986, *Story, Performance, and Event: Contextual Studies of Oral Narrative*. Cambridge: Cambridge University Press.

Benjamin, W., 1969, *Illuminations*. New York: Schocken.

Bíblia Sagrada. Lisbon: Sociedade Bíblica Britannica e Estrangeira, 1943.

Bloch, M., 1977, 'The Disconnection Between Power and Rank as a Process', *Archives Européennes de Sociologie*, 18: 107–48.

Bloch, M. and Bloch, J., 1980, 'Women and the Dialectics of Nature in Eighteenth-Century French Thought', in MacCormack, C. and Strathern, M., eds, *Nature, Culture and Gender*. Cambridge: Cambridge University Press.

Blok, A., 1981, 'Rams and Billy-Goats: a Key to the Mediterranean Code of Honour', *Man*, 16: 427–40.

Boccaccio, G., n.d. [1349–1353], *Decâmeron*. Mem-Martins: Europa-América.

Boissevain, J., 1974, *Friends of Friends: Networks, Manipulators and Coalitions*. Oxford: Blackwell.

Bourdieu, P., 1962, 'Célibat et Condition Paysanne', *Études Rurales*, 5–6: 32–135.

Bourdieu, P., 1972, *Esquisse d'une Théorie de la Pratique*. Geneva: Droz.

Bourdieu, P., 1976, 'Marriage Strategies and Strategies of Social Reproduction', in Fortes, R. and Ranum, O., eds, *Family and Society*. London: Johns Hopkins Press.

Bourdieu, P., 1977, *Outline of a Theory of Practice*. Cambridge: Cambridge University Press.

Bourdieu, P., 1980, *Le Sens Pratique*. Paris: Minuit.

Bourdieu, P., 1990, 'La Domination Masculine', *Actes de la Recherche en Sciences Sociales*, 84: 2–31.

Brandes, S., 1973, 'Social Structure and Interpersonal Relations in Navanogal (Spain)', *American Anthropologist*, 75: 750–65.

Brandes, S., 1979, 'Drinking Patterns and Alcohol Control in a Castilian Mountain Village', *Anthropology*, 3: 1–16.

Brandes, S., 1981, 'Like Wounded Stags: Male Sexual Ideology in an Andalusian Town', in Ortner, S. and Whitehead, H., eds, *Sexual Meanings: The Cultural Construction of Gender and Sexuality*. Cambridge: Cambridge University Press.

Brandes, S., 1991 [1980], *Metáforas de la Masculinidad: Sexo y Estatus en el Folklore Andaluz*. Madrid: Taurus.

Braudel, F., 1983 [1966], *O Mediterrâneo e o Mundo Mediterrânico*. Lisbon: D.Quixote, 2 vols.

Campbell, J., 1964, *Honour, Family and Patronage: A Study of Institutions and Moral Values in a Greek Mountain Community*. Oxford: Clarendon Press.

Caplan, P., ed., 1987, *The Cultural Construction of Sexuality*. London: Routledge.

Cardoso Pires, J., 1960, *Cartilha do Marialva*. Lisbon: Moraes.

Carrigan, T., Connell, R. and Lee, J., 1985, 'Toward a New Sociology of Masculinity', *Theory and Society*, 14 (5): 551–604.

Carrithers, M., Collins, S. and Lukes, S., eds, 1985, *The Category of the Person: Anthropology, Philosophy, History*. Cambridge: Cambridge University Press.

C.C.R.A. (Comissão de Coordenação da Região do Alentejo), 1983, *Projecto de Desenvolvimento Integrado dos Concelhos de Borba, Estremoz e Vila Viçosa*.

Chaucer, G., 1987 [1386?], *The Canterbury Tales*. Harmondsworth: Penguin.

Chayannov, A.V., 1966 [1925], *On the Theory of Peasant Economy*. Homewood: R.D. Irwin.

Chodorow, N., 1978, *The Reproduction of Mothering: Psychoanalysis and the Sociology of Gender*. Berkeley: University of California Press.

Clifford, J. and Marcus, G., eds, 1986, *Writing Culture*. Berkeley: University of California Press.

Cole, S., 1991, *Women of the Praia: Works and Lives in a Portuguese Coastal Community*. Princeton: Princeton University Press.

C.M.V.V. (Câmara Municipal de Vila Viçosa), 1985, *Anexo ao Plano de Actividades e Orçamento*. Vila Viçosa: Câmara Municipal.

Collier, J. and Yanagisako, S., eds, 1987, *Gender and Kinship: Essays Toward a Unified Analysis*. Stanford: Stanford University Press.

Connell, R., 1987, *Gender and Power: Society, the Person, and Sexual Politics*. Stanford: Stanford University Press.

Connerton, P., 1993 [1989], *Como as sociedades recordam*. Oeiras: Celta.

Conquergood, D., 1993, 'Embodied Meaning: Between Anthropology and Performance', *Antropologia Portuguesa*,11: 109–20.

Coombe, R., 1990, 'Barren Ground. Re-Conceiving Honour and Shame in the Field of Mediterranean Ethnography', *Anthropologica*, 32: 221–38.

Cordeiro, G., 1991, 'Jogo na cidade de Lisboa - a Laranjinha', in Pais de Brito, J., ed., vol. *Tradições*, Enciclopédia Temática Portugal Moderno. Lisbon: Pomo.

Cornwall, A. and Lindisfarne, N., eds, 1994, *Dislocating Masculinity - Comparative Ethnographies*. London: Routledge.

Cowan, J., 1991, 'Going Out for Coffee? Contesting the Grounds of Gendered Pleasures in Everyday Sociability', in Loizos, P. and Papataxiarchis, E., eds, *Contested Identities: Gender and Kinship in Modern Greece*. Princeton: Princeton University Press.

Crespo, J., 1990, *A História do Corpo*. Lisbon: Difel.

Csordas, T., 1990, 'Embodiment as a Paradigm for Anthropology', *Ethos*, 18 (1): 5–47.

Cutileiro, J., 1977 [1971], *Ricos e Pobres no Alentejo*. Lisbon: Sá da Costa.

Dalton, G., 1971, *Traditional Tribal and Peasant Economies: an Introductory Survey of Economic Anthropology*. Reading, Mass.: Addison-Wesley Modules in Anthropology.

Dalton, G., 1972, 'Peasantries in Anthropology and History', *Current Anthropology*, 13 (3–4): 385–415.

Dante Alighieri, s.d. [1265–1321], *A Divina Comédia*. São Paulo: Cultrix.

Darwin, C., 1871, *The Descent of Man and Selection in Relation to Sex*. New York: D. Appleton.

Darwin, C., 1958 [1859], *Origin of Species*. New York: New American Library, Mentor.

Davis, J., 1977, *People of the Mediterranean*. London: Routledge and Kegan Paul.

Dias, J., 1970, *O Intersexo Visto pelo Etnólogo*. Lisbon: Associação Portuguesa para o Progresso das Ciências.

Dias, M.T., 1987, *Lisboa Desaparecida*. Lisbon: Quimera.

Douglas, M., 1987, *Constructive Drinking*. Cambridge: Cambridge University Press.

Driessen, H., 1983, 'Male Sociability and Rituals of Masculinity in Rural Andalusia', *Anthropological Quarterly*, 56 (3): 125–33.

Duby, G., 1981, *Le Chevalier, la Femme et le Prêtre*. Paris: Hachette.

Duby, G., 1989, 'Prefácio à História da Vida Privada', in Ariès, Ph. and Duby, G., eds, *História da Vida Privada*, vol. 1. Porto: Afrontamento.

Duby, G., ed., 1991, *Amour et Sexualité en Occident*. Paris: Points.

Dumont, L., 1970 [1967], *Homo Hierarchicus*. Chicago: University of Chicago Press.

Dumont, L., 1982 [1977], *Homo Aequalis: Génesis y Apogeo de la Ideología Económica*. Madrid: Taurus.

Dumont, L., 1983, *Essais sur l'Individualisme.Une Perspective Anthropologique sur l'Idéologie Moderne*. Paris: Seuil.

Elias, N., 1988, 'La Cortesía del Lecho. Transformaciones en el Uso del Dormitório', *A&V-Monografías de Arquitectura y Vivienda*, 14: 18–24.

Elias, N., 1989, *O Processo Civilizacional. Investigações Sociogenéticas e Psicogenéticas*, vol. 1: *Transformações do Comportamento das Camadas Superiores Seculares do Ocidente*. Lisbon: D.Quixote.

Ellis, H., 1942 [1896–1928], *Studies in the Psychology of Sex*. New York: Random House.

Engels, F., 1976 [1884], *A Origem da Família, da Propriedade Privada e do Estado.* Lisbon: Presença.

'Epístola de São Paulo Apóstolo aos Romanos', Novo Testamento, *Bíblia Sagrada.* Lisbon: Sociedade Bíblica Britannica e Estrangeira, 1943.

Erasmus of Roterdam, [1530], *De Civilitate Morum Puerilium.*

Espanca, J.J.R., 1983 [1880], *Memórias de Vila Viçosa, ou Ensaio da História desta Vila Transtagana, Corte da Sereníssima Casa e Estado de Bragança, desde os Tempos mais Remotos até ao Presente.* Vila Viçosa: Câmara Municipal de Vila Viçosa, 32 vols.

Featherstone, Mike, ed., 1990, *Global Culture: Nationalism, Globalization and Modernity.* London: Sage.

Fernandez, J., 1974, 'The Mission of Metaphor in Expressive Culture', *Current Anthropology*, 15: 119–33.

Flandrin, J.-L., 1979 [1976], *Orígenes de la Família Moderna: La Família, el Parentesco y la Sexualidad en la Sociedad Tradicional.* Barcelona: Crítica.

Flandrin, J.-L., 1982, 'La Vie Sexuelle des Gens Mariés dans l' Ancienne Société: de la Doctrine de l' Église à la Réalité des Comportements', in Ariès, Ph. and Béjin, A., eds, *Sexualités Occidentales.* Paris: Seuil.

Fortes, M., 1949, 'Time and Social Structure', in Fortes, M., *Social Structure.* Oxford: Clarendon.

Fortes, M., 1958, 'Introduction', in Goody, J., ed., *The Developmental Cycle in Domestic Groups.* Cambridge: Cambridge University Press.

Fortes, M., 1969, *Kinship and the Social Order. The Legacy of Lewis Henry Morgan.* Chicago: Aldine Publishing Company.

Foster, G.M., 1953, 'Cofradia and Compadrazgo in Spain and Latin America', *Southwestern Journal of Anthropology*, 9: 1–28.

Foster, G.M., 1960, 'Interpersonal Relations in Peasant Society', *Human Organization*, 19: 174–78.

Foucault, M., 1972, *The Archaeology of Knowledge and the Discourse on Language.* New York: Pantheon.

Foucault, M., 1976, *Histoire de la Sexualité*, vol.1: *La Volonté de Savoir.* Paris: Gallimard.

Foucault, M., 1977 [1975], *Vigiar e Punir.* Petrópolis: Vozes.

Foucault, M. and Sennett, R., 1981, 'Sexuality and Solitude', in *Anthology* 1. London: Junction Books.

Franklin, S.H., 1969, *The European Peasantry: The Final Phase.* London: Methuen.

Freud, S., 1953–74, *The Standard Edition of the Complete Psychological Works of Sigmund Freud*, (*S.E.*) ed. James Strachey. London: Hogarth Press.

Freud, S., [1913], 'Totem and Taboo', in *S.E.* 13.

Freud, S., [1924], 'The Dissolution of the Oedipus Complex', in *S.E.* 19.

Freud, S. [1939], 'Moses and Monotheism: Three Essays', in *S.E.* 23.

Freud, S., [1940], 'An Outline of Psycho-Analysis', in *S.E.* 23.

Friedl, E., 1975, *Women and Men: an Anthropologist's View.* New York: Holt, Rinehart and Winston.

Galeski, B., 1977, 'Quelques Reflexions sur la Question Agraire dans les Démocraties Populaires (1945–1975)', in *Structures Sociales en Europe de l'Est (Notes et Études Documentaires).* Paris: La Documentation Française.

Geertz, C., 1973, 'Deep Play: Notes on the Balinese Cockfight', in Geertz, C., *The Interpretation of Cultures.* New York: Basic Books.

Geertz, C., 1983, 'Art as a Cultural System', in Geertz, C., *Local Knowledge: Further Essays in Interpretive Anthropology*. New York: Basic Books.

Gefou-Madianou, D., ed., 1992, *Alcohol, Gender and Culture*. London: Routledge and Kegan Paul.

Giddens, A., 1971, *Capitalism and Modern Social Theory*. Cambridge: Cambridge University Press.

Giddens, A., 1979, *Central Problems in Social Theory: Action, Structure and Contradiction in Social Analysis*. London: Macmillan.

Giddens, A., 1991, *Modernity and Self-Identity*. Cambridge: Polity

Giddens, A., 1992 a [1990], *As Consequências da Modernidade*. Oeiras: Celta.

Giddens, A., 1992 b, *The Transformation of Intimacy: Sexuality, Love and Eroticism in Modern Societies*. Cambridge: Polity.

Gilmore, D. and Gilmore, M., 1978, 'Sobre los Machos y los Matriarcados: el Mito Machista en Andalucía', *Ethnica*, 14: 147–59.

Gilmore, D., 1975, 'Friendship in Fuenmayor: Patterns of Integration in an Atomistic Society', *Ethnology*, 14: 311–24.

Gilmore, D., 1980, *The People of the Plain: Class and Community in Lower Andalusia*. New York: Columbia University Press.

Gilmore, D., 1982, 'Anthropology of the Mediterranean Area', *Annual Review of Anthropology*, 11: 175–205.

Gilmore, D., 1985, 'Introduction', *Anthropology* 9 (1–2): 1–10, Special Issue no. 3, *Sex and Gender in Southern Europe: Problems and Prospects*.

Gilmore, D., 1986, 'Mother-Son Intimacy and the Dual View of Woman in Andalusia: Analysis Through Oral Poetry', *Ethos*, 14 (3): 227–51.

Gilmore, D., 1990, *Manhood on the Making: Cultural Concepts of Masculinity*. New Haven: Yale University Press.

Gilmore, D., 1991, 'Commodity, Comity, Community: Male Exchange in Rural Andalusia', *Ethnology*, 30 (1): 17–30.

Godelier, M., 1982, *La Production de Grands Hommes*, Paris: Fayard.

Godelier, M. 1984, *L' Idéel et le Matériel*. Paris: Fayard.

Godelier, M., 1993, 'Espelho Meu, Espelho Meu. O Papel da Antropologia no Passado e no Futuro: uma Avaliação Provisória', *Ler História*, 23: 101–16.

Goffman, I., 1951, *The Presentation of Self in Everyday Life*. New York: Doubleday.

Goffman, I., 1988 [1963], *Estigma*. Rio de Janeiro: Guanabara.

Goldman, I., 1970, *Ancient Polynesian Society*. Chicago: University of Chicago Press.

Goody, J., ed., 1958, *The Developmental Cycle in Domestic Groups*. Cambridge: Cambridge University Press.

Goody, J., 1972, *Domestic Groups*. Reading, Mass.: Addison-Wesley Modules in Anthropology.

Goody, J., 1976, *Production and Reproduction: A Comparative Study of the Domestic Domain*. Cambridge: Cambridge University Press.

Goody, J., 1977, *The Domestication of the Savage Mind*. Cambridge: Cambridge University Press.

Goody, J., 1983, *The Development of the Family and Marriage in Europe*. Cambridge: Cambridge University Press.

Gough, K., 1971, 'The Origin of the Family', *Journal of Marriage and the Family*, 33: 760–71.

Gramsci, A., 1971, *Selections from the Prison Notebooks*. London: Lawrence and Wishart.

Gregory, J., 1984, 'The Myth of the Male Ethnographer and the Woman's World', *American Anthropologist*, 86: 316–27.

Gudeman, S., 1978, *The Demise of a Rural Economy: From Subsistence to Capitalism in a Latin American Village*. London: Routledge and Kegan Paul.

Handman, M.-E., 1983, *La Violence et la Ruse: Hommes et Femmes dans un Village Grec*. Aix-en-Provence: Édisud.

Handman, M.-E., 1991, 'Les Amitiés Féminines à Arnaia (Macédonie Grècque)', Ms. (forthcoming in *Les Amis et les Autres: Mélanges en l' Honneur de Jean Peristiany*. Paris and Athens: M.S.H. / E.K.K.E).

Hannerz, U., 1989, 'Culture Between Center and Periphery: Toward a Macroanthropology', *Ethnos*, 54: 200–16.

Harris, O. and Young, K., 1981, 'Engendered Structures: Some Problems in the Analysis of Reproduction', in Kahn, J. and Llobera, J., eds, *The Anthropology of Pre-Capitalist Societies*. Atlantic Highlands, N.J.

Herdt, G., 1981, *Guardians of the Flutes: Idioms of Masculinity*. New York: McGraw Hill.

Herzfeld, M., 1980, 'Honour and Shame: Problems in the Comparative Analysis of Moral Systems', *Man*, 15: 339–51.

Herzfeld, M., 1982, 'Disemia', in Herzfeld, M. and Lenhart, M.D., eds, *Semiotics 1980*. New York: Plenum Press.

Herzfeld, M., 1985, *The Poetics of Manhood: Contest and Identity in a Cretan Mountain Village*. Princeton: Princeton University Press.

Herzfeld, M., 1991, 'Silence, Submission, and Subversion: Toward a Poetics of Womanhood', in Loizos, P. and Papataxiarchis, E., eds, *Contested Identities: Gender and Kinship in Modern Greece*. Princeton: Princeton University Press.

Hobbes, T., 1958 [1651], *Leviathan*. New York: Liberal Art Press.

Iturra, R., 1988, 'Factores de Reproducción Social en Sistemas Rurales: Trabajo, Producción de Productores y Pecado en Aldeas Campesinas', *Arxiu d' Etnografia de Catalunya*, 6: 103–21.

Iturra, R., 1989, 'A Religião Como Teoria da Reprodução Social', *Ler História*, 15: 95–110.

Iturra, R., 1990, *Fugirás à Escola Para Trabalhar a Terra: Ensaios de Antropologia Social sobre o Insucesso Escolar*. Lisbon: Escher.

Jackson, A., 1986, *Anthropology at Home*. (ASA Monographs no. 25). London: Tavistock.

Jackson, M., 1987, ' "Facts of Life" or the Eroticization of Women's Oppression? Sexology and the Social Construction of Heterosexuality', in Caplan, P., ed., *The Cultural Construction of Sexuality*. London: Routledge.

Jameson, F., 1984, 'Post-Modernism or the Cultural Logic of Late Capitalism', *New Left Review*, 146: 53–92.

LaFontaine, J., 1981, 'The Domestication of the Savage Male', *Man*, 16: 333–49.

Lamphere, L., 1974, 'Strategies, Cooperation, and Conflict Among Women in Domestic Groups', in Rosaldo, M. and Lamphere, L., eds, *Woman, Culture, and Society*. Stanford: Stanford University Press.

Lancaster, R., 1988, 'Subject Honor and Object Shame: the Construction of Homosexuality and Stigma in Nicaragua', *Ethnology*, 27 (2): 111–25.

Laqueur, T., 1990, *Making Sex: Body and Gender from the Greeks to Freud*. Cambridge, Mass.: Harvard University Press.

Laslett, P. and Wall, R., eds, 1972, *Household and Family in Past Time*. Cambridge: Cambridge University Press.

Laslett, P., 1977, *Family and Illicit Love in Earlier Generations*. Cambridge: Cambridge University Press.

Lawrence, D., 1982, 'Reconsidering the Menstrual Taboo: A Portuguese Case', *Anthropological Quarterly*, 55 (2): 84–98.

Leacock, E., 1972, 'Introduction', in Engels, F., *The Origins of the Family, Private Property, and the State*, Leacock, E., ed., New York: International Publishers.

LeGoff, J., 1991, 'Le Refus du Plaisir', in Duby, G., ed., *Amour et Sexualité en Occident*. Paris: Points.

Lévi-Strauss, C., 1962, *La Pensée Sauvage*. Paris: Plon.

Loizos, P. and Papataxiarchis, E., eds, 1991, *Contested Identities: Gender and Kinship in Modern Greece*. Princeton: Princeton University Press.

Lucie-Smith, E., 1972, *Eroticism in Western Art*. London: Thames and Hudson.

Lutz, C. and Abu-Lughod, L., eds, 1990, *Language and the Politics of Emotion*. Cambridge: Cambridge University Press.

Lutz, C., 1990, 'Engendered Emotion: Gender, Power, and the Rhetoric of Emotional Control in American Discourse', in Lutz, C. and Abu-Lughod, L., eds, *Language and the Politics of Emotion*. Cambridge: Cambridge University Press.

MacCormack, C. and Strathern, M., eds, 1980, *Nature, Culture and Gender*. Cambridge: Cambridge University Press.

Malinowski, B., 1927 a, *Sex and Repression in Savage Society*. London.

Malinowski, B., 1927 b, *The Father in Primitive Psychology*. London.

Malinowski, B., 1962, *Sex, Culture and Myth*. New York: Harcourt, Brace and World.

Malinowski, B., 1975 [1929], *La Vida Sexual de los Salvajes del Noroeste de la Melanesia*. Madrid: Morata.

Marcus, G. and Fischer, M., eds, 1986, *Anthropology as Cultural Critique: An Experimental Moment in the Human Sciences*. Chicago: University of Chicago Press.

Marvin, G., 1984, 'The Cockfight in Andalusia, Spain: Images of the Truly Male', *Anthropological Quarterly*, 52 (2): 60–70.

Marx, K., 1978 [1845], 'The German Ideology', in Tucker, R., ed., *The Marx-Engels Reader*. New York: W.W.Norton & Co..

Marx, K., 1979 [1867], *Capital*. New York: International Publishers.

Mathieu, N.-C., 1991, *L' Anatomie Politique: Catégorisations et Idéologies du Sexe*. Paris: Côté-Femmes Éditions.

Mauss, M., 1980 [1936], 'Les Techniques du Corps', in Mauss, M., *Sociologie et Anthropologie*. Paris: P.U.F.

Mauss, M., 1980 [1938], 'Une Catégorie de l' Esprit Humain: La Notion de Personne, Celle de "Moi"', in Mauss, M., *Sociologie et Anthropologie*. Paris: P.U.F.

McLennan, J.F., 1865, *Primitive Marriage*. Edinburgh: Adam & Charles Black.

Mead, M., n.d. [1949], *O Homem e a Mulher*. Lisbon: Meridiano.

Mead, M., 1963, *Moeurs et Sexualité en Océanie*. Paris: Plon. Includes *Coming of Age in Samoa* [1928] and *Sex and Temperament in Three Primitive Societies* [1935].

Medeiros, A., 1991, 'A Praça, a Rua', in vol. *Tradições*, Enciclopédia Temática Portugal Moderno. Lisbon: Pomo.

Medick, H. and Sabean, D., eds, 1989, *Interest and Emotion: Essays on the Study of Family and Kinship*. London: Cambridge University Press.

Meillassoux, C., 1975, *Femmes, Greniers et Capitaux*. Paris: Maspero.

Melo, D.F.M., n.d. [1651], *Carta de Guia de Casados*. Mem-Martins: Europa-América.

Memória Paroquial, Pardais, 1758, vol. 27, mem. 82, pp. 523, Arquivo Nacional da Torre do Tombo.

Menèndez, Eduardo, 1993, 'Regla y Trasgresión: el Alcoholismo como Integrador Ideológico', *Janus*, 1034: 59–66

Merleau-Ponty, M., 1962, *Phenomenology of Perception*. Evanston, Ill.: Northwestern University Press.

Mill, J.S., 1912 [1869], 'The Subjection of Women', in Mill, J.S., *Three Essays*. London: Oxford University Press.

Mintz, S., 1973, 'A Note on the Definition of Peasantries', *Journal of Peasant Studies*, 1: 91–106.

Morgan, L.H., 1870, *Systems of Consanguinity and Affinity of the Human Family*. Washington: Smithsonian Institution.

Morgan, L.H., 1987 [1870], *La Sociedad Primitiva*. Madrid: Endymion.

Murphy, M., 1983, 'Coming of Age in Seville: The Structuring of a Riteless Passage to Manhood', *Journal of Anthropological Research*, 39: 376–92.

Musil, R., n.d. [1930–1943], *O Homem Sem Qualidades*. Lisbon: Livros do Brasil.

Nader, L., 1969, 'Up the Anthropologist: Perspectives Gained from Studying Up', in Hymes, D., ed., *Reinventing Anthropology*. New York: Pantheon.

Nader, L., 1989, 'Post-Interpretive Anthropology', Ms., American Anthropological Association Meetings, Phoenix, Az., November 1989.

Nash, M., 1966, *Primitive and Peasant Economic Systems*. San Francisco: Chadler Publishing Co.

Nazareth, J.M., 1988, *Princípios e Métodos de Análise da Demografia Portuguesa*. Lisbon: Presença.

Neves, J.G., 1991, *O Encarregado das Pedreiras de Extracção de Mármore*. Dissertação de Licenciatura em Sociologia, I.S.C.T.E., Lisbon.

O'Neill, B., 1984, *Proprietários, Lavradores e Jornaleiras: Desigualdade Social numa Aldeia Transmontana, 1870–1978*. Lisbon: D.Quixote.

Ortner, S., 1974, 'Is Female to Male as Nature is to Culture?', in Rosaldo, M. and Lamphere, L., eds, *Woman, Culture, and Society*. Stanford: Stanford University Press.

Ortner, S., 1984, 'Theory in Anthropology Since the Sixties', *Comparative Studies in Society and History*, 84: 126–66.

Orther, S. and Whitehead, H., eds, 1981, *Sexual Meanings: The Cultural Construction of Gender and Sexuality*. Cambridge: Cambridge University Press.

Orwell, G., 1959 [1949], *Nineteen Eighty-Four*. London: Secker & Warburg.

Pacheco Pereira, J., 1980, 'Atitudes do Trabalhador Rural Alentejano Face à Posse da Terra e ao Latifúndio', in Barros, A., ed., *A Agricultura Latifundiária na Península Ibérica*. Oeiras: Instituto Gulbenkian de Ciência - Centro de Estudos de Economia Agrária.

Panoff, M., 1974, *Malinowski y la Antropología*. Barcelona: Labor.

Papataxiarchis, E., 1991, 'Friends of the Heart: Male Commensal Solidarity, Gender, and Kinship in Aegean Greece', in Loizos, P. and Papataxiarchis, E., eds, *Contested Identities: Gender and Kinship in Modern Greece*. Princeton: Princeton University Press.

Peristiany, J., 1965, ed., *Honour and Shame: The Values of Mediterranean Society*. London: Weidenfeld and Nicholson.

Picão, J.S., 1983 [1903], *Através dos Campos: Usos e Costumes Agrícolo-Alentejanos*. Lisbon: D. Quixote.

Pina-Cabral, J., 1989 a, *Filhos de Adão, Filhas de Eva: A Visão do Mundo Camponesa no Alto Minho*. Lisbon: D.Quixote.

Pina-Cabral, J., 1989 b, 'The Mediterranean as a Category of Regional Comparison: a Critical View', *Current Anthropology*, 30 (3): 399–406.

Pitt-Rivers, J., 1971 [1954], *The People of the Sierra*. Chicago: Chicago University Press.

Pitt-Rivers, J., 1973, 'The Kith and the Kin', in Goody, J., ed., *The Character of Kinship*. Cambridge: Cambridge University Press.

Pitt-Rivers, J., 1977, *The Fate of Schechem or the Politics of Sex: Essays in the Anthropology of the Mediterranean*. Cambridge: Cambridge University Press.

Pitt-Rivers, J., 1988, *From the Love of Food to the Love of God*, Marett Lecture, Ms.

Pitt-Rivers, J., 1993, 'The Spanish Bullfight and Kindred Activities', *Anthropology Today*, 9 (4): 11–15.

Polanyi, K., 1957, 'Aristotle Discovers the Economy', in Polanyi, K., 1957, *Trade and Market in the Early Empires*. New York: Free Press.

Porto, N., 1991, 'Razão, Sexo e Sentimentos: Aprender a Ler no Estado Novo', Ms. [See also by the same author *O Corpo, a Razão, o Coração: A Construção Social da Sexualidade em Vila Ruiva*. Lisbon: Escher, 1991].

Rabinow, P. and Sullivan, W., eds, 1979, *Interpretive Social Science: A Reader*. Berkeley: University of California Press.

Reich, W., 1972 [1936], *The Sexual Revolution*. London: Vision Press.

Reiter, R., 1975, 'Men and Women in the South of France: Public and Private Domains', in Reiter, R., ed., *Toward an Anthropology of Women*. New York: Monthly Review Press.

Reiter, R., ed., 1975, *Toward an Anthropology of Women*. New York: Monthly Review Press.

Ribeiro, O., 1987 [1945], *Portugal: O Mediterrâneo e o Atlântico*. Lisbon: Sá da Costa.

Ricoeur, P., 1979, 'The Model of the Text: Meaningful Action Considered as a Text', in Rabinow, P. and Sullivan, W., eds, *Interpretive Social Science: A Reader*. Berkeley: University of California Press.

Riegelhaupt, J., 1967, 'Saloio Women: An Analysis of Informal and Formal Political and Economic Roles of Portuguese Peasant Women', *Anthropological Quarterly*, 40: 109–26.

Róis de Confessados da Freguesia de Santa Catarina de Pardais, 1828, 1844, 1859, 1867, 1891, 1900, 1911.

Rosaldo, M.,1974, 'Woman, Culture and Society: A Theoretical Overview', in Rosaldo, M. and Lamphere, L., eds, *Woman, Culture and Society*. Stanford: Stanford University Press.

Rosaldo, M., 1980, 'The Use and Abuse of Anthropology: Reflections on Feminism and Cross-Cultural Understanding', *Signs*, 5 (3): 389–417.

Rosaldo, M., 1984, 'Toward an Anthropology of Self and Feeling', in Shweder, R. and LeVine, R., eds, *Culture Theory: Essays in Mind, Self and Emotion*. Cambridge: Cambridge University Press.

Rosaldo, M. and Lamphere, L., eds, 1974, *Woman, Culture and Society*. Stanford: Stanford University Press.

Ross, E. and Rapp, R., 1984, 'Sex and Society: A Research Note from Social History and Anthropology', in Snitow, A. et al., eds, *Desire: The Politics of Sexuality*. London: Virago.

Rousseau, E., 1969 [1762], *Émile*, vol. VI of *Oeuvres Complètes*. Paris: Gallimard.

Rubin, G., 1975, 'The Traffic in Women: Notes on the "Political Economy" of Sex', in Reiter, R., ed., *Toward an Anthropology of Women*. New York: Monthly Review Press.

Rubin, G., 1984, 'Thinking Sex: Notes for a Radical Theory of the Politics of Sexuality', in Vance, C., ed., *Pleasure and Danger: Exploring Female Sexuality*. London: Routledge and Kegan Paul.

Sacks, K., 1975, 'Engels Revisited: Women, the Organization of Production, and Private Property', in Reiter, R., ed., *Toward an Anthropology of Women*. New York: Monthly Review Press.

Sahlins, M., 1972, *Stone Age Economics*. Chicago: Aldine-Atherton.

Sahlins, M., 1976, *Culture and Practical Reason*. Chicago: The University of Chicago Press.

Sahlins, M., 1985, *Islands of History*. London: Tavistock.

Sartre, M., 1991, 'L' Homosexualité dans la Grèce Antique' in Duby, G., ed., *Amour et Sexualité en Occident*. Paris: Seuil.

Schechner, Richard and W. Appel, eds, 1990, *By Means of Performance*. Cambridge: Cambridge University Press.

Schneider, J., 1971, 'Of Vigilance and Virgins: Honour, Shame, and Access to Resources in Mediterranean Society', *Ethnology*, 10: 1–24.

Segalen, M., 1986, *Historical Anthropology of the Family*. Cambridge and Paris: Cambridge University Press and Éditions de la Maison des Sciences de l' Homme.

Seidler, V., 1987, 'Reason, Desire and Male Sexuality', in Caplan, P., ed., *The Cultural Construction of Sexuality*. London: Routledge.

Sevilla-Guzmán, E., 1980, 'Reflexiones Teóricas sobre el Concepto Sociológico de Latifundismo', in Barros, A., ed., *A Agricultura Latifundiária na Península Ibérica*. Oeiras: Instituto Gulbenkian de Ciência - Centro de Estudos de Economia Agrária.

Shanin, T., 1973, 'The Nature and Logic of the Peasant Economy', *The Journal of Peasant Studies*, 1 (1): 63–80; 1 (2): 186–206.

Shorter, E., 1975, *The Making of the Modern Family*. New York: Basic Books.

Shweder, R. and LeVine, R., eds, 1984, *Essays on Mind, Self and Emotion*. Cambridge: Cambridge University Press.

Silbert, A., 1978, *Le Portugal Mediterranéen à la Fin de l' Ancien Régime*. Paris: S.E.V.P.E.N., 2 vols.

Silva, C., 1980, 'Acerca da Génese das Relações de Produção Características do Latifúndio em Portugal: Tentame de Enquadramento dos Factores da sua Formação', in Barros, A., ed., *A Agricultura Latifundiária na Península Ibérica*. Oeiras: Instituto Gulbenkian de Ciência - Centro de Estudos de Economia Agrária..

Simmel, G., 1978, *The Philosophy of Money*. London: Routledge.

Singer, M., 1988, 'Hacia una Economía Política del Alcoholismo', *Nueva Antropología*, vol. X, no. 34: 9–53.

Sperber, D., 1981, 'L' Interprétation en Anthropologie', *L' Homme*, XXI (I): 69–92.

Steinberg, L., 1983, 'The Sexuality of Christ in Renaissance Art and in Modern Oblivion', *October*, 25: 1–222.

Stocking, G., 1987, *Victorian Anthropology*. New York: Free Press.

Stoller, R., 1993, *Masculinidade e Feminilidade: apresentações do género*. Porto Alegre: Artes Médicas.

Stoller, R. and Herdt, G., 1993 'O Desenvolvimento da Masculinidade: Uma Contribuição Cultural Cruzada', in Stoller, R., *Masculinidade e Feminilidade*. Porto Alegre: Artes Médicas.

Strathern, A., ed., 1982, *Inequality in New Guinea Highlands Societies*. Cambridge: Cambridge University Press.

Strathern, M., 1981, 'Self-Interest and the Social Good: Some Implications of Hagen Gender Imagery', in Ortner, S. and Whitehead, H., eds, *Sexual Meanings: The Cultural Construction of Gender and Sexuality*. Cambridge: Cambridge University Press.

Strathern, M., 1987, 'An Awkward Relationship: The Case of Feminism and Anthropology', *Signs*, 12 (2): 276–92.

Strathern, M., 1988, *The Gender of the Gift*. Berkeley: University of California Press.

Strathern, M., 1989, 'Enterprising Kinship: Consumer Choice and the New Reproductive Technologies'. Ms., Conference at the Centre for The Study of Cultural Values, University of Lancaster, September 1989.

Synnott, A., 1992, 'Tomb, Temple, Machine and Self: The Social Construction of the Body', *British Journal of Sociology*, 43 (1): 79–110.

Taussig, M., 1980, *The Devil and Commodity Fetishism in South America*. Chapel Hill, N.C.: University of North Carolina Press.

Tepicht, J., 1975, 'A Project for Research on the Peasant Revolution of our Time', *The Journal of Peasant Studies*, 2 (3): 258–69.

Thompson, E.P., 1963, *The Making of the English Working Class*. New York: Vintage.

Turner, V., 1974 a [1969], *O Processo Ritual*. Petrópolis: Vozes.

Turner, V., 1974 b, *Dramas, Fields and Metaphors*. Ithaca: Cornell University Press.

Turner, V. and Bruner, E., eds, 1986, *The Anthropology of Experience*. Chicago: University of Illinois Press.

Tyssot, G., 1988, 'Lo Social Contra lo Doméstico. La Cultura de la Casa en los Últimos Dos Siglos', *A&V-Monografías de Arquitectura y Vivienda*, 14: 8–13.

Uhl, S., 1991, 'Forbidden Friends: Cultural Veils of Female Friendship in Andalusia', *American Ethnologist*, 18 (1): 89–103.

Vale de Almeida, M., 1983, *Festas dos Rapazes ou de Santo Estêvão*. Ms., Monografia de Licenciatura em Antropologia, Faculdade de Ciências Sociais e Humanas da Universidade Nova de Lisboa.

Vale de Almeida, M., 1985, *Social Reproduction Through Ideology: Can One Find It in Children's Drawings?*, Ms., Term paper, Master's Degree, Binghamton, N.Y.: State University of New York.

Vale de Almeida, M., 1991, 'Leitura de Um Livro de Leitura: A Sociedade Contada às Crianças e Lembrada ao Povo', in O'Neill, B. and Pais de Brito, J., eds, *Lugares d' Aqui: Actas do Seminário 'Terrenos Portugueses'*. Lisbon: D.Quixote.

Vance, C., 1991, 'Anthropology Rediscovers Sexuality: A Theoretical Comment', *Social Science and Medicine*, 33 (8): 875–84.

Vaz de Caminha, P., n.d. [1500], *Carta de Pero Vaz de Caminha a El-Rei D. Manuel sobre o Achamento do Brasil*. Mem-Martins: Europa-América.

Veiga de Oliveira, E., et al., 1976, Alfaia Agrícola Portuguesa. Lisbon: Instituto de Alta Cultura.

Veyne, P., 1982, 'L' Homosexualité à Rome', in Duby, G., ed., *Amour et Sexualité en Occident*. Paris: Points.

Viegas, S., 1991, 'Do Nascimento ao Baptismo', in vol. *Tradições*, Enciclopédia Temática Portugal Moderno. Lisbon: Pomo.

Vigarello, G., 1988, 'Higiene y Intimidad del Baño: Las Formas de la Limpieza Corporal', *A&V-Monografías de Arquitectura y Vivienda*, 14: 25–32.

Weber, M., 1958, 'Class, Status, Party', in Gerth, H.H. and Wright Mills, C., eds, *From Max Weber*. New York: Oxford University Press.

Weber, M., 1983 [1901], *A Ética Protestante e o Espírito do Capitalismo*. Lisbon: Presença.

Weeks, J., 1985, *Sexuality and Its Discontents: Meanings, Myths, and Modern Sexuality*. London: Routledge and Kegan Paul.

Weeks, J., 1987, 'Questions of Identity', in Caplan, P., ed., *The Cultural Construction of Sexuality*. London: Routledge.

Westermack, E., 1984 [1891], *Historia del Matrimonio*. Barcelona: Laertes.

Whitehead, A., 1977, 'Review of Jack Goody's *Production and Reproduction*', *Critique of Anthropology*, 3 (9–10): 153–58.

Whitehead, H., 1981, 'The Bow and the Burden Strap: A New Look at Institutionalized Homosexuality in Native North America', in Ortner, S. and Whitehead, H., eds, *Sexual Meanings: The Cultural Construction of Gender and Sexuality*. Cambridge: Cambridge University Press.

Wikan, U., 1977, 'Man Becomes Woman: Transsexualism in Oman as a Key to Gender Roles', *Man*, 12 (2): 304–19.

Willis, P., 1977, *Learning to Labour: How Working Class Kids Get Working Class Jobs*. Tiptree, Essex: Gower.

Wolf, E., 1976 [1966], *Sociedades Camponesas*. Rio de Janeiro: Zahar.

Wollstonecraft, M., 1975 [1792], *Vindication of the Rights of Women*. Harmondsworth: Penguin.

Yanagisako, S., 1979, 'Family and Household: The Analysis of Domestic Groups', *Annual Review of Anthropology*, 8: 161–205

Yanagisako, S., 1988, 'Sex and Gender: You Can't Have One Without the Other', *Ms.*, paper presented at the First Annual Meeting, Society for Cultural Anthropology.

Young, K., et al., 1981, *Of Marriage and the Market: Women's Subordination in International Perspective*. London: C.S.E. Books.

INDEX